THE THREE SITWELLS

A

THE
THREE SITWELLS

A BIOGRAPHICAL AND
CRITICAL STUDY

By

R. L. MÉGROZ

LONDON
THE RICHARDS PRESS
LIMITED
1927

Republished 1971
Scholarly Press, Inc., 22929 Industrial Drive East
St. Clair Shores, Michigan 48080

Library of Congress Catalog Card Number: 79-145174
ISBN 0-403-01102-7

To

SIR RONALD ROSS
K.C.B., M.D., F.R.S.

CONTENTS

" What a sight it is to see *Writers* committed together by the eares, for *Ceremonies, Syllables, Points, Colons, Commas, Hyphens,* and the like? fighting as for their fires, and their Altars; and angry that none are frighted at their noyses, and loud brayings under their asses' skins? "

BEN JONSON (*Discoveries*).

PREFATORY NOTE

IF I needed any justification for writing this book, apart from the importance of the Sitwells' work and its peculiar biographical interest, it would lie in the vagaries of contemporary criticism. The poets have been accused of many strange sins. Some of the accusations have been acts of merely personal warfare and as such are not worth consideration. Among the honest and unmalicious critics are some who have accused, and still accuse, the Sitwells of nihilist designs upon form and tradition. I hope such writers will find in the following pages a reasonable answer to the charge, for the most " anti-Sitwellian " cannot say that I have ignored what I believe to be the poets' faults or that I have displayed any partiality for eccentricity posing as originality. The Sitwells are important enough to be recommended to the attention of intelligent readers without any Mumbo-Jumbo. I hope especially to persuade my readers to make a certain mental adjustment to the fresh angle of vision in modern poetry, and by sympathetic understanding to realise that the Sitwells are loyal fighters on the losing side in a world where beauty has been driven back from the highways and the market-places into the depths of the still hungry spirit.

We are driven inwards because the external reality we have created is plangently ugly. The most urgent

problem confronting civilisation is not any issue between economic or political schools and parties; it
is nothing less than the corruption of all that is best
in the human mind by misdirected and degraded
mob-emotion.   Standardisation in the economic
sphere may be a material advantage, but we cannot
afford to have spiritual pabulum supplied on a
" commercial basis." Freedom and vitality of the
spirit is not to be gained for the community by
destroying tradition (a task of Tantalus, anyway)
but in ennobling it; and all those who have a care
for the things that matter should be the first to
encourage enemies of complacent and comfortable
materialism.   The genius of the individual is the
only creative force in human society, and too often
the avowed servants of beauty fight against their
friends before recognising that they are of the same
clan.

Acknowledgments and thanks are due to the
following publishers for permission to quote from
Sitwell books published by them : Messrs Duckworth
& Co., Leonard Parsons Ltd., Chatto & Windus,
" The Bomb Shop," the Hogarth Press, the Fleuron
Press, Basil Blackwell Ltd., and the publishers of this
book. The bibliographical appendix will indicate my
debts in detail.   R. L. M.

PART ONE

CHAPTER ONE

THE SITWELLS AND SACHEVERELLS

Feudal England—the beginning of the Sitwell line—
Normans in the Midlands—Walter de Boys—Simon
Sitewell—Renishaw in the thirteenth century—The
Reresbys—The break in the Sitwell male succession,
1727—Sacheverells, Sitwells and Reresbys all con-
nected—" an earlier Sir Roger de Coverley "—
" Country Life in the Seventeenth Century "—
" Letters of the Sitwells and Sacheverells "—Inter-
marriage—William Sacheverell—George Sitwell's
domestic accounts—The Copley portrait group—
Francis Hurt Sitwell—Winter evenings at Renishaw
—Connections with Archbishop Tate, Baron Wens-
leydale, and Viscount Ulleswater—Miss Wilmot
Sitwell and Byron—The Hebers—Mary Cholmondeley—Stella Benson.

I T was in that picturesque period where history,
heraldry and legend become the mingled threads
of an old tapestry of feudal England, that the
ancestors of the Sitwells, tall, blonde, blue-eyed
Norman chiefs in the midlands, were taking root in
the Celtic soil of England. In the concise summary
of Burke's Peerage, the Sitwells are descended from
the Hallamshire family of del Wode, de Boys, or de
Bosco, which intermarried early in the 14th century
with the Lords of Midhope and of Barnby, and held

13

lands in the parish of Eckington. A small portion of
the park at Renishaw (their present seat) has been in
the possession of the Sitwells for 600 years, and the
arms are identical with those of the Stutevilles,
Lords of Eckington.

The story of the beginning of the Sitwell line is
told by Sir George Sitwell in a fascinating historical
essay entitled *The Pilgrim*, which he described as
the first chapter in a family history. Of the lords
of Hallamshire in the 13th century he says they
" had surrounded themselves at Sheffield (which is
about seven miles north-west of Eckington) with a
little court of feudal tenants, of whom some were
akin to them by blood, some served as esquires in
the castle and fought under their banners when they
were called upon to appear in the field. Amongst
these families was one which bore the surname of
de Boys or del Wode, in Latin de Bosco." On Ridgeway,* a spur of high land looking over Eckington
and south-ward down the broad vale of Rother, six
and a quarter centuries ago there stood three or
four wooden houses and twice as many mud and
osier cottages. It was one of those natural tracks
used by armies and travelling chapmen long before
history was written. But on a May morning in 1299
Walter de Boys left the largest of the wooden houses
on Ridgeway, a high-roofed, double-winged hall
made of heavy oak beams, to set forth on a pilgrimage to the Holy Land.

" At the head of the village, just where the road
begins to rise towards the ridgeway," Sir George
Sitwell says, " a small crowd had gathered round a

* Now known as High Lane.

tall grey-bearded man clad in a red-brown sclavine,
or hooded robe of wool, with a cross of white cloth
sewn upon the shoulder, a purple-grey tunic, dark
hose, and broad-brimmed low-crowned hat of felt
lying upon his shoulders and fastened under the chin
with tasselled strings. By him was the old horse
which had borne him eight years before as a mounted
archer in the Scottish expedition "—after the death
of " the maid of Norway " had left the crown of
Scotland a goal for competing claimants, and Balliol
had been confirmed as Edward the First's " liege
man for Scotland." (Sir Robert de Stuteville, lord
of the manor of Eckington, was the first-named of
the great land-owners in Durham for service in
person against the Scots in June 1291.)

Walter de Boys was never to return from his pilgrimage, and after a special service in the church
and a funeral procession through the village of
Eckington it became necessary to recognise legally
his heir. In 1301 Simon Sitewell of Ridgeway, was
declared Walter de Boys' son and heir, as is shown
by a suit which Sir George Sitwell quotes in *The
Pilgrim* from the Derbyshire County Assize Rolls.
Even modernised in spelling it is still redolent of the
old feudal courts :

" Assizes taken before Adam de Crokeydayke and
Lambert de Trikyngham, justices assigned to take
Assizes in the county of Derby in the twenty-ninth
year of the reign of King Edward, son of King Henry
—Crokeydayke.

" Yet of Assizes at Derby in the twenty-ninth
year, Derbyshire, to wit. The Assize comes to recognise whether Walter de Boys, father of Simon Sitewel

of Regeweye was seized in his demesne, etc., of one
messuage and twenty acres of land, with appurten-
ances, in Barleburgh, on the day when he took the
path of pilgrimage towards the land of Jerusalem,
in which pilgrimage, etc., he died, and if, etc. which
William son of William son of Walter de Barleburgh,
and Alice his wife, hold, etc., who come not and
show no reason why the assize should remain. Therefore let the Assize be taken, etc.

"The jurors say upon their oaths that the aforesaid Walter of whose death, etc., was seized, and
it, of the aforesaid tenements in his demesne as of
fee, etc., and that the aforesaid Simon is his nearer
heir; and therefore it is considered that the aforesaid Simon do recover his seizin thereof by the view
of the recognitors, and his damages which are taxed
by them at forty shillings. And the aforesaid
William and Alice in mercy, twenty pence, etc.,
Damages 40s. A moiety to the clerks."

The change of name from de Boys to Sitwell was
probably due to Simon Sitewell, Walter de Boys'
son, being called after his mother, who may have
been the heiress of an older family bearing the name.
It occurs in neighbouring counties in the 13th cen-
tury and may be derived from Shotswell alias
'Seteweld,' in Warwickshire, Sidwell alias 'Sete-
well' in Hampshire, or Sideville in Normandy.
Regarding the last possibility, it is noteworthy that
Sideville is in the Côtentin about eight miles from
Cherbourg. Estouteville-sur-mer, from which the
Stutevilles sprang, is near Yvetot in the Côtentin.

In *The Pilgrim*, Sir George Sitwell quotes two old
charters which are preserved at Renishaw, signed by

Adam, son of Richard de Bosco of Killamarsh (which lies between Barlborough and Eckington). This Richard may have been a grandson of the first Thomas de Bosco of Sheffield who with John de Midhope, seneschal of Hallamshire, appears in a charter of the year 1246. He would then have been father or brother to Walter de Boys. The two charters of Adam de Bosco are earlier than the statute of *Quia Emptores* (1289). The first witness to them both is " Philip de Ekenton, Marescall." This Philip married a daughter and co-heir of Oliver De Stretton, the owner of Renishaw.* He lived at Eckington during the last thirty years of the 13th century. A charter of 1281 to him from his brother-in-law, William de Honeston, concerns the lands and house at " Reynaldewcahe " (an early spelling of Renishaw), and among the witnesses to it are Sir Thomas de Furnival (Lord Furnival) and Sir William de Stuteville.

One or two other glimpses into the distant past may be taken. In 1310 Roger Cytewell appears as one of the founders of the guild of St. Mary at Eckington. We find Robert Sytwell, gentleman of Staveley Netherthorpe, a descendant of Roger Cytewelle (Tem. Edward IV) subscribing £25 against the Armada, and becoming a co-founder of a grammar school at Netherthorpe. After his death, his widow Elizabeth Sytwell married Roland Eyre, of Hassop, ancestor of the titular Earls of Newburgh.

In 1693 Mary Reresby married William Sitwell of Renishaw, and by this marriage the Sitwells are

* The present Renishaw Hall, the Derbyshire home of the Sitwells, dates from 1625.

the only remaining representatives of the family of
Reresby of Thribergh.

The ancestor of the Reresbys was Hugh Fitz
Osbern (or Osbert), a baron in Cheshire in 1086.
The credit for tracing their history as far back as
this is due to the painstaking Sir George Sitwell,
who in *The Barons of Pulford* completed the useful
work done by Sir John Reresby in writing a history
of the family (which remains in manuscript in the
British Museum) to within 130 years of the "Conquest." This Sir John Reresby was M.P. for York
1634-1689 and author of the 17th century *Memoirs*
which enjoyed a popularity unprecedented until the
discovery of the absorbing diaries of Pepys and
Evelyn. In his family history he preserved an
account of a saint well known to antiquaries,
Leonard of Reresby (13th century) anciently vener-
ated at Fryberg in Yorkshire.*

Sir George Sitwell fills in the *hiatus* between the
St. Leonard story and the Conquest by the pedigree
of Isidore Fitz Alexander, a landowner in Reresby
(close to Lincoln) and the adjoining villages at the
end of the 12th and commencement of the 13th century, and by the identity of the Hugh Fitz Osbert,
already referred to, one of the Earl of Chester's
greater tenants. Hugh Fitz Osbert, Lord of Pulford,
called "Blundus" or "The Fair," had many
manors in Cheshire, and two in Lincolnshire. He
was enfeoffed by Thomas Darcy in the two fees in
Marton, Reresby, etc., after 1086. His grandson
Alexander who took revenue from the land at Marton
in the time of Henry II, married a Juliana de

* His account is quoted in Baring-Gould's *Lives of the Saints.*

Reresby. The Reresbys took their name from
Reresby (now Reasby) near Lincoln. Alexander's
son, Isore (or Isidore) Fitz Alexander, surnamed de
Reresby, became Lord of Plesley, Derbyshire, in right
of his wife. His son, Ralph de Reresby, a coroner
for Notts and Derby in 1269, married Margery, sister
and heir to Sir Adam de Normanville, Lord of
Thribergh etc., Co. York, and Stainton, Co. Lincoln.
Their son was the Sir Adam de Reresby, Lord of
Thribergh, captured at Boroughbridge, the possible
hero of the myth of St. Leonard described in Sir John
Reresby's history of the family. As ancestor of the
Reresbys, he is one of the ancestors of the Sitwells.

The direct male succession of the Sitwells was
never broken until the eventual heiress of the family,
Catherine Sitwell, in 1727 married Jonathan Hurt
of Sheffield, and her son Francis succeeded to the
Renishaw estates and assumed the name of Sitwell.

It was in 1659 that Sir John Reresby, the author
of the valuable memoirs, succeeded to a house which
had suffered seriously by plunder and sacrifices made
in the Royalist cause during the Civil War. As Sir
George Sitwell happily says, his writings give a
picture of an earlier Sir Roger de Coverley—the
hospitality and friendships, the public duties and
private quarrels of a country gentleman of the old
school; and a similar picture of the Sitwells at
Renishaw is presented by Sir George Sitwell in
Country Life in the Seventeenth Century, and more
fully in *Letters of the Sitwells and Sacheverells*.

The preface to the *Letters of the Sitwells and
Sacheverells* explains that the families were connected by two inter-marriages in 1656 and 1707, and

by other relationships, for George Sitwell in the first
half of the 17th century was cousin to Henry Sacheverell of Barton and Morley; and Mary Reresby,
who married William Sitwell in 1693, was fourth in
descent from Sir Thomas Reresby, whose wife was
grand-daughter of an earlier Henry Sacheverell.
This Henry Sacheverell must not be confused with
the later Dr. Henry Sacheverell, the notorious political preacher who provoked Defoe's irony in " The
Shortest Way with Dissenters." A man more powerful and more worthy of fame than the Tory Doctor
(whom Sarah, Duchess of Marlborough, summed up
as an " an ignorant and impudent incendiary, the
scorn of those who made him their tool ") was
William Sacheverell (1638-1691), the prime personal
influence leading to the Revolution of 1688, and the
" ablest parliament man " of Charles the Second's
reign, according to Speaker Onslow. Dr. Henry
Sacheverell was almost certainly unrelated to the
family of William Sacheverell, who was M.P. for
Derbyshire, the real force behind the Test Bill of
1673, and a powerful supporter of the motion for
the removal of James Duke of York, the future
James II from Court. Our interest in this somewhat
neglected statesman and politician springs from his
blood relation with the Sitwells of Renishaw, for he
was in the line of the Sacheverells referred to by Sir
George Sitwell, who includes in the two volumes of
the " Letters " a section on the " Life and Letters
of William Sacheverell."*

---

* This is the substance of *The First Whig,* a separate book by
the same author previously printed, but in an edition limited to
fifty-two copies.

"I have at Renishaw," says Sir George Sitwell,
"a portrait of William Sacheverell which represents
him in 1656 as a handsome and interesting boy of
eighteen years of age . . . Ever since the year 1197,
when Jolinde Saultchevreuil divided with Oliver de
Longford the large inheritance of a certain Ralph
Fitz Ertald, whose two co-heirs, were, earlier in the
century, for many years in the wardship of Geoffrey
de Clinton, King Henry's Minister, the Sacheverells
had been a family of principal note in Derby and
Nottinghamshire. Their beautiful Norman name,
disguised as Sent Cheveroll, is to be seen in the roll
of Battle Abbey; their badges are to be found on
seals of the 13th century, their arms in the Tourna-
ment rolls of Richard the Second's reign, their banners in the descriptions of that army that fought at
Terouenne and Tournay. The series of Sacheverell
and Statham brasses at Morley is acknowledged to
be 'by far the finest in the Midlands,' and in the
churches of Ratcliffe, Barton and Morley there still
remain some fifteen monumental statues in alabaster
of Knights and Esquires in richly decorated armour,
and of ladies in Court costume, who once bore the
name of Sacheverell. Amongst William's more im-
mediate predecessors, John Sacheverell was a Knight
of the Shire in the reign of Henry VI, and his son,
another John, who was represented in a memorial
window and on a brass at Morley, was a member
of that remarkable league of Knights and Esquires
who bound themselves in 1475 to sustain the famous
William Lord Hastings 'against all persons as well
in peace as in war,' and was eventually slain '*in
bello Ricardi Tertii apud Boseworth.*' Sir Richard

Sacheverell had been a courtier to Henry VII, and
a favourite councillor of Henry VIII . . . Sir Henry,
a Knight of the body to the same King, was made
a Banneret in the French war, and was one of the
principal officers employed in suppressing Aske's
rebellion."

The collection of " Letters " compiled and edited
by Sir George Sitwell constantly shows the Sacheverells and Sitwells in communication about intimate
affairs. The correspondence of George Sitwell (1657-
1723) especially, includes a big proportion of letters
to or from his Sacheverell cousins.

Space cannot be spared for quotations from this
extremely interesting correspondence " en famille "
of people whose lives reflected the standards and
ideals of people of substance and tradition in those
days. The accounts of George Sitwell from 1697
to 1707 show an average expenditure of £910 per
annum. The ordinary income of a Knight at that
time was estimated by Gregory King at £650, of an
Esquire at £450, and of a gentleman at £280 a year.
George Sitwell's income, however, increased after
1707. In the autumn of 1681 Mr. and Mrs. Sitwell
lodged at the house of the leading physician in
Derby. They brought two horses with them and
paid £17 10s. 6d. per quarter for the " Tableing "
or board of themselves and their servants. Their
first child, Francis Sitwell, was born there in April
1682.

A good deal of hospitality seems always to have
been dispensed at Renishaw, and under the regime
of Mr. George Sitwell, the " House Book " showed
an expenditure of about £200 a year on meat and

drink. The following table of wine and beer con-
sumed from 1st January, 1682-3, to 31st December,
is worth quoting:

Small Beer, 48 Hogsheads valued at -	£19	4	0
Strong Beer, 11 Hogsheads valued at -	10	10	11½
March Beer, 4 Hogsheads valued at -	9	6	2
State Beer, 4½ Hogsheads valued at -	4	9	10½
Ale, 3 Hogsheads valued at - -	5	8	0
Ale, 2.1/7 Hogsheads valued at - -	3	17	7
Ale, 132 bottles valued at - - -	1	7	10
November Ale, 120 bottles valued at -	1	12	3
March Beer, 149 quarts, 50 pints -	1	14	10
Cider, 68 bottles - - - - -	2	3	1
Claret, 221 quart and 110 pint bottles -	18	0	6
Rhenish, 2 bottles - - - -	0	3	4
White wine, 5 bottles - - - -	0	5	0
Sack, 3 gallons and 2 quarts - -	1	12	8
	£79	16	1

In January, 1683-4, Robert Sacheverell, a fifteen-
year-old cousin, visited Renishaw, and the book kept
by his father's steward, who accompanied him, shows
the following particulars:

An Accompt for Mr. Robert

1683-4 Jan. 1.	£	s.	d.
For a new hatt at Nottingham as he went to Renishall - - - -	0	9	0
A payre of gloves 7d Trimming 6d -	0	1	1

A payre of sleive buttons 1s. A combe 6d - - - - - - -	0	1	6
Charges, horses and selves goeing, and my coming back - - - -	0	2	6
Renishall to servants.			
To William, 10/-; Cook and Chambermaid, 10/-; Little butler, 2/6; One maid, 2/6; George, 2/-; Two boyes in the Yard, 2/- - - -	1	9	0
Charges, myselfe and horses goeing for him, and our charges coming home -	0	3	10

The recipient of the gratuity of 2/- named George was George Thompson, Mr. Sitwell's personal servant, whose wages were £5 per annum. The two boys in the yard were no doubt postillions or grooms, and the " little butler " a footman.

This George Sitwell had a handsome and goodnatured face, judging by the fine portrait of him entitled " Mr. Justice Sitwell " at Renishaw, said to be by Sir Godfrey Kneller. He was born at Renishaw, 1657, the eldest son of Francis Sitwell by Katherine, daughter of Henry Sacheverell of Barton and Morley, and succeeded his father in 1671, when only fourteen years of age. William Sacheverell, who was then commencing his political career, helped his sister, Mrs. Sitwell, in arranging for the education of her children.

Another particularly interesting ancestral portrait which hangs on the wall of the vast eighteenth century dining-room at Renishaw Hall is a portrait group by Copley of the Sitwell family, 1787, which was mezzotinted by Ward in the following year. This portrait marks the first break in the family's male succession. The last Sitwell heir, a blue-eyed, fair boy of about sixteen, according to his portrait which is preserved also, having been drowned (he is a family ghost who is said to haunt Renishaw), the property had passed into the hands of a Francis Hurt, who in 1776 succeeded his uncle William Sitwell, his father Jonathan Hurt having married William Sitwell's sister Catherine. The Hurts were a wealthy family who lived at Sheffield, and for many years the Sitwells at Renishaw would exchange visits as well as correspondence with the Hurts at Sheffield, as well as other branches of the family,—Sacheverells, Sitwells, Ormesbys, Phipps's, Reresbys (who were close relatives of the Hurts also) at various places in the Peak district and in the adjoining counties. For some years before William Sitwell's death Francis Hurt lived with his uncle, moving as the seasons went from Renishaw to London, or to fashionable watering places like Harrogate and Bath. After his marriage he made a custom of visiting York, which besides being a beautiful city was a great social centre. His name appears among the subscribers to the city's Assembly Rooms, which rivalled those of Bath in prestige. In his account book among the items of expenditure on his travels is the cost of a gratuity at Child's Coffee House, close to St. Paul's Cathedral, once frequented by Addison. During the winter evenings at Renishaw he would join the musical parties which frequently brightened life in the country, playing the German flute in sonatas, symphonies, and concertos set for four to six performers. Many of his music books are

preserved still at Renishaw, for although it was
nothing unusual for a country gentleman to play
some instrument, particularly the flute, he seems to
have displayed a more than ordinary taste and talent
for music, and the violin was another of his instruments.

When his uncle William Sitwell died, Francis Hurt
inherited something like half a million pounds ster-
ling, the equivalent of a fortune of about three times
that figure today.* His income was estimated at
£22,000 a year. In 1777 he took the name and arms
of Sitwell by Royal Sign-manual. His children
appear in the Copley Portrait group referred to.
They are: Mary Sitwell, aged sixteen, her two
younger brothers, Francis (aged twelve) and Hurt
(aged nine), and Sitwell Sitwell, the eldest. Mary
married Sir William Wake, whose daughter-in-law,
Charlotte Lady Wake, was the sister of Archbishop
Tate.† Sitwell Sitwell became engaged to Mary
Parke, daughter of a Liverpool merchant, Thomas
Parke, whose wife came of a Lancashire family, the
Prestons of Preston. One of Thomas Parke's sons
became Sir James Parke, the famous judge, afterwards Baron Wensleydale of Walton (Lancs.).
James Parke was a brilliant scholar at Cambridge
and showed early a promise of the career awaiting
him. His daughter, the Hon. Charlotte Alice, mar-
ried in 1853 the Hon. William Lowther, and was the

* The Hurts, a family which settled in Nottinghamshire in the
15th century were not wealthy iron-founders as stated in Lady
Wake's Memoirs, and were never as rich as the Sitwells until
they succeeded to the Sitwell Estates.

† Another sister of Archbishop Tate was Lady Sitwell, wife of
the second baronet and grandmother to Sir George Sitwell, the
4th baronet.

mother of Viscount Ulleswater, the late Speaker of the House of Commons.

Mary, the wife of Francis Hurt Sitwell, died in 1792, a year before her husband, at their town house in Audley Square, which they had been in the habit of occupying for prolonged visits to London.* It is interesting to observe the record in a notebook of Francis Hurt Sitwell of a stay in London from March to August 1786, during which he went to various Exhibitions ("Desenfans pictures," "Ansell's Exhibition," "Exhibition, Oxford Street," and "Exhibition of stain'd glass," are among the items noted; also, he heard Babini at the Opera; attended "Hick's benefit" and other plays, and the "rehearsal, Messiah").

The mention of Audley Square is a reminder that the Miss Wilmot Sitwell living in South Audley Street, with whom Byron corresponded and to whom he wrote one of his best poems ("She walks in Beauty like the Night"), was a cousin of the Sitwells of Renishaw. Byron first met her at the town house of the Hurt Sitwells.

The Hebers, an old Yorkshire family, were also closely related to the ancestors of Sir George Sitwell on his mother's side, and two of them, Reginald Heber (1783-1826) and Richard Heber (1773-1833) his half-brother, call for special notice. They were the sons of Reginald Heber (d. 1804) who held a

* She was Miss Mary Warneford, daughter of Canon Warneford of York. Her husband met her at Bath, where she was a noted beauty and also known as a clever "precieuse." Canon Warneford was the son of Henry Warneford, by Mary, daughter of Sir Henry Goodriche, who came of an ancient Wiltshire family, from which Mrs. Hurt's descent could be traced to reigning Dukes of Normandy, Counts of Britanny and many English baronial houses.

moiety of the living of Malpas. He inherited from
his mother the estate and living of Hodnet in Shropshire. His son Reginald, who became Bishop of Cal-
cutta, was the eldest child of his second marriage.

Reginald Heber, the Bishop, was born at Malpas,
Cheshire. At Brasenose College, Oxford, where his
father had been a Fellow, he won in his first year
the prize for the *Carmen Seculare*, with a Latin poem
on the commencement of the new century; and in
1803 the English prize for a poem on " Palestine,"
which was set to music nine years later and has been
several times reprinted—a rather lonely example of
a prize poem which survived its day. An Indian
Civil servant who wrote a pamphlet on *The Missionary Bishop and Sweet Singer* after the Bishop's
lamented death, tells us that before the poem was
quite completed, Sir Walter Scott was one morning
in Heber's room at Brasenose, at a breakfast party.
The conversation turned to the subject of the poem,
which was then read aloud. Sir Walter Scott praised
it heartily, and remarked that no reference had been
made to the fact that tools were supposed not to
have been used in building the temple of Solomon.
Heber, retiring for a few minutes, wrote the lines
which are part of the best passage in the poem :

No hammer fell, no ponderous axes rung ;
Like some tall palm the mystic fabric sprung.
Majestic silence !

These lines were subsequently revised, and in
*Oxford Prize Poems** appear as :

* 4th Edition, Oxford, 1810.

No wórkman steel, no ponderous axes rung,
Like some tall palm the noiseless fabric sprung.
Majestic silence !

He was a great traveller, as well as a popular hymn
writer, and knew how to describe his travels. His
*Narrativé of a Journey through the Upper Provinces
of India* is noteworthy. In 1811 he published the
first specimens of his hymns in the *Christian Obser-
ver*. The collection was one of the first attempts to
write systematically a set of hymns adapted to the
Christian seasons.* The best known is " From
Greenland's Icy Mountains," written while he was
on a visit to his father-in-law, for a service at Wrex-
ham Church, where his father was to preach on
behalf of the Society for the Propagation of the
Gospel. His collected *Poetical Works* were published
in 1841, and includes the well known piece to Mrs.
Heber, " If thou wert by my side, love." When
Heber died in India from an apoplectic seizure,
Southey and other poets expressed the universal
regret in elegiac verse.

Richard Heber also was a remarkable man. Grad-
uating M.A. at Oxford, he projected editing Latin
poets, and printed part of an edition of *Claudian*.
The writings and personal friendship of the Whar-
tons, George Steevens, Ellis, Percy and Malone
formed his taste for early English dramatic and
poetic literature, and the accidental purchase of a
copy of Henry Peacham's *Vallie of Varietie* (1638),
is said to have been the beginning of his collection
of rarities in these classes. That collection became

* The Rev. Canon Overton on *Reginald Heber,* in *N.D.B.*

world famous, and when he died, although no mention of books occurred in his will, he possessed eight houses dotted about England and the Continent, in which books of all kinds overflowed the rooms, passages and corridors. These books were gradually disposed of in a series of memorable sales. One of the maxims of this great bibliophile and scholar .was charming :

" No gentleman can be without three copies of a book; one for show, one for use, and one for borrowers ! "*

Heber was a lifelong friend of Sir Walter Scott, who referred to him in writing to Ellis as ' the magnificent, whose library and cellar are so superior to all others in the world,' and the sixth canto of ' Marmion ' was affectionately dedicated to him, while the Notes to the Waverley Novels contain frequent allusions to him.

Mary Cholmondeley, who died in July 1925, the popular author of *Red Pottage, The Danvers Jewels* and other novels, was related to the Hebers. Her father, the Rev. R. H. Cholmondeley, like Reginald Heber, was a Rector of Hodnet, Shropshire. His mother was a sister of the Hebers. Mary Cholmondeley was his eldest daughter, while Caroline, the second daughter, who married Mr. R. B. Benson, of Lutwyche Hall, Shropshire, became the mother of the well-known writer, Stella Benson.

* H. R. Tedder, *Richard Heber*, in *N.D.B.*

CHAPTER TWO

LONDESBOROUGHS AND BEAUFORTS

Henry Conyngham and his wife—the Prince Regent—
The Brighton Pavilion—William Joseph Denison—
Albert Denison, first Lord Londesborough—The
first Earl Londesborough—Lady Edith Somerset—
Admiral Boscawen—Arabella Churchill—The Duke
of Berwick—The Duke of Wellington—The origin
of the Beaufort line—Autobiography in " Colonel
Fantock " and in Miss Sitwell's prose.

SIR GEORGE SITWELL'S children can claim
an ancestry even more striking, if less remarkably consistent, than that of their father, for
they add to his lineage that of their mother, Lady
Ida Denison, whom he married in 1886.

Lady Ida Denison was the daughter of the second
Lord Londesborough whose father, the first Lord
Londesborough, was Albert Denison (1805-1860), or
Lord Albert Conyngham, a very interesting man,
and the son of Henry Conyngham, first Marquis
Conyngham.

Henry Conyngham (1766-1832) came of an old Norman family in Ireland. He succeeded as third Baron
Conyngham in 1787, and became in 1816 a Marquis
in the Irish peerage. In 1821 he was made Baron
Minster in the British peerage and Lord Steward of
the Household. His rise in the peerage and at the

English court was due to the influence of his wife over the virtuous and misunderstood Prince Regent, afterwards George IV. This lady, Elizabeth Denison, whom Conyngham married in 1794, was the daughter of William Joseph Denison (1770-1849) of Denbies, Surrey, a millionaire banker, partner in the Lombard Street House of Denison, Heywood and Kennard. Fortunately William Joseph Denison left the bulk of his vast wealth to his nephew Albert, the son of Henry Conyngham, who was to become Lord Albert Conyngham and then Albert Denison first Baron Londesborough. Henry Conyngham before his arrival in London was already known as a vigorous supporter of the Union in the Irish House of Lords, and after the passing of the Union generally voted for the Ministerial party. He does not appear to have been an active politician, and but for his wife's friendship with the Prince Regent, might not have been heard of. In 1821, besides being created Lord Minster of Minster Abbey, Kent, in the British peerage, he was in the same year sworn of the Privy Chamber and made Lord Steward of the Household and Captain, Constable and Lieutenant of Windsor Castle. The Conyngham influence remained supreme at Court until the death of George IV, when it collapsed, after Elizabeth Conyngham's unseemly looting of the Brighton Pavilion. The Brighton Pavilion and the King's complaisant attitude to his mistress enter into the Greville Memoirs. Lady Conyngham had on a notable occasion ordered the Pavilion to be lighted up, and this was questioned and brought to the King. He said, according to Greville: " Thank you, thank you, my dear, you always do what is right; you cannot please me so much as by doing everything you please, everything to show you are mistress here." The same authority tells us that she used the King's carriages and horses when she wished, and that the dinners she gave at her town house were cooked at St. James' Palace.

It is pleasant to turn to the third son of Henry Conyngham and Elizabeth Denison, Lord Albert Conyngham (the first Baron Londesborough) (1805-1860) whose first wife, a famous beauty who died young, was the sister of Lady Chesterfield and of Lady Bradford. Disraeli's friendship with Lady Bradford is well known; it will be found recorded, with Disraeli's correspondence, in Monypenny's "Life." A clause in the will of his uncle, William Joseph Denison, who bequeathed to him his property, stipulated that Lord Albert Conyngham should assume the surname of Denison. Albert Conyngham, afterwards Denison, was educated at Eton, became secretary of the Legation at Florence in 1826, at the age of twenty-one; was created a K.C.H. in 1829 by George IV; was Secretary of the Legation at Berlin, 1829-31; Deputy Lieutenant of West Riding of Yorkshire; M.P. for Canterbury 1835-41 and 1847-50. He was created Baron Londesborough in 1850, a year after his assumption of the surname of Denison. Lady Ida Denison's grandfather was an original thinker and scholar; his studies of Anglo-Saxon antiquities are among the memorable things in the history of archæology. After his inheritance of his uncle's wealth, he had ample opportunity to satisfy his bent. Besides the domains of Londesborough, near Market Weighton,

c

and Grimston Park, near Tadcaster, he became the owner of the Manor of Selby in Yorkshire, and held over altogether 60,000 acres of land. With Ackerman, another famous antiquarian, he made contributions to the *Archæologia* on the contents of the Saxon tumuli on Breach downs and in the neighbourhood which became a valuable part of our knowledge of the Anglo-Saxons. He was an F.S.A. and an F.R.S., a President of the British Archæological Association, and a President of the London and Middlesex Archæological Society.

The eldest son of Lord Albert Denison was William Henry Forester Denison, second Lord and first Earl Londesborough, who married Lady Edith Somerset, youngest daughter of Henry, seventh Duke of Beaufort. Lady Ida Denison was their third daughter. Her father's mother was the daughter of the famous Admiral Boscawen, and her paternal grandmother was Arabella Churchill, sister of the Duke of Marlborough and the mother by James II of the Duke of Berwick, another instance of active leadership in the same family. Her mother's mother was the sister of the first Duke of Wellington.

Return for a moment to Lady Edith Somerset, daughter of the seventh Duke of Beaufort. We have here the long Norman lineage of the Beauforts, who are descended on the male side from Edward III, for the Beaufort line sprang from the union of John of Gaunt and Katherine Swynford, widow of Sir Hugh Swynford. The eldest son of this union was John Beaufort (1373-1410) Earl of Somerset, and a son of his, also named John (1403-1444), first Duke of Somerset, was the famous military commander. At

the age of seventeen he fought with Henry V in
France, and in 1421, serving under the Duke of
Clarence, was captured during an advance against
the Dauphin in Anjou. He was soon ransomed and
fighting again under Henry VI. He was made Duke
for his services in France, and the family name of
Beaufort was taken from a castle in Anjou which
belonged to John of Gaunt. Another Duke of Somerset, Edward Beaufort, in the 16th century, showed
that the family could turn their brains to other things
than fighting, for he invented what was assuredly the
first steam engine.

Before leaving this branch of the family it is not
necessary to resist the temptation to note that
Katherine Swynford, the first mother of the Beauforts, is believed to have been a sister of Phillippa,
Chaucer's wife. Phillippa was a Maid of Honour at
Edward III's Court, and she is usually said to have
been one of two daughters of a Sir Payne Roet, the
other being Katherine, who after the death of her
first husband, Sir Hugh de Swynford, in 1372, became governess to John of Gaunt's children and subsequently his mistress and then his wife. It is possible, however, that Phillippa was sister to Sir Hugh
and sister-in-law to Katherine, in which case the
blood-connection does not exist.

These references to the common ancestors of three
living poets are not irrelevant even if the reader
attaches little importance to ancestral inheritance in
the present state of our knowledge. There is ample
evidence that the poets themselves have been influenced by their family traditions, so that in addition to the cheering discovery of distinguished men

and women here and there in a long and extensive
lineage, and the less problematical value of " race,"
the Sitwells have secured for themselves the real
advantage of a spiritual inheritance rich in romance
and stimulating to the critical intellect. That they
are conscious of this inheritance, one poem alone will
demonstrate. " Colonel Fantock " in Miss Sitwell's
Troy Park is valuable as a deliberately personal
confession. It is dedicated to her brothers Osbert
and Sacheverell. It is based not only upon biographical facts, but is a re-written version of a passage
occurring in a prose autogiography, from which the
poet quoted an extract in the volume of verse entitled *Bucolic Comedies.*   Colonel Fantock, the
" military ghost," was a very real character in the
childhood of the poets, acting as tutor and generally assisting their parents. He lived at Scarborough
in a yellow brick house engirdled by rose-bushes,
for he was enthusiastic gardener, and during visits
to Renishaw his attention would be divided between
his charges and some of the great flower beds which
his efforts had crowded with blooms. When Sacheverell, the youngest, was approaching an age beyond
the reach of tutoring he was a queer vivid figure,
with burnt-brick complexion, white downward-
curling moustachios, a bald head and an eternal
pair of canary yellow boots.* He could remember
seeing the Duke of Wellington lying in state, and
this recollection of his youth would be a sort of
supplement to the memories of the children's maternal grandmother whose maternal grandmother was
the Iron Duke's sister, for she had many a time seen

* See *All Summer in a Day,* Part I, Chap. 2, by Sacheverell Sitwell.

the Duke in his yellow nankeen trousers and light
blue coat with silver buttons. Had the old lady's
mind not been bewildered by the press of years she
might have linked up the centuries in talking with
her grandchildren, for her paternal grandmother, as
we have seen, was daughter of Admiral Boscawen,
and from this mother-in-law was but another step
backwards of two generations to Arabella Churchill.
Some stories of these things would certainly have
been related to the children, if not by either of their
grandmothers, by their parents or Colonel Fantock.
A greater proportion of their childhood was spent
at Scarborough than at Renishaw, but Renishaw remained the home of the family traditions, and Renishaw was to them haunted by the past much as is
the palace in Miss Sitwell's story of " The Sleeping
Beauty," so it is that memories of those days mingle
in "Colonel Fantock" with an avowed pride of
ancestry. The poet's mother or grandmother is
referred to in:

" Thus spoke the lady underneath the trees:
    I was a member of a family
    Whose legend was of hunting (all the rare
    And unattainable brightness of the air)—
    A race whose fabled skill in falconry
    Was used on the small song-birds and a winged
    And blinded Destiny . . .

    There in a land austere and elegant
    The castle seemed an arabesque in music;

Time passed " suavely, imperceptibly," the poet
says,

" But Dagobert and Peregrine and I
  Were children then . . .

The poem calls up Colonel Fantock, the " old military ghost with mayfly whiskers " and then again
introduces the poet and her brothers, Dagobert
(Osbert) and Peregrine (Sacheverell):

" All day within the sweet and ancient gardens
  He* had my childish self for audience—
  Whose body flat and strange, whose pale straight
      hair
  Made me appear as though I had been drowned—
  (We all have the remote air of a legend)
  And Dagobert my brother, whose large strength
  Great body and grave beauty still reflect
  The Angevin dead kings from whom we spring;
  And sweet as the young tender winds that stir
  In thickets when the earliest flower-bells sing
  Upon the boughs, was his just character;
  And Peregrine the youngest with a naive
  Shy grace like a fawn's whose slant eyes seemed
  The warm green light beneath eternal boughs.
  His hair was like the fronds of feathers, life
  In him was changing ever, springing fresh
  As the dark songs of birds . . . the furry warmth
  And purring sound of fires was in his voice
  Which never failed to warm and comfort me.

" And there were haunted summers in Troy Park
  When all the stillness budded into leaves;
  We listened, like Ophelia drowned in blond
  And fluid hair, beneath stag-antlered trees;
                    * Colonel Fantock.

Then in the ancient park the country-pleasant
Shadows fell brown as any pheasant,
And Colonel Fantock seemed like one of these."

The poet, dreaming of childhood, roams from Scarborough to Renishaw, and mingles memories of
Renishaw Park with memories of Troy Park, a real
place in Wales. Miss Sitwell's great-grandmother,
Lady Edith Somerset's mother, is referred to in her
poetry, especially in " The Sleeping Beauty." The
old lady owned a loved parrot, and when she was
very old the parrot died and was stuffed, but its
mistress could not see then the difference and would
talk to the stuffed bird.*

At Troy Park lived two aunts of the poet whose
family were the heirs of the first Lord Bacon. Those
two aunts like " twin pagodas " also come into her
poetry. .

A piece of Miss Sitwell's characteristic prose recalling, or rather, building up memories which properly belong to her mother's childhood, links the
last two centuries with to-day, as well as reveals
the first stage of some of the poetry in " The Sleeping
Beauty." It is a passage from an essay in autobiography, of which only a small portion has appeared
in print : †

" By the flat-pearled shore of winter, in a land
elegant and austere as her body, my great-grandmother, the Duchess of Troy, is driving with a little
girl, my mother. The trees have a noble and austere

---

* See Section V of " The Sleeping Beauty."
† In " The New Age," July 6th, 1922. This essay is quoted again
in succeeding chapters.

beauty like that of crucifixes; the thin, dark-papered leaves are sounding drearily; and the mulberries upon the trees are dark as tunes upon a musical box. The peruked waves curl fantastically; sometimes sheep, as periwigged as King William and Queen Mary, run aimlessly through the fields, and my great-grandmother, the Duchess of Troy, looks at them rainily. She is very old. The little girl's hair is black as the Bohea she sipped with Sir Horace Walpole . . . she has slipped away again into the past; she is drowned beneath a deep still lake of sleep. Every day she gives that little girl a present, bribing her. 'Take me,' she would say, 'for a strange new drive' ! Every day they leave the Castle of Troy by the same gateway, drive by the empty, fantastically curling waves;—there is only one drive, and only one view, but she does not know it, for everything would be strange and fresh if only she could see it through the somnambulism of age. This is now her only pleasure,—this and her parrot. The parrot had died many years before, but none had dared to tell her; so the brilliant if speechless bird was stuffed into the semblance of a lifeless immortality, and restored to its gilded cage. The Duchess even rallied it for its lack of animation and failure to respond to her vague and windy affections; but she never· discovered that the bird's soul had flown. So indeed was it with Destiny, which, though powerfully winged and beaked like a harpy, appeared to her only as a bird of brilliant plumage, to be imprisoned in a gilded cage among the perfumes on her dressing-table, opposite the menacing photograph of dead Queen Anne, about whose fate I, as

a little girl, was warned not to ask. (Alas, poor
lady, she sleeps now under the strawberry-beds, and
her surprising end is only a subject for my family's
conversation."

The wonderful and eccentric Lady Septuagesima
Goodley of Dodderingham Old Hall, in Osbert Sitwell's " Triple Fugue," is too good not to be also
true, or partly true. Surely the lists of items " Lost "
on her country walks, which were pasted up in the
village sweet shop, are not entirely the invention of
the satirical Osbert ? He must at least have invented
them under provocation. Perhaps she was a near
relative of the lady referred to in Miss Sitwell's autobiography already quoted, and now quoted once
more : " My grandmother, her daughter the Countess
of B . . . When I first remember her, she was a
fantastic wave-like Chinoiserie, a Laideronette, Princess des Pagodes."

More generally available at present is the metrical
version in " The Sleeping Beauty " :

" Who is this now who comes ? " Dark words reply
    and swoon
Through all the high cold arbours of the moon :

" The slighted Laidronette, the unbidden fay,
    Princess of the Pagodas . . . Shades; make way ! "

The sedan-chair that hides her shade is mellow
As the trees' great fruit-jewels glittering yellow,

And round it the old turbanned ladies flock
Like apes that try to pluck an apricock."

It is as if figures from some old tapestries hanging on the walls of the Dining Room and Ball Room at Renishaw have stirred into life. They have joined the company of revivified bewigged ancestors whose portraits stared so strangely at the three children predestined to add laurels to the family's heraldic arms.

CHAPTER THREE

Sir George Sitwell

Renishaw—His succession—Boyhood and youth at
Renishaw—Discovery of historical materials—and
brocaded dresses and eighteenth century prints—
" Who's Who's " little joke—The capture of a
spirit—The old country gentleman and Macaulay—
" Country Life in the seventeenth century "—" The
letters of the Sitwells and Sacheverells "—" The
Barons of Pulford "—" On the Making of Gardens "—The Sitwellian Eden—Dark trees and sobbing fountains—Periwegs and 18th century quaintness—Mental travelling—" Fountains."

SIR GEORGE RERESBY SITWELL, the 4th
Baronet, was born in 1860, the eldest son of
the 3rd Baronet and Louisa, daughter of
Colonel the Hon. H. Hely Hutchinson, herself a
descendant and heiress of Welsh princes. Renishaw,
his seat at Chesterfield, Derbyshire, is set in a fine
old Park. There are all the elements of different
eras of horticultural history within the wide bounds
of Renishaw Park, from the " gardens for all months
of the year; in which severally, things of beauty may
be then in season," to the rounded sward and noble
avenues, and statued arbours beloved of the Augustan poets. The house itself contains an extraordinary
variety of antiquarian relics and styles in archi-

43

tecture and furniture, besides old books and pictures.
Sir George Sitwell has been zealous in building
additions to the Hall and in improving the park.
The house, like the park, is beautiful with age, and
yet heavy with things that have passed away, incon-
gruously mingling but failing to mix the inspiration
and the moribundity of tradition. To this home,
which was also part of the earliest environment of
his children, Sir George Sitwell succeeded his father
at the somewhat immature age of two. His boyhood, under the guardianship of Archbishop Tate,
was divided between school and Renishaw.

" My father died when I was two years old," he
writes in the Introduction to the *Letters of the
Sitwells and Sacheverells*, " and at the time I first
went to school we used to spend but a few months
in the summer at our old home in Derbyshire. The
buildings of great size, giving an impression of past
wealth and power, the ' old richesse ' which Chaucer
tells is the foundation of ' genterye,' and the
Jacobean plasterwork and stone-tiled roof bear witness to its antiquity . . . I remember finding, on
one of my holiday visits, the old books in the hall,
a Greek grammar of the days when Shakespeare was
at school, and in it my own name, written by an
earlier George Sitwell just three hundred years
before. The lumber room, with its Georgian panel-
ling and arched windows looking out upon the staircase, had always excited my curiosity, and being
allowed to poke about it on rainy days, I came upon
many strange and dusty relics of the past . . . old
portraits and brocaded dresses, portfolios of eighteenth century prints . . . and, most precious of all,

a few old chests, heaped up with manuscripts, parch-
ments and books." Among these papers were tradesmen's bills of Queen Anne's reign, inventories, alman-
acs, wills and charters. "Curiosity and the rather
wild hope of hitting upon autographs of Cromwell
or Shakespeare," led him to examine these docu-
ments, and by the end of his second year at Eton
he had learnt to read them. Thus was slowly gathered the main part of the material for the two big
volumes of the *Letters.* Among the items he discovered concerning the Francis Sitwell, "Mr. Justice
Sitwell," whose portrait is at Renishaw, for instance,
were fifteen Pocket Almanacks, dated from 1692 to
1721, full of entries in his handwriting; the Renishaw
household book, showing the cost of housekeeping
down to 1685; tradesmen's bills; estate accounts,
and his book of notes upon Justices' justice. Such
details fill in the picture of country life in the seventeenth century preserved in the memoirs of Sir John
Reresby, and help to explain the interest of the
three poets' in the picturesque centuries of history
between 1600 and 1800, a period in Europe of a class
culture which was doomed to the way of all things
when the age of machinery dawned; but which
nevertheless left a spiritual legacy of revolt against
the standardisation of thought in a machine-con-
trolled society.

The student of *Who's Who* may learn that Sir
George Sitwell contested Scarborough in 1884, 1886,
1895 and 1900; M.P. for Scarborough 1885-86, and
1892-95; captured a spirit at the headquarters of the
Spiritualists, London, 1880; travelled a good deal
and was present at the coronation of the late Czar,

Moscow, 1883; formerly Captain Yorkshire Dragoons, Lieutenant-Colonel commanding 2nd Vol. Batt. P.W.O. Yorkshire Regiment 1904-8; retired on disbanding of battalion with rank of Colonel; during the war, being unfit for service, farmed over 2000 acres, producing great quantities of wheat and potatoes. Owns about 6000 acres; Lord of the Manors of Eckington, Derbyshire; Whiston, S. Yorks.; and Long Itchington, Yorks. Pub.: *The First Whig, Country Life in the Seventeenth Century; An Essay on the Making of Gardens; Who Killed Cock Robin?* Recreations: when younger, golf, cricket, hunting, cycling, lawn tennis. Heir: Osbert. Address: Castle of Montegufoni, Montagnana, Val di Pesa, Florence, Italy; Renishaw Hall, Derbyshire.

It is needless to tell any reader of Osbert's violent little book, *Who Killed Cock Robin?* (the answer of course to be found in the name of a well-known critic), that the inclusion of this title among the publications of Sir George Sitwell is* one of the brightest jokes in *Who's Who*. "Captured a spirit at the headquarters of the spiritualists, London, 1880," is, however, intriguing, and there is, as a matter of fact, a story behind it. Sir George Sitwell combined a rigid Puritanism in ethics with an almost equally rigid atheism in philosophy, and while an undergraduate at Christ Church, Oxford, in 1880, he and a friend agreed to attend one of the seances which just then were causing no little stir in society. Sir George went as a sceptic determined to expose a fraud. In due course the lights were turned down

*Or was, in 1925.

and a ghostly pale form " materialised " in front of
the curtain which stretched across one end of the
room. Not at all impressed, Sir George Sitwell and
his friend rushed forward; his friend pulled the curtain away while he got a firm grip on the " spirit,"
which so soon as lights were turned up proved to be
a frightened woman in a high degree of nudity. She
had left her clothes in the next room, the door leading to which was behind the curtains. The disturb-
ance, as may be supposed, rippled in widening cir-
cles over the press, and the *Graphic* of that time
came out with a detailed story and a front page
covered with drawings illustrating the capture of the
" Spirit." Spiritualists were very angry about the
affair then, though nowadays they would perhaps
with their modern broadmindedness profess grati-
tude for the exposure of quackery.

For the rest of the *Who's Who* entry, does not that
laconic inventory reveal all the outstanding marks
of a surprising survival of " the country gentleman
of the old school," of the school, indeed, of Sir George
Sitwell's ancestors? Not entirely, for no country
gentleman of the old school should be quite so skilled
a writer as he, despite the weight of urbane tradition,
reveals himself to be in his historical reconstructions
of the past and in his discussions on gardens. And
yet this is but a slavish subjection to the influence
of Macaulay's brilliant Whig partisanship which in
the *History* is betrayed in one sentence : " The gross,
uneducated, untravelled country gentleman was
usually a Tory." Macaulay was referring to the
country gentleman of Charles the Second's reign,
whose " ignorance and uncouthness, whose low tastes

and gross phrases would, in our time, be considered
as indicating a nature and a breeding thoroughly
plebeian." Sir George Sitwell himself in *Country
Life in the Seventeenth Century*, and again in his
learned and gracefully written notes to the *Letters
of the Sitwells and Sacheverells* has not much difficulty in disposing of Macaulay's estimate by setting
contemporary evidence against it. And in writing
about gardens and travel as well as family history
he is not less true to a fine type than several other
old country gentleman in the seventeenth and eighteenth centuries, of the ilk of Sir Thomas Browne,
John Evelyn, Sir William Temple and Sir John
Reresby. The *Memoirs* of Sir John Reresby, an
ancestor of Sir George Sitwell, have been referred
to in the previous chapter.

Sir George Sitwell's historical studies and the
published results of them have also been referred
to. The full title of *The Barons of Pulford* is interesting enough to quote in full : *The Barons of Pulford, in the eleventh and twelfth centuries and their
Descendants the Reresbys of Thrybergh and Ash-
over, The Ormesbys of South Ormesby, and the Pul-
fords of Pulford Castle, being an Historical Account
of the lost Baronies of Pulford and Dodleston in
Cheshire, of seven Knights' Fees in Lincolnshire
attached to them, and of many Manors, Townships
and Families in Both Counties, by Sir George R.
Sitwell, Bt., F.S.A., F.S.S. Printed and sold by
Sir George Sitwell at his Press in Scarborough,*
MDCCCLXXXIX."

The author refers to the record as justifying its
existence for students of the early history of Cheshire,

because it deals with a race of soldiers whose arms were well known throughout the middle ages. By his intensive study of one province, he hoped to throw new light on the origin and development of English institutions, particularly English palatinates, and he shows how Cheshire, though not a palatinate, remained as a province under Home Rule until the reign of Henry the Eighth, Norman still in spirit and divorced from the political evolution of the nation.

The book is as a matter of fact a model of careful writing and conscientious research, and the same must be said of *The Letters of the Sitwells and Sacheverells.*

When we come to his book *On the Making of Gardens,* we are reminded of that other address of his: Castle of Montegufoni, Montagnana, Val de Pisa, Florence, and also of the fact that his sons reveal an absorbed interest in many things he writes of like a lover. Turn to the section on " Gardens of Italy," and at once will be found some of the nectar his children have imbibed. Read his hurrying sentences about the " domes and meres of Mantua in the blue Lombardic plain, and a sea of ruddy-brown roofs breaking round about ancient towers and spires." Or of the canephoræ of Caprarola— " the giant guard of sylvan divinities, playing, quarrelling, laughing the long centuries away." Or of " Isola Bella . . . a thing by itself, not a garden, but a mirage in a lake of dreams, a great galleon with flower-laden terraces and fantastic pinnacles which has anchored here against a background of purple mountains on its return to the realms of rococo."

D

He writes of the lemon-grove at Florence: " It is an oval lake encompassed by a broad pathway in the shadow of a mighty wall of ilex. Marble seats are set under the green canopy, and quaint baroque fountains from curving shells and gullets of sea-monsters drop tiny rills into the lake, where merman and sea-nymph on water-horses are wildly urging their steeds towards the shore. In the centre of the island a gigantic basin of stone supports three seated figures bracketed against the pedestal of John of Bologna's splendid statue of Oceanus. But the glory of the Isolotto is in its balustrade; where instead of pilasters we have sweeping curves cut away to admit great red garden-vases, which with their burden of green and gold are doubled upon the water-film, far above the clouds that are sailing through the blue gulf below."

The further one reads the more deeply one penetrates the enchanted Eden which haunts Sitwellian poetry. The author goes on to describe Villa Torlonia at Frascati, which " is not like Villa d'Este where the great heart of the Anio throbs through the garden and every grove and thicket and alley is filled with a tumult of sobbing sound. It is a place of mysterious silence, of low-weeping fountains and muffled footfalls; a garden of sleep." He describes the great slanting staircase, the sombre ilex avenues and mossy fountains. Beyond an opening in the woodland before the central staircase of the house there is a lawn and pool below a cascade. " The main fall drops from a balcony between two tall umbrageous ilexes which rise on either hand like the horns of an Addisonian periwig; from basin to basin

it drops in a silver fringe, held in by low serpentine
walls that curve and re-curve like the arches of a
bridge or the edges of a shell." One is tempted to
quote at inordinate length from this enchanting
book; but perhaps enough has been quoted to show
the source of much of the clear, strange, bright
imagery and even an attitude of mind, a readiness
to be pleased by Rococo, and a sort of eighteenth
century quaintness, to be found in the work of our
poets. Ilexes like a periwig might have been anywhere in *Bucolic Comedies* or *The Sleeping Beauty*;
the bold lines that draw balustrades and staircases,
and the delicate observations of water and watery
reflections, as well as the abandonment to a magic
atmosphere, are like an anticipation of *Southern
Baroque Art* and certain lyrical garden songs in *The
Hundred and One Harlequins* and *The Thirteenth
Cæsar*. The love of a landscape, and of playing with
centuries of time as if they were toys is particularly
a gift of the author of *Discussions on Travel, Art
and Life*. Indeed one is tempted over much to quote
once more, just to show better Sir George Sitwell
as a mental traveller. After finely describing some
magnificent garden vistas at Bergamo, he says:

"But it is in Brescia, above all places, that the
painted vista reigns, for here a southern imagination
has run riot, and the stranger may make his choice
of time and place and season, of Goth or Roman,
of spring or autumn, or tropic palms or Arctic snows.
Here beyond the palace courts are great pointed
vaults and ruined castle halls, Renaissance loggias,
wild rococo fantasies of pillared porticoes, of crumbling theatres, or interminable arcades. Here are lake

scenes with vast planes of stubborn rock lifting themselves into the sky, tiny hamlets clustering round
a church tower upon the mountain side, bright
palaces gleaming on the water edges, while all the
landscape seems to swoon in a white haze of heat.
Here on the bosom of a mystic river, leading from
nowhere to nowhere, a slow boatman with averted
face is ever seeking to raise an unprofitable sail; and
here are dreams of the old Roman world before the
fall which make one tremble at the sound of a church
bell, for by stream or cataract the shepherd is piping
to his flock, and under the shadow of the great stone
pines shine out the marble statues and temples of
the gods.

" Of the principles which guided the great Renaissance garden-makers it is not so easy to speak, for
it was in poetry, in imagination that they reigned
supreme, and inspiration is a breath of the Muses
which may not be brought within the rules of art.
Their first thought was for the æsthetic impression
upon the individual, for sentiment and emotion, for
intellectual suggestion, for chords struck upon those
vague, nebulous, spectral feelings which are ever
trembling upon the threshold of consciousness. To
them the garden seemed to be only half the problem,
the other half was that blundering ghost-haunted
miracle, the human mind."

He finds in the garden magic of Italy a psychology
and a witchery by which we are at one with the
surroundings, and find our own emotions in nature
" in the radiant happiness of the plants whose flowering is the expression of a desire to live, a sigh of
well-being, a smile of thankfulness, a hymn of praise,

whose blossom is as laughter, and whose perfume is
a song."

Fountains and fountain-masks, which have so
often occurred in Sacheverell's first two volumes of
verse are among Sir George Sitwell's favourite subjects. His rhapsodies about them constantly contain or suggest Sitwellian imagery. For the sake of
any unlucky reader who does not yet know the work
of Sir George Sitwell's children, a single example may
be given here of the common fund of interest. In
Osbert Sitwell's *Argonaut and Juggernaut* is a piece
entitled " Fountains." Not only interesting as an
original poem, it captures our attention by its extraordinary harmony with the mood and mentality of
" On the Making of Gardens." Furthermore, it is
prefaced by four lines from another poem on fountains which is to be found in Sacheverell Sitwell's
The People's Palace. The lines so quoted by Osbert
are these, and they might have been directly inspired
by a passage in " On the Making of Gardens " :—

" The graven fountain-masks suffer and weep.
  Carved with a smile, the poor mouths clutch
  At a half-remembered song,
  Striving to forget the agony of ever laughing."

Osbert Sitwell's poem begins :—

" Some fountains sing of love
  In full and flute-like notes that charge the night
  With all the red-mouthed essence of the rose;
  Then turn to voices murmuring above,
  Among the trees,
  Of hidden sweet delight.

Another fountain flows
With the faint music of a first spring breeze;
Each falling drop is jewelled by the moon
To some fine luminous ecstasy of light.
It sings of noon,
Of sunlit blossoms on a first spring day
And all things sweet and pleasant to the sight."

The poem sings of other fountains, one that sobs
and one that fears, and concludes:—

" Those graven fountain-masks are white with woe!
Carved with a happy smile
They strive to weep . . .
End their eternal laughing—for awhile
To loose themselves in sleep
Or in the silver peacefulness of death."

CHAPTER FOUR

CHILDHOOD MEMORIES

Edith, Osbert and Sacheverell—Normans in appearance
—Their portrayal by artists—Children of Renishaw
Hall—The Peak country—Bolsover—Renishaw in-
terior—Scarborough—Their communal memories—
Arnold Bennett's pen sketch—" the curve of their
nostrils "—Rebels and Leaders.

EDITH, Osbert and Sacheverell Sitwell offer
some evidence of that persistence of inherited characteristics which is often summed
up in the word " race." It is not merely that their
appearance is eloquent of a long Norman lineage,
but that they are obviously of the same strongly
marked stock. All three of them are about six feet
in height, and blond. They all have the long, sharp-
featured face, high-bridged nose, straight, pale hair
and light eyes—grey, grey-blue and grey-green of a
well recognised type. They have been made the subjects of several efforts at portrayal by contemporary
artists; notably in paintings by Sargent,* Alvaro
Guevara, and C. R. W. Nevinson, drawings by Walter
Sickert, Max Beerbohm and Wyndham Lewis, and a
clever sculpture by Frank Dobson. Miss Sitwell in
Mr. Lewis' drawings outvies the austere angularity of

* Sargent's portrait group of the Sitwells was painted when
Edith was 11½, Osbert 6½ and Sacheverell 1½ (the little boy
playing with bricks).

55

Queen Elizabeth and in Signor Guevara's brilliant painting in the Tate Gallery is more fay than human; while the sculptured head of Osbert Sitwell by Mr. Dobson, at anyrate as it appears in the two casts of brass taken of it, seems to me (though many people like it) to be a caricature.

It will be agreed that here is an extraordinary trio (I have seen them described as a Triumvirate) of poets and personages; probably they are the most remarkable trio belonging to the same generation of the same family in the history of English literature. They all spent much of their youth in the seclusion of the ancestral home at Renishaw Park, and like returning migrants, regularly go back there from their life in London and their long and busy visits to the south of Europe. Renishaw indeed may be regarded as a symbolic as well as actual background to their lives, a token of the Past from which they spring.

Their earliest memories of this great, rambling, fan-shaped edifice and the surrounding meadows, valleys, steep hills and rugged moors, would be coloured sombrely with the white mists, cloudy skies and silver curtains of rain with which every dweller among the hills of Derbyshire is too familiar. Sunshine of the summer days would appear with magical brightness, transmuting green to lucent gold and bathing the dulled, sad brick and stone of the Hall in warm though evanescent radiance. The contrast of sober hues and melancholy prospects with such temporary brightness would later on in their lives be repeated but far more vividly as they began to accompany their parents to Florence and to spend a part of the year wandering under the skies of Italy and Spain.

Renishaw Hall faces east and the sunlight strikes the front of the house only in the early morning and at an angle which casts the lengthening shadow of the south wing across it. This perpetuates the heaviness of its mood to the eye of one approaching along the drive of the Park through avenues of elm and lime, though on the garden-girdled west and south sides of the house the children must have gathered many memories of golden afternoons. One may leave the house from the front and follow the drive through the Park, as the youthful Sitwells must often have done when sallying on excursions, black-berrying, or boating on the lake or the canal which runs through Eckington to the north-west, where the vale of the Mosbecke joins that of the Rother. One then passes sheep-inhabited meadows and reaches the sloping side of the Rother valley. Just outside the confines of the Park the drive meets an ascending road which has come from the north-east and has crossed the little river twisting through the country's green cupped hands. Along this road groups of dusky miners pass twice a day, reminding one of the colliery chimneys and black slag heaps on the opposite slopes, the seal of the industrial age upon a land heavy with memories of feudal England. Beyond those broken hills and high moors ten or twelve miles away to the north Sheffield lies belching energetically. The twentieth century cannot be avoided for long, even here, and perhaps a sign of this were the miners' meetings held in Renishaw Park during the protracted dispute between colliery own-

ers and miners, meetings at which some of the most
bellicose utterances of the quarrel were made.

Seeking less troubled vistas, instead of going north
and east one may leave Renishaw on the west, and
from the crest of the rocky spur on which it seems to
guard the Rother valley, look southward and see the
rich land cut up by hedgerows like a chessboard into
cattle-dotted fields with streams ribboning silver
through distant green, every mountainous hill standing clear and hard above the clusters of forest. A
little farther round the compass towards the east is
a prominent ridge of moorland on which stand the
two Elizabethan strongholds, Hardwicke and Bolsover, the latter, surrounded by great elms, tower-
ing on the cliff-edge of the plateau. No reader of
Sacheverell Sitwell's garden poems in *The Thirteenth
Cæsar* has any excuse for being unmoved by the name
of Bolsover Castle. This long-enduring monument of
Elizabethan splendour which haunted his boyhood
is immortalised in " The Venus of Bolsover Castle "
and less indisputably (but more graphically) in
" Bolsover Castle." In the latter the poet imagines
the Cavaliers riding their horses round the castle
yard for practice ; and then while the horses feed,
standing to rest under the trees, and

" Looking at the Castle built between the boughs,
For it springs up all the trees' height with its four
tall towers
Leaping from branch to branch with its windows
like flashing mirrors,
Till it comes to the pavilion standing higher than
the towers

Whose lattices might make a cage for the crooning
  turtles,
For their soft and rumbling murmur comes down
  out of the cloudy tree tops.

Venus flashes, naked, from her conch of water
High above the hedges in the garden
She stands out, treading the blue waters of the sky,
Her hair held boldly as a sail to blow her on
The fountain, as it plays on her,
Will make her naked body glitter out between the
  leaves
As she stands among the clouds that look like little
  breaking waves . . ."

His poetry is ample excuse for wandering a few miles
from Renishaw, but there is more reason for returning. Tramping across the uneven open forest land
northward once more, one may pass occasional
groups of old Jacobean stone houses, strangely con-
trasting with the double line of railway running
through this quiet country parallel, at one stage,
with the canal which meanders past the picturesque
manor park of Eckington. Nearing the almost closed
lips of the valley and bearing north-west and uphill
all the time one may approach the house through
the Great Orchard, which in the time of Charles the
First occupied a crowded four-and-half acres. Viewed
across the gardens thus from the south-west the Hall
appears to be an accidental agglomeration of buildings and styles, for in its long history many different
owners have made additions and undertaken repairs.
The centre portion, the oldest, like the knot in the

middle of a broad bow, holds two great wings reaching out north-east and south-east. The porch and front door are in this central Jacobean section, which was built out of the savings of his minority for Mr. George Sitwell (1600-1667) in place of a manor house at Eckington already named Renishaw. The house was garrisoned for King Charles in the Civil War, though Mr. Sitwell, notwithstanding that he was mulcted in common with other country gentlemen, including his relative the first Sir John Reresby of Thribergh, served the State as Sheriff and in other ways under the Rump Parliament and the Commonwealth. He received a grant of arms in 1647, and the heraldic grant was regranted after the Restoration. But if this is not a divagation from Renishaw it is at least the dangerous first steps along a path which might lose itself in the drama of English history, and so, travel in time as well as space being severely restricted, let us enter Renishaw as it stands to-day, after passing along the drive through the Park, instead of by the orchards and gardens on the other side.

From the lofty hall one goes through a lobby, and reaches one of the two great rooms which give the house its definite character. This is the drawing-room, a long, high apartment with an Adams' ceiling and an ormolu chandelier recalling the Prince Regent and the Brighton Pavilion. A row of tall windows stare steadily along one side of the room, and facing them two high mahogany doors break up the expanse of wall. At one end of the room is a tall Georgian mantelpiece and another of the mahogany doors on each side of it. These lead into an ante-room,

formerly called the little parlour, which opens on the
far side into an apartment vaster and more lofty than
the dining-room—the ball-room. On the walls of this
room three tapestries hang similar to two hanging
in the dining-room. The panels of tapestry had an
extraordinary fascination for the children as they
wandered through these great apartments.* The
seventeenth century designer evidently tried to
crowd into them every suggestion of " Indian "
opulence he could imagine. Black slaves, elephants,
pagodas, fantastically clipped trees, terraces and
balustrades loaded with pots of orange trees, eter-
nally jetting fountains, galleon-like fleets of cloud—
indeed a goodly percentage of Sitwellian images—
are in these panels. There is also a princess, non-
chalant, in plumed head-dress, attended by a slave,
and on the baroque stone steps folios lie negligently
open waiting to be picked up again and read. In the
ball-room, where this Princess forever waits the fulfilment of her command, is another tall eighteenth
century mantelpiece, and drawn up to the leaping
fire, the children would have tea here of a winter
evening, and see the light go dim until, escaping from
the cupboard of their nurse's memory " the whimpering sad ghosts " would come forth. Of these was

" the Princess Jehanne, long since dead
    Whose hair was of costly long gold thread."

Readers of " The Sleeping Beauty " will remember
how she

* *All in a Summer Day.*

"Would slip her flat body, like a gleaming
Quivering fish in a clear pool dreaming,
Through the deep mesh of a conversation,
Making some ghostly imputation."

By a rather sudden transposition we must turn
now to Scarborough, that cul-de-sac of sea-side
respectability, invalidism, clubs, churches, and bath
chairs. The Sitwells spent a considerable portion
of their time for many years at Scarborough, where
"Colonel Fantock" as well as their parents owned
a house. It is therefore another locality where their
youthful memories have been tinctured with similar
colours, and the result is seen once more in the use
they make of those memories, drawing on this common pool for poetic furniture. Except in the last
poem in *The People's Palace*, and indirectly, by some
satirical references, Sacheverell Sitwell has not paid
much attention to Scarborough in his poetry, but in
the first instalment of his autobiography* this sea-
side town comes to life again, with its curious end-
of-the-world atmosphere, perhaps suggested by the
way it runs up to the very edge of the cliffed land,
and drops down in asphalt paths and sudden stone
stairs to the "front."

The sea-front and the municipal band inspired
several of Edith Sitwell's earlier poems (I am, however, relying only on internal evidence for such an
assertion) and it is clearly the same place named
"Newborough," described in Osbert Sitwell's story,
"Low Tide," the first piece in the *Triple Fugue*
volume, and in *Before the Bombardment*.   The

* *All Summer in A Day.*

town provided our satirist with irresistible openings
for generalising in a non-realistic way, but the setting
for " Low Tide," the pathetic story of the Misses
Cantrell-Cooksey, is full of facts remembered.

" The two little figures at the top of the steps,
though put in on a large and crowded canvas, inevitably and entirely dominated the scene at this
precise moment of the day. Behind them under the
pale blue canopy of the sky rose the intricate perspective of steep cliffs, trim but wind-cut trees, and
dells of a cultivated wildness; while the sharp cries
of the children, as they raced round these, falling
down, laughing, and dropping wooden spade or
metallic pail, gave a certain poignancy to the otherwise flat blur of the band wafted up from below.
The staircase was the culmination of the garden.
On to it led every dell, dingle, and asphalt path.
With heavy stone balustrades, crushed-down beneath
rows of weighty clumsily-carved stone vases over-
flowing with purple petunias and a new, very municipal variety of dwarf sweetpea—salmon-pink in
tone—it held its own with any other feature of the
town. It competed successfully for the attention
with funicular-trams, which by their movement continually caught the eye as they performed their
geometrical operations up and down the cliff with
the precision of a drill-sergeant; it outshone the
flashing eyes of the bandstand, encased in panes of
glass, and even outvied in interest the lion-coloured
sands flecked with moving, gaily dressed people, and
spotted with trestles, centres of little groups, on
which white-clad figures gesticulated, or opened and

shut soundless mouths. On each side of this imposing structure, set in wide sloping surfaces of grass,
smooth and green as baize, two enormous five-
pointed stars—frilled out at the edges with varie-
gated leaves of iodine-brown, ochre, green-white and
lemon-yellow, lined again within by lobelias of a
copper-sulphate blue that in their turn enclosed a
round pupil of coral pink begonias and red and purple
fuschias—glowered out to sea like two bloodshot
eyes; one Cyclops guarding each side of the steps."

The temptation to go on quoting must be resisted,
though the remainder of the description of the front,
and of the people haunting it is just as vivid and
definite. Among the residents of the town, " the
old military gentlemen " are all Colonel Fantocks,
" rather red and puffing, with long white mustachios,
and heavy walking-sticks." They " are pacing up
and down, their elbows out-turned, the two joints
of the arm forming a right angle; they are continually pulling at their cuffs—stiff, white cuffs with
coloured lines on them—as if on the point of con-
juring, the verge of exhibiting, an alive but miraculous white rabbit. All the summer days they spend
here, in-the-open-air-damn-it, and all the winter on
the cliff above, with eyes fixed to the end of a gigantic telescope, pointed like a gun at the sea, in the
bow-window of the commodious Gentlemen's Club,
the exterior of which is painted a thick but appropriate magenta."
All of which is nearly photographic in accuracy,
as are the similar descriptive passages in *Before the
Bombardment.*

The point of these observations is the communal use which the Sitwells make of their common memories. They have developed certain tastes and inclinations which contrast notably with what is fashionable, and their culture is also to some extent communal, like their memories, because it largely springs from similar experiences. The only qualification to this summary which is necessary is that they are strongly individual, and will tend to become less like one another as the external antagonism of an astonished world is softened into critical appreciation.

Since it is not possible to ignore a passage which their distinguished contemporary, Mr. Arnold Bennett, wrote about the three young poets before their genius was recognised by more than a handful of people—indeed while they were still being pursued by a good deal of malicious abuse as well as honestly adverse criticism—it will be best to quote it, and then suggest how it ought to be qualified (so far as concerns the personal element) before it goes down to posterity.

" The Sitwells sister and brothers have each published a book of verse within the last twelve months, and the latest volume is Osbert Sitwell's *Out of the Flame* which has set my thoughts flowing around the triune phenomenon. The Sitwells can all write. They are educated in words. They are interested in words; they have an affection for words—even if they have a greater affection for images. This, at any rate, cannot be denied of them. To my mind— and I have said it before—Edith is the most accom-

E

plished technician in verse (unless it be Robert
Bridges) now writing. Her skill dazzles me, who once
attempted rhyme. Further, the Sitwells are all personages. See them in the flesh. See Edith's portrait in the Tate. Further, they all afflict the public
—I mean the poetical public—which is a grand thing
to do. They seldom or never deal with love. They
exult in a scrap. Battle is in the curve of their
nostrils. They issue forth from their bright pavilions
and demand trouble. And few spectacles are more
touching than their gentle, quiet, surprised, ruthless
demeanour when they get it, as they generally do.
Under the leadership of Osbert they have printed
themselves on the map. Osbert is a born impresario
—The Charles B. Cochran of the muse (and let no
high-brow frown disdainfully upon Charles B. Cochran, who has real taste in various arts). Osbert
' presents ' the family, and does it with originality.
Edith is the chief gladiator and, like Eclipse, has
never been beaten. Sacheverell's sole volume, published last year, *The One Hundred and One Harlequins*, attracted, I fear, little notice from the man-
darins. Ninety-three harlequins were omitted from
it (why ?); but despite the vast omission it appeared
to me to be a wonderful portent. It is most damn-
ably difficult, though it seems less difficult to me
this year than it did last. I can still make scarcely
anything of the sixth Harlequin, for example, or of
several other pieces. And when you have finished
the book you feel like nothing at all. But I will
stand till I fall dead by the positive assertion that
there is a very considerable amount of new beauty
in this book. You don't see it clearly. It tantalises

you by its shyness. You see it moving dimly at the ends of misty glades. It exists, however; it is a characteristically Sitwellian Beauty. And more than any other Sitwell book or manifestation *The Hundred and One Harlequins* persuades you to be convinced that the Sitwells live in a world of perceptions and sensations of their own, extraordinarily, insultingly different from anybody else's. Their idiom, perhaps, comprises too many unicorns, harlequins and Kinfoots; it, perhaps, is too busy with the mischief of making one sense do the work of another (seeing sounds, hearing colours, etc., etc.); but the idiom may be modified, is being modified; and, anyhow, it is only the vehicle, not the content. Osbert's *Out of the Flame* is the longest stride forward by the Sitwells up to date. It made me reflect that the trio is still quite young and may develop in astonishing ways. It really excited me; for, in my shortsightedness, I had really looked upon Osbert as simply a satirist, as the slayer of Kinfoots and their kind. And lo ! he is now creating ideal beauty. "Out of the Flame " and " Two Garden Pieces " in particular are lovely and original poems. The satirical part of the volume, while it contains the best satire that Osbert has yet done, is inferior in essential quality to the first part. And I am inclined to think that Mrs. Kinfoot is definitely slain and should be buried."*

What is true of the Sitwells is that they are " insultingly different " from many worthy and possibly quite as intelligent people who happen to resemble

* " Adelphi," August, 1923.

more closely the majority of the English literary world, whether as writers or as readers. The Sitwellian trio's common level of intelligence is indisputably a high one, which of course makes their peculiarities so exasperating to many people who prefer to condemn their work without reading it.

It is not true that the Sitwells " exult in a scrap " as Mr. Bennett so brightly put it, or that they " demand trouble," though battle is certainly " in the curve of their nostrils " and they would make bad enemies, for there is a steely hardness at the core of their amiable personalities. I suspect that the bellicose reputation of these generous hearted and usually rather shy and sensitive people has been created by Osbert Sitwell's impetuous onslaughts on critics who have attacked his sister with offensive personalities which are generally considered to be ill-mannered as well as alien to the spirit of modern criticism.

So there is this much truth in Mr. Bennett's observation. The Sitwells have shown no reluctance for " a scrap " when first attacked. I am not prepared to maintain that they have not sometimes been too impatient under adverse criticism. But the Sitwells have experienced not only artful depreciation of malicious parody; they have had to endure also some nasty-minded slander. And one cannot easily deal with poisonous flies by wielding a sword, though even against the flies they (especially Miss Sitwell) have wasted much energy. Such noisome insects should be left to frosty Time.

CHAPTER FIVE

THREE PERSONALITIES

" Wheels "—the " Façade " recital—Poetry and verse-speaking—Humour and child-like seriousness—Edith Sitwell begins—Osbert and Sacheverell's schooling—War and " peace "—" The Winstonburg Line "—Sacheverell a classical poet; Edith and Osbert romantics—Unicorns—Futurism—Sun, Moon and Wind, symbols of three temperaments.

THE Sitwells constitute as a trio of forces an irritant " foreign body " in the corpus of contemporary English literature, where personality (and still more plausibility) plays as big a part·as merit in making reputations. The irritation is less acute than it was, and a certain measure of approval and even cordial appreciation is extended to some of their work. A part of their peculiarity as writers, which has caused them to be regarded almost as a separate school, can be explained by the biographical facts already mentioned. They have a desire for leadership in their blood, and finding themselves landed in the post-war twentieth century equipped with the intelligence of poets they very naturally are among the most caustic critics of the traditions which their own ancestors helped to establish. As artists they

69

try both to revolt and to lead. Poetry becomes an instrument of power and prestige, and probably the desire to make themselves felt as independent personalities provided their earliest and strongest stimulus to artistic development. But if they have leadership in their blood, it does not come out as the arrogance of the aristocrat of melodrama, but as the arrogance of the warring artist; and, since (as we shall see later in examining their poetic imagery) their literary activity is due largely to a striving to get out of themselves, the artistic arrogance leaves room for the simplicity of nature and a generous fervour which they all possess in varying degrees. They have their full share of the child-like capacity for seeing life as an adventurous game, which belongs conspicuously though not exclusively to artists. The heritage of their ancestral memories is food for their phantasy not less than the materials of common experience. It is fortunate for us that they were born with poetic genius as well as striking personalities, so that their adventures, intellectual and spiritual, strike fresh and clear notes in the diapason of modern thought. Their influence, which is bound to increase, is on the side of internationalism in art. It is in sharp opposition to pettifogging " highbrow " affectations as well as the more dangerous because more popular conservatism of dull or jealous literary Nabobs. It is endlessly at war with the stereotyped and that respectable (and profitable) mediocrity which I once heard a popular novelist urge upon an audience of young writers.

The Sitwells raised their banner with the first publication in 1916 of *Wheels*, an " Annual Anthol-

ogy of Verse " which lasted until 1921 and was intended as a platform for a group of young poets.
" Wheels " was edited by Miss Sitwell, and she and
her brothers were the most frequent contributors to
the anthology which should be regarded as a sowing
of wild oats, though even so the venture was justified. It has now gone the way of all such barriers
of blissful and youthful folly erected against " materialism and the world."

The public recital of " Façade " through Stengerphones in the London Aeolian Hall on June 12, 1923,
was a more startling experiment which again was
but a natural expression of an unusual artistic personality. The idea behind this recital was two-fold;
first, that verse, especially verse with strong rhythms
such as the " Façade " series and other poems in
Bucolic Comedies being an appeal to the ear, should
be *heard*; secondly, that the audience should not be
distracted from hearing the verse by the personality
of the reciter and a sentimental eloquence of enun-
ciation. Accordingly the audience found itself confronted, not with the poet, a lectern, a table and
a carafe, but a strange curtain painted by Mr. Frank
Dobson with a design of three primitive archways,
and a mask in two of these through the mouth of
which stengerphones were pointed at the audience.
Behind the centre masque, of a huge female with
closed eyes and open mouth, Miss Sitwell was
stationed, while Mr. Osbert Sitwell stood behind the
smaller mask. Mr. Sitwell's task was to make an-
nouncements and explanations. Miss Sitwell's recitations were accompanied by a kind of musical
decoration composed by Mr. W. T. Walton. For

the effect of this strange performance, the opinion of the late Gerald Cumberland,* a clever critic of music as well as a poet, is worth quoting. He wrote of it:

" Miss Sitwell half spoke, half shouted, her poems, in strict monotone, emphasising the metre rather than the rhythm, and permitting her voice no expressiveness save on rare occasions when, because of its unexpectedness, and because of the sudden relief it afforded, it had a deeply emotional effect. Her voice, beautiful in tone, full, resonant and clear, could without effort, be heard above the din of the music. It was only by variations in the speed of her delivery that she sought to give additional expressiveness to her words; her command of a fluid *rubato* was consummate; and though I failed sometimes to follow her in the application of her method, I have no doubt that my failure was due to the novelty and the daring of that method. Sometimes she spoke with the rushing rapidity that Bernhardt used to give us twenty years ago in scenes of angry passion, at other times she dropped heavily on a word, remained upon it, giving it a static emphasis. Many of the poems she recited are familiar to me, but her interpretation of them disclosed implications that previously had not been apparent. To this hour I am by no means sure what some of her poems mean, but if I do not understand their beauty, I divine it, and for that reason am all the more attracted, drawn, seduced.

" Mr. Walton's music was clever. It had intuition,

* In *Vogue*, July, 1923.

it understood the words. Its office seemed to be to sprinkle jewels and flowers with an apt hand on the pathway of Miss Sitwell's poetry. Only once did I observe it to fail, and it failed by becoming obvious . . .

" Miss Sitwell, then, has discovered and tried a new method of interpretation. The experiment was well worth making; but I am inclined to think that her success was in no small measure due to the strangeness and beauty of her poetry . . . No other poetry known to me would survive this particular kind of presentation . . .

" And did the audience succeed ? " Cumberland asked finally, and concluded that ' a previous knowledge of Miss Sitwell's work would have helped it to an understanding; but being without that knowledge, it applauded often in the wrong place, spoiling picture after picture by its anxiety to assert and prove its enthusiasm. For a full appreciation of Miss Sitwell's poetry one must have a mind both alert and sensitive :

For only the gay hosannas of flowers
Sound, loud as brass bands, in those heavenly
    bowers.

Not all who visited the Eeolian Hall heard the brazen call of the tiger-lily or saw the gleaming purple of the nightingale's song."

Although the performance was a sign of Sitwellian originality, it is a nice problem whether such a recitation illustrates any sound principle of communica-

tion between poet and audience. Poetry, it is true,
among other things, is musical language; but the
verbal music is purely mental to a cultured reader,
and the experience of listening to a poem spoken is
different in important respects from the experience
of reading it silently. Vocal reading may serve a
purpose similar to the dance and chant of the savage,
but is dancing and chanting (or stengerphone recitation) necessary any more?   The most interesting
point in Gerald Cumberland's criticism of the recital
at the Aeolian Hall was that certain qualities in Miss
Sitwell's poems were manifested for the first time.
But in any poem one may discover something new
during a private reading. It depends upon the reactions set up in the mind of the reader, and these
are influenced by mood. One might argue that such
a recitation induces the right frame of mind, especially when accompanied by decorative music; but
one may ask whether it is not likely to reveal something which is not in the poem at all, but in the
combination of the human voice and the instrumental
music.

These recitations are undoubtedly experiments of
great interest, but how should poetry like the following be spoken, in what tone, with what inflexions
and what emphasis or departures from the metrical
beat?

> Summer, who play about the wood,
> Sway not the branches, fix your mood,
> Deep silence, like the grave, conspire
> Then slant your beams and move your fire.

Let not the shadow of your leaves
Dropping like water from high eaves
Hide from me the sight I've seen
Through changing windows in the green.

Here at the stream side climb down steep
With no noise save where springs do weep
Their sweet tears welling up to join
New coolness with the stream's hot loin.

Out of that glass world heaped breast high
The nymphs climb for your beams to dry,
Then trail your fire down sharp and fine
And let no shadow mar your shine.

These are the opening stanzas of a poem entitled
" Actæon " by Sacheverell Sitwell,* and the reason
for my curiosity about how it should be read is that
I heard the poet read it himself in a recital at the
New Chenil Galleries. He read it badly, I thought,
though in that he was not exceptional among poets,
unfortunately. How many poets can read their own
work aloud effectively? And how many poems ought
to be read aloud? These are questions worthy of
attention; it is possible that the speaking of poetry
is one of the most important as well as the most
neglected of arts.

Certain subtleties of visual imagery, such as the
gleaming hint of the nymphs in sunlit, beryl-green
waters which Mr. Sitwell reveals in the fourth of the
above stanzas, may possibly be gathered up by the

* "Poor Young People" by Edith, Osbert and Sacheverell Sitwell.

mind of a silent reader better than by the ears of a
listener, even if the words are spoken with more art
than the poet displayed. Earlier in 1926 there was
another stengerphone recital of " Façade," the group
of pieces in the *Bucolic Comedies* volume. The
" Façade " poems are nearly all witty nonsense in
witty and clever metrical forms which produce a sort
of jazz music with obvious rhythms and rhymes.
They therefore lent themselves admirably to the purpose of the recital, which was more successful than
the speaking of their own poems by the poets, and
the favourable judgment of Gerald Cumberland in
1923 was corroborated in 1926 by Mr. Ernest Newman in the *Sunday Times.*

" When I read this of Miss Sitwell's," wrote Mr.
Newman :

> " Long steel grass—
>   The white soldiers pass—
>   The light is braying like an ass.
>   See
>   The tall Spanish jade
>   With hair black as nightshade
>   Worn as a cockade !
>   Flee
>   Her eyes' gasconade
>   And her gown's parade
>   (as stiff as a brigade)
>   Tee-hee !

" or this—

> Beside the castanetted sea
> Where stalks Il Capitaneo
> Swaggart braggodocio
> Sword and moustachio—
> He
> Is green as a casada
> And his hair is an Armada,

" or this—

> When,
> Sir
>
> Beelzebub called for his syllabub in the
>   hotel in Hell,

the device of the broken line misses fire with me,
because I am not used to that sort of thing in the
poetry I was brought up on. But when the megaphone bellows the words at me with a sledge-hammer
insistence on the *See, Flee, When* and *Sir*, I get the
poet's idea, and, I must confess, enjoy it."

The poet's idea which **Mr. Newman** appears to
have " got " is just the nursery-rhyme delight of
metre and joyous nonsense, with hints of satre, an
important and characteristic element of Miss Sitwell's work. The poet herself is a keen student of
music as well as of merely verbal sonority and she
uses rhyme constantly to strengthen rhythm and to
produce effects belonging to music rather than to
verse. The extension of the boundaries of verse
towards those of modern music is part of her individual technical achievement. Pieces like " Fox-
Trot," " Hornpipe," " Sir Beelzebub," " Water
Party," " When Don Pasquito," " Something lies

beyond the Scene " are clever musical compositions in verse.

But the reader will perceive that the Sitwellian recitation through a funnel projecting from a painted mask on a painted screen concealing the speaker is only a suggestive text on a wider theme, the theme of the speaking of verse as a public entertainment. The Sitwells had special reasons for the special and original " Façade " recital. When they gave subsequently a personal reading of their own poems, they were, as I have more than hinted, less than satisfying. Indeed only Miss Sitwell, who has a fine and subtle voice well under control, managed, I think, to get her verse and its poetic content across to the audience. It is useful to remember that the Sitwellian reason for the masks, the painted curtain, the musical decoration, and the megaphone was the necessity to be impersonal, to do away with the usual intrusion of the reciter's personality. A hasty person might see the solution of the problem in making each poet recite his own poems. But besides the lamentable fact that few poets can speak beautifully the words they can compose beautifully, there is another important consideration. The personality of the poet responsible for the poem is quite other than the every-day personality which stands on a public platform and recites.

It happens sometimes, by a fortunate coincidence of gifts, that the poet can speak verse well, and is able to speak his own verse in such a way that the majority of people in the audience may get a finer pleasure than could be obtained from silent reading. Mr. Vachell Lindsay, whose verse lends itself admirably to the purposes of public recital, has done excellent propaganda work in the States. Messrs. Gordon Bottomley, John Drinkwater, John Masefield and Harold Munro among others are good speakers of verse, whose public readings advance the cause alike of poetry and of musical speech. Until, however, I heard Miss Marjory Gullan and her Scottish Verse Speaking Choir I still lacked, as most people must lack, the necessary data for estimating the possibilities of verse-speaking. Not only are the poets few who speak verse well, but their selections are usually narrow in range, consisting either of a selection from their own work or of illustrations to a discourse. But apart from this *rara avis*, the reciting poet, I knew only of the performance of so-called " elocutionists " until I had heard the Gullan Choir, and I was therefore a confirmed sceptic about verse-speaking. The colour and sound and movement of words had always seemed to me, as it does to most readers of poetry, a purely mental experience, not dependent upon sensation. But not only did the Choir trained by Miss Gullan speak the words most beautifully of a selection of poetry as wide in range as is suggested by the intervals between Milton and Flecker, Euripides (according to Gilbert Murray) and Robert Bridges; but they gave their audience the full pleasure of metre and rhythm in interplay, which is precisely what few actors on the stage will ever condescend to do when they have to speak verse instead of prose. How many Shakespeare performers allow the audience to feel the music of the verse?

To conclude, it is certain that if people will be

content to speak beautifully and to interpret poems instead of their own emotions, verse-speaking has unlimited possibilities as an entertainment. It will revitalise the spirit of poetry in the modern world, and the poet of to-day may once more become a powerful prophet of to-morrow. Perhaps the final subtleties of lyrical verse must remain beyond the capacity of the human voice, and the most elusive colorature which can be imparted to language, is very likely to be experienced only by the inner ear and eye. At any rate it is early yet to estimate the possibilities of what amounts to a new art in the modern world; that it can make new converts to poetry and intensify the enjoyment of those who already have the imaginative franchise of Parnassus is a fact of such importance that no intelligent reader ought to ignore it. And if I prefer quoting two distinguished music critics on the Façade recitals to praising them myself without severe reservations, nevertheless for her courage and skill in an art so experimental Miss Sitwell has my devout admiration. The virtues of the Sitwell recitals and the quantity of cheap wit which the mere rumour of them evoked afford a useful test on one phase, at least, of Sitwell-ism in the nondescript " literary " world of to-day.

Some of the public appearances of the Sitwells may have given an impression that they are always striking an attitude lest they should be seen as ordinary people. The fact is, and a sympathetic study of their work should convince anybody of this, that they are generally remarkably free from affectation, though they have a peace-disturbing tendency to attack affectation in other people. None of them

lacks a sense of humour, which is somewhat inimical
to pose. Their satirical and adventurous spirit as
artists is closely related to the play impulse. There
is much of the child's directness about their methods.
How well Miss Sitwell understands the childlikeness
of the artist may be seen in the " Introduction " to
her *Children's Tales from the Russian Ballet*, where
she says :

" To a child, logic does not exist, therefore circumstances cannot be the logical outcome of certain acts,
but appear to be extraneous and marvellous growths
. . . much as if a flower could be born without
springing from dark roots in our conventional earth.
To these strange beings, half seraph and half animal,
the simplest things are a matter for wonder, and
are stared at with eyes as fresh as a flower's eyes,
completely unjaded by civilisation."

It is possible to be serious and playful at the same
time, like the child ; or, let us say, the rococo crafts-
man, Jacques Caffieri, because we shall be concerned
with rococo soon.

A fact to be noted, since it has been implied by
more than one writer in the press that the Sitwells
have trodden an effortless and flowery path to fame,
is that they have fought every step of the way into
public recognition. Miss Sitwell's first published
work appeared in the London *Daily Mirror*, thanks
to Mr. Richard Jennings. " Drowned Suns," which
will be found in the *Wooden Pegasus* volume was
actually the first of the many little poems which
appeared in the *Mirror*. The most ambitious piece
in Miss Sitwell's earliest collection of verse, " The

F

Mother," was written at the age of 25, within a year after she began writing. Grimm, with Hans Andersen a good second, provides the staple diet of her imagination from the age of four. At fourteen years of age she did not know of any poets except Shakespeare and Shelley, who happened to be in the library at Renishaw. She had not even heard of Keats until some years later when she saw an edition of him in a shop in Germany and bought it out of a small allowance of pocket-money. At the age of seventeen she suddenly discovered Swinburne. Looking for a birthday present to buy a friend she noticed a copy of *Poems and Ballads*. Unfortunately for the friend's birthday she began to read *Poems and Ballads* and was unable to part with the volume. Poetry now began to occupy in her mind a place rivalling that of music. From early childhood she had studied the piano and was, and still is, a brilliant performer. After Swinburne she made a similarly exciting discovery of modern French poetry, in which of course Baudelaire's work loomed like a dark enchanted forest. I believe Baudelaire has still first place among poets in her mind. The first poem she ever wrote was " Serenade " (in *The Wooden Pegasus*) " during a bout of measles " at the age of twenty-four ! The passion for poetry now sent her away from Renishaw to find congenial soil in London for her aspirations. If Edith Sitwell was thus the family's poetic pioneer, her elder brother seems to have dashed first where many angels fear to tread, composing a horrific drama on Jezebel, which his sister, luckily for him, tore up, advising him to bide a wee.

Both Osbert and Sacheverell Sitwell went through
the usual private school (St. David's, Reigate, in
their case) to prepare for Eton (Tatham's House),
but while Sacheverell went to Balliol for two terms,
Osbert entered the Sherwood Rangers, a yeomanry
regiment, in 1911, at the age of nineteen, and was
attached to the 11th Hussars.   His biographer,
recalling 1914, has mixed memories of " The Cherry
Pickers," as the 11th were called, but as a trooper,
while the subject of this record was of course a member of the " regular Army " officers' mess.   Fortunately for Osbert Sitwell he was able to exchange the
cavalry for the Grenadier Guards at the end of 1912,
and I imagine that he was not a little relieved to
find that one could—with moderation, of course—
reveal there an interest in the lines of a building, the
art of a painter or the style of a writer.   He was
something of an iconoclast even at Eton, for he con-
trived to read enormously.   I have heard that one
of the feats which amused his friends was the reading
of all Shakespeare's works in a week.   He went to
France with the Guards in December 1914 and was
at the battle of Loos.   He returned in May 1916 on
leave and developed blood poisoning from a cut on
a finger got while in the trenches, and was ill for
several years from complications.   One is struck by
the force of individuality which preserved (though
in a sense made) the Osbert Sitwell we know from
that standardisation of public school and British
Army, which is an expression of the importance of
being heir to a baronetcy and scion of an ancient
county family : he ought to be dividing his interest
between hunting, agricultural and golf.   And then

came the dissipating effects of active military service to delay the fulfilment of the culture he had acquired. " Peace-time " found him very angry with the muddlers and the profiteers, the scamps, the fools, and the selfish sentimentalists.   His attempt to enter Parliament in 1918 as a member of a party which was to fare so badly was no doubt the result of a coincidence of his new mood with the traditional convention for one in his position and social class to dabble in politics.   It is not necessary to say that he was in no mood for dabbling or dilettantism.   His sentiments must often have been extremely " Red " in hue, and it is scarcely an accident that one of his first efforts at authorship after the war was the virulent attack (in Bolshevistic free verse) on Mr. Winston Churchill's scheme of a campaign in North Russia.   And *The Winstonburg Line* was published appropriately from " The Bomb Shop " in Charing Cross Road.   It began :

> I think, myself,
> That my new war
> Is one of the nicest we've had ;
> It is not war really,
> It is only a training for the next one,
> And saves the expense
> Of Army Manœuvres.
>
> Besides we have not declared war,
> We are merely restoring order—
> As the Germans did in Belgium,
> And as I hope to do later
> In Ireland.

Some still more unpleasant reflections are put into Mr. Churchill's mouth, and the satirist becomes indiscriminate when he reaches the subject of Gallipoli, because he is already approaching the generalisation of satire and making of Mr. Churchill a type. In the beginning of the seventeenth century the ancestors of the present generation of Sitwells were connected by marriage with the ancestors of Mr. Winston Churchill. Can family tradition have stepped in here to reinforce the opposition of sentiment?

Sacheverell Sitwell was only seventeen when war broke out, and joined the Special Reserve of the Grenadiers. The last piece in his brother's volume, *Argonaut and Juggernaut* is dedicated to him. It reveals Osbert Sitwell's after-the-war sentiments expressed in a mood of apprehension for a brother who seemed very much more than the actual five years younger that the calendar declared. All men who experienced the war as soldiers, however youthful, had such a feeling for those too young to do so. The very title of " The Next War " is a promise of the ferocity of the satire in it.

The youngest of the three Sitwells is intellectually the best trained poet. His studies in Baroque, and of art under the Holy Roman Empire, reveal him as the biggest reader and student of the three, and his description of himself as " mainly self-educated " is not invalidated by a brief period at Oxford. Probably the British Museum Library has meant much more to him than Eton and Balliol combined. Like his brother and sister, he has travelled wide-eyed, but his observations are threaded on abstractions of thought, and he has escaped much of the emotional complication which early experience produced in his brother and sister. In this and other characteristics he is the furthest away from the average centre of the trio. He is the only classically-minded poet of the three. The clear, bright, still, unexpected imagery of his sister and his brother's vehement satire belong to the type of poetry which can be recognised if not easily defined by the label " romantic "; the cultivation of artificiality and a peculiar stage-property by these instinctively romantic poets accounts for the alien atmosphere and occasional self-contradiction in their work. But they are able to cast a dream-light over the most obvious stage-properties, whereas Sacheverell Sitwell has often made his work baldly eccentric by introducing the very same artificialities. Comparatively untroubled (and unstimulated) by the conflicts which have engaged the energies of his brother and sister, he is to a lesser degree a poet who obeys, or can command, the dreaming mind, though the consequences of his intellect being ignited, as " The Venus of Bolsover Castle " proved, are most important to English poetry.

" Stone Venus, fixed and still
　　Holding your raven hair,
　　Who stood you naked there?
　　Who carved you, tracing down those lines
　　Each lover thought his only care
　　Sure that your gold lay hid in mines?

But all your gilding is the Sun
Who paints you with his glorious light :
Your clothes, the shadows, turn and run
Till hidden treasures have you none :
If with your hair a sail you make
You'll float there, naked, on a golden lake.

Now, working with their webbed oars
The swans ride near to where you float :
With steady wing a huge cloud soars
Anchored in Heaven like a boat :
Water and sky, above, below,
Are cool and shining like a bed of snow.

Two apples tumbled from a bough
Your breasts show, lying clear
And straight the swans begin to plough
Till furrows do appear :
Now with their beaks the fruit they try
And air, like glass, breaks with a cry.

Your legs like stems of flowers are seen
All naked from your ankles thin,
The leaves have fallen that were green
And foam lies where the flowers begin :
His plumes and white wings are no cover
And all the world can see your lover.

Gone is the cloud, the swans have flown,
Waiting, you hold your raven hair,
Your naked limbs by sun are shown
For human lover to climb the stair :
You stand above the fountain ledge
For all to see without a hedge.

Know the cruel stratagem to keep you safe !
Hair like a raven's wing, and limbs cool white
Are guarded from us, though they're still in sight,
Down pour the waters in a chilled flood
To damp all those who are not flaming quite,
While he who carved you burns with fiery blood."

This is, however, less explicitly a record of something seen than the long piece in *vers libre* entitled " Bolsover Castle " which is charged with regretful memories of the vanished Past. The note which prefaces the poem shows that his literary and historical interest in Bolsover has combined with the recollections of childhood to evoke his mood. The note runs :

" William Cavendish, first Duke of Newcastle, entertained Charles I at Bolsover Castle in 1634 with a performance of Ben Jonson's Masque of Love's Welcome, for which Inigo Jones designed an elaborate stage-setting."

Obviously this long piece of carefully cut free-verse is an elaboration of history, another of the " variations " he is fond of. But " The Venus of Bolsover Castle " is the result of a fiery fusion of these elements of experience, in which the Venus is a living symbol born from an artist's fiery heart. Childhood and manhood meet to lift the poet into an intenser air.

On the subject of certain eccentric imagery in his verse, he replied to insistent questioning why he had put so many unicorns (not to mention snow and glass) into his *Hundred and One Harlequins* volume :

" Well, they are delightful things. Writers like
Dekker and Greene used them very effectively, I
think . . . What is wrong with ornament ? Every
great poet, including Shakespeare, has his own stage
property. One could go through the works of Keats
and Shelley and lay a finger on all the images and
turns of speech peculiar to them. You could take a
fine passage from ' Prometheus Unbound ' and image
by image, word by word, pick out the Shelleyan
stage-property."

His special liking for the Caroline poets and the
minor Elizabethans, has left marks on his verse,
notably in the metrical neatness of his poems in
stanzaic form, as well as in " stage-property." The
reader will observe that minor Elizabethans, Caroline
poets—and Pope, belong to eras closely involved
with family history.

All three Sitwells seem to remember their early
youth as a period of monotony menacing originality
of thought, and no doubt their reactions against
environment before they found an outlet in poetry
contributed to those qualities which make their work
peculiar and distinct to-day. When the exuberant
Marinetti invaded these shores he quickly made a
devoted convert of Sacheverell Sitwell. Futurism
seemed like a tonic, a means of escape from the
bluntness of familiar experience. It offered violent
brevities and a new keenness of expression. And
though the maturer mind of the present Sacheverell
Sitwell might now feel qualms about its former idol,
the poet gained in experience.

" The reliance of the Italian upon metaphor is

indeed most encouraging counsel for any young poet," he has declared, " since it teaches expansion of the imagination as against rural contraction into which it is so easy to fall in this country . . . I believe also that ' free-verse ' when it is not mangled and cut into arbitrary lengths is a much more sure method of learning the true music of poetry—the use of rhyme than the customary method of beginning one's first attempts at poetry with this adornment.''*

About the same period, from the age of fifteen to, say, eighteen, he was an enthusiastic reader of Chinese classical poetry (in translation) and " Lil-Tai Pe " in *The People's Palace* (1918) is perhaps a keepsake of that time, from memory's reliquary. His tastes in pictorial art also roamed away from the accustomed, finding a resting place in the contemporary novelties of Hokusai's prints, and as an alternative, for a change of mood, the German Primitives.

The personalities of the three poets may appear more distinctly if a general impression is gleaned from their work, an impression which may be summarised in their employment of a single favourite image. The selected image, while it is as representative as possible of something quintessential, must not be regarded as more than a convenient symbol for the striking individuality which belongs to each of the poets notwithstanding that the human weakness for affixing labels and certain qualities which they do share have combined to give them a sort of three-in-one and one-in-three existence in the public eye.

The favourite imagery of Edith Sitwell, speaking

* *All in a Summer Day.*

generally, is, tactile and audile, Osbert's is visual and audile, while Sacheverell's is predominently motile and visual, especially motile, probably a characteristic usual to the philosophic mind which plays with abstractions. To take now a single image, it may be said that Osbert favours the moon, Edith the sun and Sacheverell the wind.

Edith Sitwell, unlike Osbert, has no exuberance or combative energy and is not driven like him to let off steam by waving a banner or stalking down examples of unconscious humour, stupidity or beastliness in society; and whenever she is personally satirical her attack is either self-defensive, or to champion victims of injustice; but it is laboured, and never impetuous. Her energy is mainly devoted to living at a high nervous tension in the service of poetry. In constant contact with the world she remains forlornly outside it. Of her the confession in her poem " Colonel Fantock," " We all have the remote air of a legend " is especially true. If the moon may be regarded as Osbert Sitwell's favourite image, hers is sunlight. Sunlight is to her so beneficent and lovely that she is never weary of inventing for it richly sensuous images. But note it is sunshine rather than the sun; a warmth, a softness and a brightness, as of " gold brocade " rather than a mighty god, an elemental power. Texture, colour and music to preserve her from the dark deeps of thought she knows too well, rather than abstract ideas or the analytical processes of satire constitute her poetic material. For her the sun is not a symbol of vital force merely, but with other vivid images expresses the hunger for colour in life, intense and

refined experience, and revolt from monotony and
spiritual moribundity. And fire is generally associated in her poems with images of animal warmth—
it " purrs " and is " furry."

Osbert Sitwell is the most constantly satirical of
the three poets : his collection of short stories, *Triple
Fugue*, with a fine display of poetic perception, contains some of the best English satire written this
century. This must be due to temperament as well
as experiences like the war. How does his temperament stand revealed by the employment of the moon,
assuming this to be a favourite image ? Among the
attributes of the satirist's paradise, calmness and
coolness are prominent. Fiery, emotional, nervous
and impulsive, he is quickly irritated by the dis-
agreeable things in the world, and seems to turn
gratefully to the quiet of the moon, the impersonal
peace of the night. Notwithstanding a tendency in
the early verse to revel in night-born horrors, the
following youthful couplet from " Spring Hours " is
truer to his mind :

> " Ah ! It is worth full many a sun-gilt hour
> To see the heavens bursting into flower."

The imagery in " Pierrot at the War " is characteristic. Pierrot was happy before the " hurricane of
death " dashed down " the blossoms of the world,"

Dancing throughout the warm moon-haunted night.
Swan-like his floating sleeves, so long and white,
Sailed the blue waters of the dusk.

And in " Nocturne ";

> The sighing woods are still
> Wrapp'd in their age-long boon
> Of mystery and sleep.

Sacheverell Sitwell, the most intellectual of the
three poets, in whose mind conflicting theories play
out ironic comedies, and whose imagination, like
Shelley's, is motile, gives to wind the place in his
poetic heaven, and more than the importance, which
the moon is given in his brother's.   Wind in his
poetry is generally an interfering, personal influence,
a kind of benevolent Mercury moving things and
thoughts.   It serves to spread life, and to refresh
earth and the spirit wearied by the sun's great fire;
it moves the clouds like cloaks above them, or brings
the benison of rain.   Turn to the section entitled
" Hortus Conclusus " in *The Thirteenth Cæsar* and to
certain pieces in *The Hundred and One Harlequins*,
and there, beside a new poetic vision, find what he
does with wind and sun, this sceptical Shelley who
is coming to maturity as the " great war " and the
Russian revolution subside into history.   It is an
object lesson in the eternal youth of poetry and its
immemorial antiquity.   The spirit of youth blossom-
ing on the ancestral tree of time—that is an image
expressing something of the meaning of all three Sitwells of this generation.

CHAPTER SIX

The Meaning of Sitwellism

Norman brigands and adventurous connoisseurs—The
" Who's Who " entries—Baroque and Eighteenth
Century Taste—The Sitwells' Historical Sense—The
Meaning of Baroque and Rococo—Pre-Renaissance
Europe—Modern Psychology—Sitwells not Nihilists
—Refinements of Experience—Pater—Baudelaire—
Rimbaud—Laforgue—Tradition married to Futur-
ism.

BEYOND saying that the Sitwells owe their
artistic personalities in part to an unusual
inheritance it is not easy to fix on any racial
characteristics peculiar to their work except the
adventurous restlessness of their roving Norse ancestors in the dawn of European civilisation. The Sitwells loot Italy, Sicily and Spain with brain and pen
as hungrily as Norse brigands did with fire and
sword. Their characteristics and influence as artists
and critics of life are the logical result of adding
their mental environment to that tradition and culture which they share. They are debtors as well as
contributors to modern European civilisation; and
perhaps some account of their debts will make an
appreciation of their contributions easier.

The entries in *Who's Who*, as regards all three
Sitwells of this generation, are the brightest reading
in that not unamusing work of reference. Those

entries are the logical and illuminating consequence
of the Sitwells being themselves. Sacheverell Sitwell's recreations are: " Listening-in; Mr. J. C.
Squire; and catching that *rara avis* the London
motor omnibus "; Edith Sitwell " in early youth
took an intense dislike to simplicity, Morris dancing,
a sense of humour, and every kind of sport except
reviewer-baiting; and has continued these distastes
ever since." Osbert Sitwell, " The Charles B.
Cochran of the muse," contested Scarborough as a
Liberal at the 1918 General Election, and much
reduced the Conservative majority in this Tory
stronghold which his father used to represent. In
Who's Who he declares that his spare time is spent
" regretting the Bourbons, repartee, and *Tu Quoque*,
and that he " Founded the Rememba Bomba
League, 1924," a piece of information which needs
to be taken with a grain of salt, but which even as
a joke becomes intelligible after a reading of the
section on King Bomba (the last King of the Two
Sicilies) in the entrancing *Discursions on Travel, Art
and Life*. He is also a director of the New Chenil
Galleries in Chelsea and he was a member of the
Committee of the Burlington Fine Arts Club which
organised the memorable exhibition in London in
the summer of 1925 of Seventeenth Century Italian
Art. He contributed to the Club's catalogue of the
Exhibition a breezy Introduction to the paintings,
reproducing a little out of the mass of information
in his brother's *Southern Baroque Art*. The pictures,
most of which came from famous old English country
houses, included some specimens lent by him, for
on a modern scale he is a connoisseur. Although his

tastes are not confined in painting to seventeenth
century work he has a strong partiality for Italian
painters, and so far as is compatible with due admiration for the Titians and Tintorettos, he would rather
praise a della Francesca, or a Carlo Dolci, for besides
honestly admiring these he can wage a battle against
their detractors. One remembers also that the *raison
d'être* of the Magnasco Society, of which Sacheverell
Sitwell was the founder and is the Secretary, is to
encourage the public appreciation of seventeenth and
eighteenth century Italian art. The Magnasco
Society's first exhibition, held in London in October
1924, was a furtherance of the revival which began
with the exhibition of late Italian portraits at the
Palazzo Vecchio in Florence and an exhibition of
eighteenth century Venetian art at the Burlington
Fine Arts Club, before the war; and a fine display
of Seicento and Settocento pictures at the Pitti
Palace in 1921. This revival should succeed in
England. The exhibition in London last summer by
the Burlington Fine Arts Club proved that England
is very rich in the private ownership of late Italian
works, and Osbert Sitwell's Introduction in the
Club's Catalogue clearly revealed how the Sitwells
have taken seventeenth and eighteenth century art
to their bosom, without however losing a sense of
proportion. Osbert Sitwell showed there how, like
the author of *Southern Baroque Art*, he is captivated
by the virtuosity and variety of artists of the type
of Caraveggio and Domenichino, Gentileschi, Strozzi,
" and a hundred others "; but his language never
flares up into hyperbole. " The Baroque epoch was,
in truth, an age of experiment," he says, " and if

for that reason alone, the present generation should
find in those new stirrings much of interest and sympathy.   The classic tradition of Raphael, though
nobly upheld by Guido Reni and the Carracci, was by
others . . . submitted to a thousand modifications."

If he finds in the baroque style a refuge from the
dullness of the stereotyped and unchallenged ver-
dicts of criticism about the Golden Age, his taste
remains valid, like that of his less propagandist
brother and sister, who are equally ready to turn
back from the aftermath of Ruskin to the autumnal
hues of the seventeenth and the enamelled pagodas
of the eighteenth century.   Such epochal styles in
art cannot be limited to painting; they are reflections
of the atmosphere of their own age, in sculpture,
architecture, furniture, literature and music also.
The peculiar inclination of the Sitwells' interest to
Italian artistic expression is due largely to their historical sense.   They are accustomed to think in centuries and in civilisations.   Italy was the source of
that secondary renaissance which reached its most
various expression in seventeenth century pictorial
art.   With the decay of the Italian states and the
dispersal of Italian civilisation, Italian architecture
and painting were taken by the wandering craftsmen
across the whole of civilised Europe.   That Sir
George Sitwell should have a " castle " in Florence
was a factor not less important to the cultivation
of their tastes than his own interest in Italian and
Spanish gardens and art.   They must be as familiar
with architecture and painting in Italy and Spain
as they are with these in England. Possibly more
familiar.

G

The Sitwells' recognition of this historical perspective confirms the interest which they all share in that " Venetian oligarchy " as Disraeli called it, which English society solidified into with the advent of the Hanoverians. The present revival of interest in seventeenth century Italian art is a looking back to the taste of the cultured section of eighteenth century English society. No gentleman's education was complete until he had made the grand tour and returned with the spoils of Italy. And as Osbert Sitwell does not fail to remind us, " the pictures of Guido Reni and Carlo Dolci were the chief trophies of this æsthetic chase."

Lord Chesterfield's epistolary advice to his son not to buy Titians in Italy was explicit enough, and it reflected a taste which persisted until Ruskin became an oracle. Several of these eighteenth century travellers put some of the fruit gleaned in their travels into memoirs and letters, like the rather insular-minded Smollett, who displayed a Sitwellian flair for unjustly neglected works and an equally Sitwellian impatience with much-praised fashionable masterpieces. But Smollet was an uninstructed, bigoted and dirty-minded critic.

In earlier chapters we have seen a historical centering of family interest in the period between the Revolution of 1688, which William Sacheverell helped to bring about, and the decay of the " Venetian oligarchy " under George IV, who showered honours on the husband of Lady Conyngham, the mother of the first Lord Londesborough. During that century and a quarter the principal manifestations of rococo taste and Augustan poetry appeared and

faded. There is no harm in reminding ourselves that
rococo (like Augustan poetics) came to this country
from France, and that the source of this taste for
the ornate and bizarre was baroque art, which came
from Spain and Italy. Baroque and Rococo both
originally were terms referring to applied art;
barroco (Portuguese) or *barrueco* (Spanish) meaning
a rough pearl, being a craft of the jeweller, while
rocaille (French for " rock-work ") was a style of
decoration in furniture and architecture. The essence
of baroque art was decorative elaboration, while that
of Rococo was *imitation* of nature in the toy-like
medium of shells, mother-of-pearl, metal scrolls,
wooden foliage, and miniature Rockies. Such imitation quickly develops into conventional symbolism
and at the root of both Rococo and Baroque, it may
be suspected, was an obedience to elaborate convention pretending to the dignity of human reason.
So in English poetry from Dryden to Pope, the
tendency of a hardening convention was to deepen
the gulf between art and reality,—the reality of
imagination not less than of natural phenomena.
Truth whether to nature or to human dreams was
ousted by arbitrary rules and capricious fancies. In
the literature of France may be seen on a more complete scale the conditions which produced in England
as a masterpiece " The Rape of the Lock." All was
mannerism and imitation with less than the original
contributions of genius which were made in England.*

* Cf. Remy de Gourmont: " Ce qui caracterise la poèsie du
XVIII siècle, c'est l'esprit d'imitation. Ce siècle est romain par
l'imitation. Il imite avec fureur, avec grace, avec tendresse, avec

Baroque and Rococo represented something that
was a reaction against classical harmony and simplicity. They came as an aftermath of the renaissance, and were a partial relapse to the pre-renaissance florid Gothic manner. Racial memories never
die; the renaissance was absorbed by a Europe
whose soul was, and is, mainly the child of that
mediæval mixture of Hebraic religion, Arabian
romance, Roman paganism, and Teutonic democracy.† When Osbert Sitwell freshly discovers merit
in artistic manifestations in Sicily or in Bayreuth,
he is really doing much more than react against
classical æsthetics, although his satirical manner,
directed now against Ruskin and the next moment
against American steel-kings might lend plausibility
to critics who see in the essays of the Sitwell brothers
only a perverse championship of styles condemned
long ago as cheap and florid. Their prose criticism
has a mainly poetic import; it is what a wit of our
day has called a " memory of the future "; it is an
advance report of a " frisson " of deeper self-consciousness coming over Europe. The present reaction
of taste for baroque art, which the Sitwell brothers
have encouraged by the influence of their attention

ironie, avec bêtise; il imite avec conscience; il est chinois en même
tamps que romains. Il y a des modèles. Le mot est imperatif.
Il ne s' agit pas qu'un poète dise l'impression que lui fait la vie:
il faut qu'il regarde Racine et qu'il escalade la montagne." (" La
Culture des Idées: Mallarmé et l'Idée de Decadence.")

† Athenian democracy was dead before Plato and Aristotle
immortalised it. Norse brigands with their incurable conviction
that " an Englishman's home is his castle " resurrected constitu-
tional government on a democratic basis. Serfs were to take the
place of slaves, but the basis even of feudalism was representative
Government. The mixture of Pagan and Christian elements in
European poetry is examined in my study of Francis Thompson.

to a field neglected for nearly a century, is only a
wave on the surface of a current that seems to be
moving across the æsthetic consciousness of Western
civilisation. So far as Western literature is concerned
the movement may be regarded as starting in France
with Baudelaire, though all such delimitations can
never be more than convenient landmarks set up
arbitrarily. But if we take Baudelaire as an original
source, the new æsthetic movement will be seen as
only incidentally a return to certain characteristics
of post-renaissance* Europe. The nineteenth century
brought a psychological *finesse* to poetry which
makes anything like a resurrection of the past impossible. The Sitwellian restlessness is a sign of the
hunger of English poetry for fresh stage-property,
more recondite wit, and the new refinements of sensory experience.

I do not think anything could be more false therefore than to group these conscientious literary craftsmen with a hypothetical class of poets which
" eschews all thought of texture as being another of
those heavy chains clamped on the naked limbs of
poetry," †though it is true that the Sitwells, together
with the rest of Mr. Graves's " Left Wing " act on
the principle that new rhythms, new rhymes, and
new imagery are essential to express the adventurous
experiences of the modern mind. Mr. Graves's analysis is at fault also in its insistence on the revolutionary character of their thought. Just as they pay
careful attention to form, they also are far too well
tutored in the European tradition to be philosophical

* Also pre-renaissance.
† Robert Graves, in " Contemporary Techniques of Poetry."

nihilists.   They are not " expressing their dissatisfaction with all the means at their disposal in metre,
texture, diction " with anything so dull as orthodox
opinions in philosophy and religion; that is at most
occasionally implicit in their search for new poetic
material.   Let them find that material and they are
then merely sensitive human beings with personal
likes and dislikes rooted in emotional experiences
which go back to a childhood unusually rich in historical atmosphere.

The Sitwells, particularly Edith Sitwell, have tried
to obtain more subtle refinements of expression by
confusing the sensory dialects, translating colours in
terms of sound, or sound in terms of touch, for
instance, and what they have all been aiming at is
an escape from the familiar, not to the inexplicable,
like Walter de la Mare, but to the unrecorded.   They
might, with Walter Pater say: " To burn always
with this hard, gem-like flame, to maintain this
ecstasy, is success in life.   In a sense it might even
be said that our failure is to form habits; for, after
all, habit is relative to a stereotyped world, and
meantime it is only the roughness of the eye that
makes any two persons, things, situations, seem
alike . . . With this sense of the splendour of our
experience and of its awful brevity, gathering all we
are into one desperate effort to see and touch, we
shall hardly have time to make theories about the
things we see and touch.   What we have to do is to
be for ever curiously testing new opinions and court-
ing new impressions, never acquiescing in a facile
orthodoxy . . ."

But whereas Baudelaire makes researches into

pathological psychology of set artistic purpose, like his true modern disciple Proust, Sitwellian curiosity is more preoccupied with the æsthetic consequences of experiments in all the arts. They might almost be described as scientists of sensory experience. And it is not impossible to trace their preoccupations and artistic personalities to biographical facts. They leapt out of the bosom of mid-Victorian society into the arms of French Decadence and post-impressionism, Italian futurism and a quite cosmopolitan incoherence. It is a weighty proof of their innate sanity that they so soon found their feet as artists!

In France Rimbaud was one of the disciples of Baudelaire with whom Edith Sitwell has shown much artistic affinity, and by whom she may have been made conscious of her proclivity for enhancing the expressiveness of language by the confusion of the senses. Rimbaud was a decorative poet whose artifice did not exclude vision; it was rather an attempt to record a new vision. In an interesting letter translated by Mr. Rickword* he writes:

" I say that one must be a visionary (voyant), make oneself a VISIONARY. The Poet makes himself a *visionary* by a long immense and reasoned *derangement of all the senses*." He says also : " to examine the unseen and to listen to the unheard being another matter than bringing back the spirit of dead things, Baudelaire is the *first of visionaries*, king of poets, *a true God*."

But if any parallel to the personal and artistic experience of the Sitwells were called for, I should

* " Rimbaud: the boy and the poet: Appendix," by Edgell Rickword.

be inclined to point out Jules Laforgue, the French
poet and contemporary of Rimbaud who died in 1887
at the age twenty-seven.   Born at Montevideo, he
left Uruguay at the age of six, and was taken on
a long sea voyage by his father, who then settled
down at Tarbes.   According to his biographer and
critic M. Ruchon,* this change from a stimulating
and hot climate to the mountainous country of the
Hautes-Pyrenees where he lived until adolescence,
had a profound effect upon Laforgue and led to an
unsettlement of his nature (" une sorte de rupture
d'equilibre ").   From Tarbes the young poet went
to Berlin, to work and to study, and while there
was never free of a nostaglia for the ocean and for
Uruguay, which in the " Fleurs de Bonne Volonté "
he refers to as his homeland.   The nostaglia was,
however, something deeper than this ostensible desire
to revisit a " patrie."   Laforgue soon found a temporary spiritual companionship in philosophers of
disillusionment like Schopenhauer and Hartmann,
but as a consequence of the dislocation between his
early experiences and his later perceptions he becomes the herald of the new tendency of decadent
art : he is the first coherent exponent of free association as a means to the new sensationalism formu-
lated by Pater, and he practised and preached, with
considerable effect upon French poetry, the artist's
duty merely to externalise his sensibility instead of
rendering allegiance to the classical principle of an
Absolute Truth and Beauty.   His objection to the
classical ideal was that it assumed the function of

* Jules Laforgue : " Sa Vie—Son Oeuvre," par François Ruchon
(1924).

art to be the correction of nature, " comme s'il
pouvait être d'autres lois d'harmonie que celles du
tel quel de la vie." The interesting consequence of
trying to put the " *tel quel* de la vie," which may be
translated as, the slice of life, into art is, in its ex-
treme results, as seen in some of the work of Gertrude
Stein, James Joyce and Marcel Proust, to set up a
new artificial *imitation* of nature, very similar in
effect though far more subtle than the reactions
against the classical ideal which produced Baroque
and Rococo. The " slice of life " becomes the " slice
of day-dream," minus intellectual elaboration.

This is of course a highly controversial and debat-
able verdict, and it is offered here as a tentative
explanation of the phenomenon of Sitwellism rather
than as an adequate explanation of contemporary
æsthetic standards and tendencies.*

Such a theory at least sheds some light on the
Sitwellian cult of seventeenth and eighteenth century civilisation, a cult which may have originated
in their interest in family history but which could
not have survived their poetic development without
some æsthetic sustenance in the psychology of
modern artists. But Sitwellism is also a freak product of centuries of bucolic culture and continuously
augmented tradition such as only the English county
family can boast to-day, married to this evanescent
spirit of futurism which is so apt when left single
to degenerate into incoherence and sterile nihilism.

* Although only literature is referred to here, similar movements
are apparent in painting and music, and the tendency is referred
to again in Chapters 8, 9 and 10, Section 2, below.

PART TWO

CHAPTER ONE

THE SLEEPING BEAUTY

For who sleeps once and sees the secret light
   Whereby sleep shows the soul a fairer way
Between the rise and rest of day and night,
   Shall care no more to fare as all men may
But be his place of pain or of delight
   There shall he dwell, beholding night as day.
                     (Swinburne)

    Or is it some more humble lay,
    Familiar matter of to-day?
    Some natural sorrow, loss or pain
    That has been, and may be again?
                  (Wordsworth)

    A secret world of wonders in thyself.
                (James Thompson)

"THE Sleeping Beauty " is a poem of about fifteen hundred lines divided into twenty-six cantos. It is not a purely narrative poem, although it retells Perrault's version of the old legend up to the point where the Prince approaches the sleeping Princess. Quite half of it is lyrical dream poetry inspired by the main theme, which in the hands of this poet, as it did in the hands of Walter de la Mare,* becomes more than was dreamt of in Perrault's philosophy. There is also a decorative element in the poem which only the luxurious Keats has rivalled in modern narrative verse; but the reader accustomed to the melodious coherence of the " Eve of St. Agnes " is likely to find " The Sleeping Beauty " difficult to read with enjoyment. The internal unity of the piece can be felt only vaguely until the disparate elements have been intellectually co-ordinated. Dream-associations of imagery, conscious reflections on life, unexpected names and characters, subtle musical effects of rhythm and metre, and occasional obscurities, sometimes due to free-association and sometimes to the language may well bewilder the reader at first blush. " The Sleeping Beauty," however, is not a denial of the tradition of poetic beauty : it is a renewal of that tradition in much the same sense that the Church of Rome is renewed from epoch to epoch by innovations that are assimilated to the existing code. This question of the rapprochement of poetry and the modern intelligence must be postponed for consideration later. " The Sleeping Beauty " is an outstanding example of poetry which represents the mind diving down into itself, seeking for the lost heaven of childhood, and in its passionate quest flashing thought across the sensory world and rearranging the images of experience. All experience is thought, and all thought is expressed by imagination (in the true sense of this word).

The first canto of the poem is unfortunately obscure from the beginning, and this difficulty for

* In " Henry Brocken."

the reader is heightened by the unexplained introduction of elements which belong to the autobiography of the poet.*   The Queen and the Dowager
Queen (there is no King in Edith Sitwell's story)
are not so much fairy-tale people as those elderly
females who are queer or solemn memories of childhood, and they will readily be identified with the
Duchess of Troy and the Countess, the great grandmother and the grandmother of the poetess.   That
the grandmother is also the wicked fairy Laidronette
means   only   that   the   original   autobiographical
material has been slightly rearranged according to
the principles of poetic licence.   The dark house,
the old gardener, the flat foliage-green water, the
the orchards, the dark wood itself all belong on one
side to the memories which woven together are the
poet's own childhood—a blending of Troy Park,
Renishaw and Scarborough.

   This is an unusual way to approach a narrative
poem; generally these biographical clues are eluci-
dated after a description of the story and the verse.
But the poet is most discouraging to a reader at the
outset, and to clear away some ambiguities now will
make the going easier.   The first passage with the
gardener's song is a kind of *motif* for the whole
poem; it returns at the conclusion.   It suggests at
once the superstitious countryside; the nature-sane
peasant whose mind is nevertheless hospitable to
tales of wonder; the primitive atmosphere in which
folk songs and fairy tales flourish; and the passing
on of an ancient dream to the dreaming mind of a
child.   Interwoven with this fairy-tale element is the

* See quotation on Page 39, above.

historical element, for we find that the gardener is telling the child about her own ancestors while she watches him gathering the plums and figs:

" Beneath those laden boughs," the gardener sighs,
" Dreaming in endlessness, forgotten beauty lies."

and we may suppose that this gardener has a delicate ear for the dream language of Walter de la Mare, as well as a knowledge of Miss Sitwell's family history.

The ancient man, " Wrinkled like old moonlight beneath dark boughs," says the poetess, " told me this old tale of Beauty's mournful christening," and the reader might suppose that until Canto 26 is reached the gardener will be telling the old story. But the opening of Canto 3 shows that the poet has forgotten this little detail:—

Then through the broad green leaves the gardener
    came
With a basket filled with honeyed fruits of dawn
Plucked from the thickest leaves. They heard him
    sing . . .

Of course Miss Sitwell might retort that this is another gardener, and why should not an old gardener tell a fairy story with a still older gardener in it? To which the proper reply would be that she has made one perfect fairy-tale gardener in the first Canto and it would be easier to believe that Shakespeare is Bacon than that the singing gardener in Canto 3 is not the ancient we have already met,

" wrinkled like old moonlight beneath dark boughs."

Let us be warned therefore that Miss Sitwell has little respect for our commonsense notions of the laws of narrative. There is no evidence in this poem that she has ever heard of them. If now we read from beginning to end it will not be very difficult to follow the story and to take note of the poetic largesse scattered on the way.

Canto One, after introducing the gardener, who was

> old as nightingale
> That in the wide leaves tell a thousand Grecian tales

recalls the pomp of a festive occasion long ago at the dark house. The fairies, who step out of eighteenth-century prints into the story,

> ordered their sedan-chairs with great elation

and

> descend from each dark palanquin
> with fanfares and with lute sounds . . .

and walk into the shade where are assembled the country gentlemen,

> so countrified
> That in their rustic grace they try to hide
>
> Their fingers sprouting into leaves; we see
> Them sweet as cherries growing from a tree—
>
> All fire and snow; they grow and never move,
> Each in the grace of his Pan-haunted grove.

H

This is a quite unnecessary but amusing and un-forgettable divagation, from which the reader returns to find the fairies bestowing their gifts on the infant. But

> The slighted Laidronette, the unbidden fay,
> Princess of the Pagodas

follows " a great fanfare." Now the airs tremble, the moonlight seems to blench,

> The apricocks have turned to amber,
> Cold as from the bright nymph Thetis' chamber,

and the far away fountains sigh. Those eighteenth century prints are surely lit up now by a lurid light from German romanticism of the early nineteenth century! Mopping and mowing, in her wide-hooped petticoat and silks, the wicked fay descends. The verse breaks its accustomed movement and screams out her imprecation in a quickened and ejaculatory rhythm very finely aided by repetitions and plangent rhymes. Then she retires to her own palace, is " un-wigged for the night " by black slaves who might owe something of their being to Verlaine. She is revealed ugly as her thoughts. Indeed this Laidron-ette becomes more than the simple wicked fairy of childhood :

> Her dwarfs as round as oranges of amber
> Among the tall trees of the shadow clamber

> And in Night's deep domain she monstrous lies
> With every little wicked dream that flies
> And crawls; with old Bacchantes black with wine,
> Whose very hair has changed into a vine,

And ancient satyrs whose wry wig of roses
Nothing but little rotting shames discloses.
They lie where shadows, cold as the night breeze,
Seem cast by rocks, and never by kind trees.

The poet hates wickedness sunken into effete sensuality. She hates the individuals of that gaudy and artificial society which died out with the reign of the "good Queen," and to which she nevertheless is driven for a spiritual or poetic refuge from "this newer aristocracy, that is an aristocracy neither of brains nor of traditions—a race of dwarfs on stilts, inhabiting hotels carved to look like clouds, clouds carved to look like hotels."*

In Canto Two the chamberlain warns the housekeeper's daughter Malinn (whose name is rather inconsequently introduced later in the poem) that no spindle must remain in the palace. The verse then alters rhythmically to suggest the agitated chattering of the maids. Cross Poll Troy, the housekeeper, chides them, and another lyrical piece follows which reminds one of De la Mare, and also of the songs in Elizabethan plays. It is the housekeeper instructing Anne, a milkmaid, and though it recalls older poets, the poetic individuality is as clear as the metrical skill which converts a song into the staccato orders of "Cross Poll Troy." In the last four lines the stream of the old dame's wrath is turned from Anne to Phœbe.

In Canto Three is the dream gardener's song, which concludes by moving the story forward a little.

* Autobiographical fragment in "New Age," op. cit.

Now in the palace the maidens knead
And bake the little loaves of the bread,
Gold as the sun; they sighing said,
' When will the sun begin to seed
And waken the old Dead—

(cold Dead)?

The first part of Canto Four is a lullaby for the baby Princess (" Do, Do " is of course the Flemish sleep-word, pronounced doe). Presumably the angels come to her while she sleeps, but the concluding portion of the Canto, from

" And when the Queen called for her child, they brought
Only her image, formed to please the Court . . ."

to the end is an example of the poet's obscurity where consecutive thought is needed to describe briefly a sequence of events. And the language is also muddled. Observe the singularly awkward repetition of " her " and " lies " in the four lines which follow the above couplet, and the unnecessary change of tense in an execrable sentence:

An old man with a gardener's hat and red
Poll parrot nose brought her a tiny bed

Whereon lies folded a small poppet rose
That in her dark leaves like a little babe lies close.

The remainder of this Canto is nearly as badly written as the above, and the reader's bewilderment at the whisking off of the Princess to lands of snow until she was weaned from milk of doves and her whisking back again to Court is not lessened by the opening of the following Canto. But since the Dowager Queen reads Latin missals to the peaches she would probably read them to the Princess, and we can understand why the angels' promises to the baby have included

"You shall not say your prayers in Latin."

All Canto Five is indeed recollections of a George the Fourth grande-dame in her old age, of a Georgian manor house and an eighteenth century interior. It follows closely the prose autobiography already quoted in which the picture of Queen Anne, the strawberry beds, the quilted satin (in the prose it is the country house which is of quilted red satin—a vivid image) appear, as well as the stuffed parrot which the old lady believes is still alive. Our Sleeping Beauty seems far away.

In Canto Six she returns in the last line, as Princess Cydalise, after some more recollections. Nobody could understand the following six lines in the first part of this Canto without clues:

The Dowager Queen, a curling Korin wave
That flows for ever past a coral cave

With Dido Queen of Carthage slowly drives
(Her griffin dog that has a thousand lives)

Upon the flat-pearled and fantastic shore
Where curled and turbanned waves sigh "Never-
more,"

Here is another passage from the prose:

" As a small and lonely child, I had my friends.
There was, for instance, Dido, Queen of Carthage
(my little griffin dog)—another dog like a schooner
in full sail, a puffin whose leg had been broken and
who stumped along by my side like a sailorman with
a wooden leg, and a crowned and radiant peacock."

So much for Dido. The curling Korin wave that
flows for ever, and the curled and turbanned waves,
are a reminiscence of a Chinese painting. They can
be found in another piece of Miss Sitwell's prose, the
Introduction to " Children's Tales from the Russian
Ballet," where she writes: " So we sit, in the loneliness of identity, watching the movements growing
and ripening like fruit, or curling with the fantastic
inevitability of waves seen by a Chinese painter."
Immediately after this obscure passage the verse
becomes fine poetry. The contemplation of the old
Dowager Queen

> " sunk beneath a clear still lake
> Of sleep,—so frail with age she cannot wake . . .

produces the thought:

> A strange horizon and a soundless sea
> Must separate wise age from you and me—

and the poetess bursts into a lamenting music that
has the sure freedom of the finest couplets in " Endymion " and a reflective sadness more poignant than

is common with Keats, more in tune with the dominant mood of a poet like Gordon Bottomley.

> O people building castles on the sand
> And taking one another by the hand,
>
> What do you find within each other's eyes?
> What wisdom unknown of the lonely wise?
>
> The promise of what spring, the certainty
> Of what eternal life to come,—what lie?
>
> Only the sound of Time's small muffled drum,
> The sound of footsteps that will never come,
>
> And little marches all beribboned gay
> That lead down the lime avenues away
>
> To the dark grave . . . we for a little weep,
> Then pray a little, sinking into sleep.

The expression of the mood has a tenderness and an unerring delicacy which are characteristics of truly feminine poetry.

The opening lines of Canto Seven suggest the vastness of the Palace nursery:

> In the great nursery where the poppet maids
> Seem small round fruits that grow in leafy glades,
>
> The Princess grew in beauty till she seemed
> That gentle maid of whom Endymion dreamed.

The Princess played " Bo-peep " with the clouds,
the moon would sing to her

Of lovely ladies and forgotten wrongs :

And once she whispered that within the wood
An ancient satyr, wiser than the brood

From which he sprang, within a cloudy cave
Teaches philosophies, both old and grave.

The Princess said, ' With my light step I will be
    gone
To peep within that far cave—but alone.'

Yet in the darkness, her gazelle-like footsteps ran
Far from the cave of that wise satyr-man.

In Canto Fourteen, after she has pricked her finger,
the memory of this dream returns, a very fine poetical
device :

> Her room now seems like some pale cave
> Haunted by a goatish wave . . .

But this is skipping. Cantos Eight and Nine are
preoccupied with " the lost and terrible innocence "
which " bruise the heart and sense " when we gaze
at flowers. The last stanza of Canto Seven is a
pleasing echo of Omar-Fitzgerald :—

Who knows what beauty ripens from dark mould
After the sad wind and the winter's cold ?
But a small wind sighed, colder than the rose
Blooming in desolation, " No one knows."

The pleasing variability of the verse is noticeable in passing from this to the next Canto :

The Princess was young as the innocent flowers
That bloom and love through the bright spring hours.

An evocative passage follows, describing how the ghosts, whimpering and sad, would, like Princess Jehanne, sometimes escape from the cupboard in which Mrs. Troy kept them locked. But the dream-atmosphere is not intensified as the poet intended when we are told that Princess Jehanne seems

> as she glimmers round the room,
> Like a lovely milk-white unicorn
> In a forestial thicket of thorn.

The reader will justly suspect this to be a Sit-wellian trick, and sure enough in the " Children's Tales " the description of the Dance Prelude to Kiki-mora contains a " sewing-machine worked by a nurse like a benevolent white unicorn." Personally, I don't mind the big-boned and placid old nurse of childhood likened to a unicorn (and the unicorn of heraldry is generally benevolent-looking !).   But this fabulous creature is merely a poetic mannerism as an image of a ghostly princess.

Miss Sitwell's extraordinary power of making vivid imagery is clear in Canto Ten, where the Princess visits the farm, and poor Dobbin is the occasion of some sly fun. The next Canto is another nostalgic reflection on the lost paradise of childhood conclud-ing with some weak lines and a very banal final one. The same *motif* flows into the beginning of Canto

Twelve where the Princess playing in the garden at Troy Town addresses the governess as " Mademoiselle Fantoche," which may be considered the feminine gender of " Colonel Fantock." The " Governante " gives advice contrary to the moon's :

> Look not on the infinite wave,
> Dream not of the siren cave,
> Nor hear the cold wind in the tree
> Sigh of worlds we cannot see.

Another remarkable metrical variation, charged with rhythmical echoes of old popular doggerels, and then the Princess is told to go and find Malinn in the still-room and to eat her " creamy curd." But Malinn's fox-red hair has sent the verse of the next Canto into a tumultuous rush of new melody and beautiful images, concluding with a passage like a final bravura, which can be enjoyed without a reduction to commonsense :

> But Malinn's reynard-coloured hair
> Amid the world grown sere
> Still seemed the Javanese sunrise
> Whose wandering music will surprise
> Into cold bird-chattering cries
> The Emperor of China
> Lying on his bier.

In Canto Fourteen Poll Troy is cross. From the still-room window she can hear " The gossiping Naiad of the water " giggling. She chases the maids and rates the Naiad for not working as she does, though her own heart often " flutters like a bird all dream-dark." Malinn meanwhile sits and muses, and sings before the fire. Then she cries out to the Naiad that she has torn her dress. The wicked fairy re-appears through the foliage round the still-room with a spindle, tempting Malinn with promise of a mar-vellous dress. Malinn invites her in. Many things occur suddenly, and the verse responds :

Far off, the Martha-coloured scabious
Grew among dust as old Eusebius,

And underneath the cotton-nightcap trees
Wanders a little cold pig-snouted breeze.

Then in a gown all frilled with foliage like hell's
   fires
And quilled like nests of cockatrices, with the
   light's gold wires

Sewing it stiff, old Laidronette the fairy
Crept through the window of the woodland dairy.

Butter and cream
Turn hard as a jewel,
The shrill flames scream,
The leaves mutter " cruel."

Through the dark jewelled leaves
See the Princess peep
As lovely as eve's
Soft wind of sleep.

She picks up the spindle. ' Oh, the curious bliss ! . .
It pricks my finger now.   How strange this is,—
For I am like that lovely fawn-queen dead
Long since,—pierced through the pool-clear heart,'
   she said.

The last two lines almost make one accept that
image of Princess Jehanne as a glimmering milk-
white unicorn.   Indeed Edith Sitwell constantly
achieves the seemingly impossible like this.

The remainder of the Canto shows still more variations in verse rhythm, the ever changing music ever
throwing up foam-like images :

> Her room now seems like some pale cave
> Haunted by a goatish wave.
>
> Through the curtains—waves of water—
> Comes the housekeeper's young daughter
>
> Where like coral-branches seems
> The candles' light, the candles' gleam.
>
> " Does Echo mourn her lost love there ? "
> Echo is a courtly air
>
> Sighing the name of Cydalise
> Beside clear pools of sleep ; she sees
>
> Her like a nymph in some deep grot
> (Where the wave whispers not)
>
> Like a rose bush in that cave
> Haunted by a goatish wave.

A lovely sleep-song follows this, then we have Canto Sixteen, a remarkable divagation from the story, inspired by rather than describing a country Fair in progress " far from snow-soft sleep." This bucolic world

> seemed a low-hung country of the blind,—
> A sensual touch upon the heart and mind.

And there is more about country gentlemen rooted in earth, like " kind red strawberries " dead to all that is not obvious except when deep asleep, and who therefore

> " wander, aiming with their gun
> At mocking feathered creatures that have learnt
> That movement is but groping into life—"

—a characteristic thought.

But the music " like harsh and crackling rags of laughter" from the loaded roundabouts shrieks " Too late, too late ! " " Life goes, Death never comes " sigh the hollow-hearted people,

> while the bright music like a wave
> Sings of far lands and many a siren cave,

and the blank verse that follows cries upon the "dead innocence and youth that were our own " :—

> But age has brought a little subtle change
> Like the withdrawal caused by the slow dropping
> Of cold sad water on some vast stone image :

A slow withdrawal, a sad gradual change
O'er tragic masks through which strange gods have
    cried.
Till seen through death-cold rents in saturnine
    leaves
They seem, almost, to echo in their form
The saturnine cold laughter of the water.

Which proves Miss Sitwell's ability to write blank
verse when she will. An example of her habit of
using images over again, is afforded by another passage :

And we remember nursery afternoons
When the small music-box of the sweet snow
Gave half-forgotten tunes, and our nurse told
Us tales that fell with the same tinkling notes . . .
" Once on a time," she said, " and long ago,"
Her voice was sweet as the bright-sparkling rime,
The fruits are cold as that sweet music's time—
Yet all those fruits like the bright snow will fade.

The Canto ends in profound pessimism, a hopeless
lament, for

the snow lies cold
Upon our heart, though Midsummer is here

The music-box as an image of half-forgotten childhood occurs in the Introduction to " Children's
Tales " : " The very name ' Children's Tales ' evokes
memories of nursery afternoons when we listened to
the snow's little old musical box, giving out half-

forgotten tunes; afternoons when our old nurse told
us stories that fell with the same tinkling notes as
the snow's tunes . . . 'long ago, and once upon a
time.' "

Canto Seventeen shows us the Court where the
ladies' maids once talked with a gentle malice and
now only the fairies are awake, and the fairies' coach-
men provide a kind of chorus, talking of the great
ladies, the Duchess of Bohea, Madam Cards, the
Marchioness of Gout, who haunted these Palace
gardens, but

> Listen . . . Who is it hearkens at their doors,
> In the vast rooms and endless corridors?

It is Death, and they hit him with their fan. They
are " Chinoiseries, old ghosts of red and white smooth
lacquer."

> What would these ghosts do if the truths they
>   knew,
> That were served up like snow-cold jewelled fruits
> And the enfeathered air of lutes,
> Could be their guests in cold reality?
> They would be shivering,
> Wide-eyed as a negro king
> Seeing the evanescent mirage snow,—
> They would be silenced by the cold
> That is of the spirit, endlessly
> Unfabled and untold.

It is as if the dim Palace of the Sleeping Beauty
has begun to swarm with other memories that belong
to time:

> The daughters of the Silence now are dead,
> And these Chinoiserie ghosts,
> These mummies in dim hosts,
> Tread the long mournful avenues instead,
> Alarm the soul by their cold interest—
> For what can be the purpose of their quest?

What indeed, except to claim the mind of the poet? They are her ancestors* and in sleep she dreams not of heaven but of those lonely Dead. They harry the Soul, their quarry, and " dwindle the bright world down to the gilded glooms of dust," and

> No one knows
> The end there is to dust—it is the soul that
> shall survive them at the last.

Subjective as the poem is now seen to be (in a mood which haunts the later lovely " Elegy on Dead Fashion "), it does return once more to the fairy tale, for two travellers from very far—two dark kings, appear—and sing. One of them, a Soldan, " like le Roi Soleil in all his pride " (a strange retention of the eighteenth century) sings of a lady fair

* The prose autobiographical fragment says: " This story shall be as honest as I can allow it to be, but there is no such thing as truth, there are only points of view; and I have no nature and no character,—only personality and gusts of cold air in the midst of the blackest loneliness. I had, however, roots, and I will tell some stories of these roots of mine because they are significant; some because they give the life of a time that can never come again—the reign of an aristocracy ' bête d'une élégance fabuleuse,' that has faded like the ladies on an ancient Flemish tapestry; some because they show why I am, above all things, a spiritual adventurer, never a spiritual parvenu."

as Daphne. Is he not a dream relative of Heine's
" Count of the Ganges " ? The other traveller, " The
Man from a Far Countree," " will be content with
some far-lesser maid."

> Thus sang these plumed kings, and the winds that
> flow
> Whispered of lands no waking heart may know.

In Canto Nineteen this singing chorus is taken up
by nymphs in their " silk pavilions of the seas,"
another reminder of Heine's " Ideas." The floating
and fantastic images are borne on verse light as
thistle-down that releases fresh rhymes at the lightest
breath of thought.

In Canto Twenty :

> "The Soldan and the King of Ethiop's land "

approach the Queen as suitors of the Princess. Only
a naiad voice sings through " water-rippling leaves,"
while

> The day grew water-pale and cool as eves . . .
> But no one heard the great Magnifico
> Or this pale song, for underneath the low
> Deep bough the Queen slept, while the flowers that
> fall
> Seemed Ariadne's starry coronal.

The singing voice of the naiad is a device adopted
by Walter de la Mare when Henry Brocken penetrates the sleeping forest and finds the wan Prince

I

Ennui at the palace. It was said above that Miss Sitwell's story included no King, but he momentarily appears in the ending of the naiad's song which contains a haunting image:

> The King bows and mutters . . .
> His eyelids seem shutters
> Of a palace pavilion
> Deserted a million
>
> Echoing years ago.

In Heine's "Ideas," the King of the enchanted palace savours more of Grimm, with the rats nosing his nose.

The old queen's dwarfs "drinking their bohea" and the portrait of Queen Anne, which will not answer to "Where is the King's daughter"? occupy Canto Twenty-two, but in the next Canto Mrs. Troy the indefatigable appears, trying to light a fire!

> But suddenly the flames turn green and red
> As unripe fruit; their shrilling fills her head.

Laidronette leaps from the fire and "wags from her chin a cockatrice's beard." Laidronette exults and the unfortunate Mrs. Troy rises up "like a thin shriek." She forgets the Latin for her prayer and her "quilted satin is beyond repair." She thinks of her harmless life and of her youth when

> noises from the sharp green wood
> Burnt and bit my satyr blood

and of her burdensome days.

The shrill flames nodded, beckoned, then lay dead ;
Her wig awry, cross Poll Troy nods her head.

The long dark corridors seem shadow-groves
Wherein a little courtier air still roves . . .

Hours pass and " the soft melodious moonlight
grows," and

Across the silver grass the powdered ghosts
Are wandering in dim and scattered hosts . . .

They pick bunches

Of ghostly flowers all poignant with spring rain
Smelling of youth that will not come again.

The rain has been described several times at intervals, and it appears at this point as a symbol of the
spring, the eternal spring which visited the Princess
in her unfathomable sleep. So too, images like the
" shadow-groves," the " little courtier air " recur as
if they were phrases in a musical composition. The
repeated dream of the princess of the "goatish cave"
has been noticed already. Mrs. Troy's memories of
her youth are almost exactly a repetition of her
daughter Malinn's thoughts as she sat before the fire.
Malinn sang :

The purring fire has a bear's dull fur,
. . . . . .
All night I hear my animal blood
Cry to my youth, " Come to the wood . . .

In the next Canto appear " the public scribe, Noc-
tambulo " ; " Doctor Gradus," representing the
Law ; and " Il Dottore," culling the simples. One is
trying to discover the truth by learning, one seeks
to gain by legal formula an earthly reality out of
what is a lost dream, and the doctor would restore
it by—should we say now psycho-analysis ? Miss
Sitwell says " physic " :

> And the mandarins in Asia,
> In the silken palace of the moon,
> Are all who are left to drink this physic
> That will restore them from a swoon.

Canto Twenty-four brings the dawn to " that world
of leaves," and all things sing an aubade, " cold,
forlorn," with the refrain

> Jane, Jane,
> Forget the pain
> In your heart. Go work again.

By the most surprising ingenuity when in this
mood of infinite regret the poet will bring back the
eighteenth century :

> Like beaux and belles about the Court
> King James the Second held, athwart
>
> The field the sheep run,—foolish graces,
> Periwigs, long Stuart faces . . .

Did ever chanticleer crow to a sleepful maid in

stranger fashion that the world of nature was already
astir ?   But

No answer came. No footsteps now will climb
Down from Jane's attic. She forgets the time,
Her wages, plainness, and how none could love
A maid with cockscomb hair, in Sleep's dark grove.

Canto Twenty-five is brief, but it is beautiful.

And now the brutish forests close around
The beauty sleeping in enchanted ground.

All night, the harsh bucolic winds that grunt
Through those green curtains, help me in my hunt.

Oh the swinish hairy beasts
Of the rough wind
(Wild boars tearing through the forests);
Nothing they will find

But stars like empty wooden nuts
In leaves green and shrill.
Home they go to their rough stye
The clouds . . . and home go I.

Above the wooden shutters
Of my room at morn,
Like bunches of the country flowers
Seem the fresh dawn hours.

And the young dawn creeps
Tiptoe through my room . . .
Never speaks of one who sleeps
In the forest's gloom.

The story in the poem ends here, and the next Canto is an Epilogue which includes the prologue. One might spin several theories out to explain the gardener's song of Jonah who had four-and-twenty daughters, the satyr crone, Jonah's fate, and the gardener's advice to " shun the wave

> Nor ever sigh for a strange land
> And songs no heart can understand,

just as out of my fairy tales a metaphysical mountain can be built.

It is sufficient for an appreciation of the poem to feel the conflict running through it between the blind security of simple happiness and the infinite pain of those who remember the light that never was on sea or land.   Four lines in the First Canto before the story begins show the poet's consciousness of the endless conflict :

> But I will seek again the palace in the wood
> Where never bird shall rouse our sleepy blood
>
> Within the bear-dark forests, far beyond
> This hopeless hunting, or Time's sleepy bond.

The poet in this mood, as in the mood of the " Elegy on Dead Fashions " is more than half in love with death ; but in the elegy there is a serenity born of contemplation, and mortality is crowned with the immortality of memory. Those ephemeral figures dwell in an eternity of the spirit, like the forms which Keats perceived on the Greek vase.

CHAPTER TWO

Terrible Gaiety

" The longing to be out of the world has proved to be the most creative impulse."—*Count Herman Keyserling.*

" Un homme pendant son sommeil est transporté rapidement dans une île au milieu de la mer vaste, sous le grand ciel, seul. Le lendemain il se reveille, il se voit seul, sous le ciel au milieu de la mer bleu . . . Il se demande avec angoisse : où suis-je ? il court, il cherche, il reflêchit, il n'a pas de repos qu'il ne sache où il est.

" Eh bien, l'homme nait, grandit : il regarde, il se trouve sur un iliot isolé dans l'azur et emporté : cependant, il vit, mange, se reproduit, etc., et meurt, sans se demander : où suis-je ? sans s'étonner de rien."—*Jules Laforgue.*

" THE Sleeping Beauty " is not only Miss Sitwell's longest and except for the " Elegy," most ambitious poem, but it interestingly occurs midway in her poetic evolution, which has been much more adventurous than that of her brothers. It embraces the different phases of that evolution, for in " The Sleeping Beauty " are traces of a melodious tenderness and a feminine romanticism, which characterises the earliest work in *The Wooden Pegasus*; the toying with imagery found first in *Clowns' Houses*, which begins as a new vehicle for the mood of hopeless nostalgia, and culminates in the ingenuity and searching wit of *Bucolic Comedies*; there is also at times in "The Sleeping Beauty" a promise of that wise maturity which the attentive reader may find not fully expressed in *Troy Park*, but informing the frequently incoherent imagery. The poems in *Troy Park* lack generally the co-ordinating control of the intellect: the vision of life is much more comprehensive and profound, but remains often implicit.

The earliest work included in *The Wooden Pegasus* appeared first in *The Mother and Other Poems*, a slim, paper-covered volume published in 1915. Never did a destined leader of a school of poetry start a career more modestly. The half-dozen or so pieces in *The Mother*, for the publication of two of which the author made acknowledgments to the *Daily Mirror*, have the imitative melody and occasional happy originality of a highly gifted and immature poet who has studied lovingly the work of other artists. But the artists whose influence lurks in those snatches of melody, wisps of old moonlight, sometimes green glare of melodramatic arc-lamps, are French poets*; probably the poets she discovered for herself and accompanied into what must have been a wonderful new world,—the poets who succeeded the romantics—the Parnassians, Symbolists, and Decadents. Some of the titles alone of the earliest pieces—"Drowned Suns," "The Web of Eros," "Serenade," "The Drunkard," evoke a particular enchanted forest to which Baudelaire cleared

* Not more than one early piece ("Lullaby," which appears in *Twentieth Century Harlequinade* and in *The Wooden Pegasus*) closely resembles any Elizabethan lyric, although Miss Sitwell regards most of these as imitations of the Elizabethans.

a pioneer path in the broken trail of forlorn Edgar
Allen Poe. It is a peculiar spirit which young poets
during the last thirty years have been tempted to
pursue, a spirit of " ivresse "—in poetry a new
flowering of the ancient dark magic, a Dionysian
impulse provided with modern " nerves " and trembling in the control of artistic form, troubling the
mind with exotic beauty. Running through such
poetry is often a vein of sardonic humour and of
irony which may find relief in fierce sarcasm. Swinburne, Beardsley, Dowson and Davidson in England
offer illustrations of all this in their divers manners.
At its extremes of expression, however controlled
the poet's style (and severe technique is often a
decadent corollary of Dionysian inspiration) it becomes frenzied, as in " La Saison en Enfer " when
the perverse Rimbaud screams : " Faim, soif, cris,
danse, danse, danse, danse ! "

" The Mother " and " The Drunkard " are the
most important of Miss Sitwell's earliest pieces,
though the influence of modern French poetry is less
evident in them than in some rather later work in
The Wooden Pegasus.

" The Drunkard " is certainly a remarkable exercise in macabre psychology, or as one might (greatly
daring) say : " neuropathic psychology." A drunken
man having stabbed his wife to death stands before
her in besotted and hysterical rumination :

> Her eyes
> Still watch in wide surprise
>
> The thirsty knife that pitied her,
> But those lids never stir,

> Though creeping Fear still gnaws like pain
> The hollow of her brain."

The drunkard's crazy reflections end in dread of the
unseen :

> And still she never speaks to me.
> She only smiles to see
>
> How in dark corners secret-sly
> New-born Eternity,
>
> All spider-like, doth spin and cast
> Strange threads to hold Time fast.

An ending which will bear comparison with that of
" Porphyria's Lover," although the complete poem
does not touch the heart as Browning's does : it is
melodramatic instead of dramatic. "The Drunkard"
would probably never have been written if the poet
had not admired Baudelaire ; it is significant of Miss
Sitwell's dramatic sense therefore that it reminds one
of " Porphyria's Lover " rather than of " Le Vin de
l'Assassin."

" The Mother " is macabre and yet it does not
leave the reader unmoved. The simplicity of statement and the poignant music of the language bring
this monologue of a murdered mother almost to the
level of tragedy, certainly redeeming the melodramatic element. The poem does not quite succeed
because in the simplicity there is a meagreness suggesting a deficient instead of a reserved force. It
was nevertheless an extraordinarily interesting fail-

ure to find in a first book of verse. The woman whose
thoughts fill the poem has been murdered by her son
for the sake of a paramour. Dead, she must endure
complete knowledge. Undying memory traverses the
anguish of bearing children and of giving them

> Our blood to drink, our hearts for food;

although

> They live to curse us; then they die.

The woman drinks her agony to the dregs, realising
that her son has murdered and robbed her for a
woman who does not even love him. Knowing, too,
that he has paid the penalty of murder. "Little
wicked thoughts" that feed on the helpless Dead
whisper:

> The child she bore with bloody sweat
> And agony has paid his debt.
> Through that bleak face the stark winds play;
> The crows have chased his soul away.

> 'His body is a blackened rag
> Upon the tree—a monstrous flag—.'
> Thus one worm to the other saith.
> Those slow mean servitors of Death.

> They chuckling said: 'Your soul, grown blind
> With anguish, is the shrieking wind
> That blows the flame that never dies
> About his empty, lidless eyes.'

I tore them from my heart, I said :
' The life-blood that my son's hand shed,
That from my broken heart outburst,
I'd give again, to quench his thirst.

' He did no sin.   But cold blind earth
The body was that gave him birth.
All mine, all mine the sin ; the love
I bore him was not deep enough.'

The horrible story in the poem might have been
culled from any criminal record, from the Newgate
Calendar, for instance, like " The Little Ghost Who
Died for Love " in *Troy Park* ; but the choice and
the treatment of the theme are characteristic of post-
Baudelairean decadent poetry.   It is nightmare for
the sake of strangeness.   But Miss Sitwell's style
lacks here the force of inevitable utterance which
Mr. W. H. Davies knows how to impart to so simple
a ballad as " Nell Barnes."   Only a few other poems
—nearly all of them in *The Wooden Pegasus*—appear
to own so directly the formative influence of Baudelaire and his spiritual children, but a mood sometimes
of nostaglia and often sardonic, a mood inspired by
the irony of going on living, so prevalent in modern
French poetry, and occasionally found earlier in the
nineteenth century in German poetry, has found a
ready soil in the poet of *Clowns' Houses* and *The
Wooden Pagasus*.   The mood often receives a dramatic treatment, but it occurs under many guises, often
in playful verses.   It receives a direct though drama-
tised expression in " Duckie," the first of the " Two
Drunkard Songs " in *Clowns' Houses*.   This is as

shocking to the reader's feelings as the most mordant examples of Baudelaire's " spleen." Despairing disillusionment was never voiced by a woman poet, or perhaps by a man, with the simple-hearted and ferocious anguish of Duckie, a drunken and starving prostitute. That terrible refrain

> " Houp-la ! the world is gay ! "

beats on the nerves like the crazy monotony of an African tom-tom, with a merciless insistence hammering at the drunken woman's plight of a trapped animal. " The streets are dancing " with her glee ; " the black streets hurl their stones " at her. The muslined windows " dance like little girls at holiday," and

> " The old are young, the young are old,
> The sunlight pours all whisky-gold !
> Houp-la ! the world is gay ! . . .

She is "a puppet on the string of Chance," dancing through " winds of misery."

> " I was so young and debonair :
> My gay feet trod the summer air,
> Houp-la ! the world is gay !
>
> And now I gnaw my bones for bread
> And lying on my naked bed—
> Houp-la ! the world is gay !
>
> I wish I had a wealth of flesh
> To sell for bread or gnaw afresh.
> Houp-la ! the world is gay ! "

One must go back to " La Belle Heaulmière " for anything like this, but Villon offers regret in place of anguish, remorse in place of this despair.   There is wild remorse in " Duckie "—

" I was so young and debonair "—

but it is overlaid by the desperation of the sensual self threatened with extinction.

The poet of *Clowns' Houses* often passes from poetry of nightmare to a delight in the superficial glister of things.   She reaches this *via* the sombre decoration of decadent poetry and the phantastic art of Beardsley.   " Black coffee," says the author, in a footnote to this poem, " was derived from a drawing by Aubrey Beardsley "; and it is not her only piece inspired by his dainty weirdness and eighteenth-centuryish elegance.   But for a time the sensual world, rather than the sensory, seems to haunt the poet, producing fierce comment and rejection. " Thaïs in Heaven," in *The Wooden Pegasus*, is a verdict upon the climax of Anatole France's novel. The poet asks Thaïs, who, dying weeping, has said " yet only flesh sold we ! "

" if love
Is really Heaven—where *you* rove—
Your kind of love . . . or mine, Thaïs ? "

And if the mud still clings, and if the stars shine like street-lamps, gilding the gutters

" And lighting up your small face where
Thin powder, like a trail of dust,
Shows the mortality of lust . . .
Still black as hissing rain, your hair?

Your body had become your soul . . .
Thaïs,—do spirits crumble whole?

When one thinks how male poets have generally
run to sentimentality in contemplating the women
whose bodies had become their soul, does it not seem
as if only a woman poet could have made so pungent
an answer to the cowardly irony of Anatole France?

The " Four Nocturnes " in *The Wooden Pegasus*
seem to be directly inspired by the *Flowers of Evil*;
but they are not mere pastiche and the careful
carving of the form leaves a soul of flame in at least
three of them. " Vacuum " is surely as good as
anything which the English eighteen-nineties produced in this vein: it is one of the most Baudelairean of English poems. The piece which follows
it, entitled " Et l'on Entend à Peine Leurs Paroles "
expresses the despair of love fallen to lust and converted into hate with an astonishing economy of
means and a quiet violence which puts one in mind
of Lamb's comment on Wordsworth's image of the
sky as " a wide-open eye." It was too violent for
art, he said. One can understand what the mistaken
critic meant reading " Et L'on Entend à Peine Leurs
Paroles " and perhaps indeed several other poems
in this manner by Edith Sitwell. It reminds us of
that remarkable piece of dramatic blank verse at the
end of *Clowns' Houses*, " The Madness of Saul,"

which was an exciting promise—not yet fulfilled—
of an escape of the poet into something quite different
from the work she has published since. " The Madness of Saul " stages : Saul ; Atarah (mother of Saul)
and Tiras ; Amasa (their old nurse) and Chorus of
Ethiopian women.   The dramatic situation is the
meeting of Atarah and Saul after the latter has murdered his brother for the sake of a woman whose
lips " burned the world."   There is much beauty,
as of some dark tropical dream-picture in this strange
Syrian vignette, where the Victorian conventions of
imagery and sonorous verse, exemplified eloquently
in our day by Mr. Sturge Moore, break out into a
fire of images that belong to the young poet herself.
Here are a few of the finely rhetorical lines which
occur in this fiery dramatic poem :

> And then She came, the music of the air,
> And all the old worlds died away like dew.
>
> .   .   .   .   .   .
>
> Behold me broken on the wheel of light.
> My footsteps are the tread of blinded Doom.
>
> .   .   .   .   .   .
>
> And thou art clothed with trembling like the grass.
>
> .   .   .   .   .   .
>
> O thou art veiled with tears like some sad river.

It is the following words of Saul's curse on the
woman who bewitched him which recall the mood
of " Et L'on Entend à Peine Leurs Paroles " and
serve as another reminder that this poet has by no
means escaped the imaginative complexities of sex.

O you are very pale—
White with the dust of æons is your face—
Things ground to powder by the mills of lust,—
And I will sift your dust like whitened ash
From craters of my hate.

These fragmentary quotations must fail to suggest
the exciting effect on the mind of the complete poem,
but the two following extracts may be given on the
ground that they especially reveal the individuality
which this poet was developing in her imagery:

The palaces of light are overthrown
And broken lie the rainbows, their great harps,
With burning music muted by the dust.

.   .   .   .   .   .

Bull-throated now the fires of madness blast.
All space becomes one golden wheel of flame—
The agony of endless moons and suns;
That giant red hole that was the ancient sea
Is filled with wreckage of the ruined sky, . . .

One can only lament the poet's failure to follow
this line of her art, which promised to express certain
emotions of tragic drama in a fresh and striking
imagery. Meanwhile we may go seeking the lines
of poetic development which she has followed, passing from the various lyrical expressions of a tragic
irony through increasingly deliberate essays in decoration to the crystal clarity of a child-like regard of
the world, in which entirely new relations are perceived between the objects of the visible world.

The new decorative element, a kind of playing with
words and images, appears to have resulted in a

K

stumbling upon new aspects of truth, much as a child learns its way about the world by playful experiments. Edith Sitwell's work is often a potent argument for the creative possibilities of that greater freedom of association which has been so misapplied by ultra-futurist poets and novelists and occasionally by herself. She moves towards her new style in *Clowns' Houses* and *The Wooden Pegasus* by cloaking sombre moods in vivid colour and light, and then in lighter moments using these to ornament phantasies. "Fireworks," for example, begins:

> Pink faces—(worlds or flowers or seas or stars)
> You all alike are patterned with hot bars
>
> Of coloured light, and falling where I stand,
> The sharp and rainbow splinters from the band
>
> Seem fireworks, splinters of the Infinite—
> (Glitter of leaves the echoes). And the night
>
> Will weld this dust of bright Infinity
> To forms that we may touch and call and see:—

A further step towards the sophistication of the *Bucolic Comedies* is "Minstrels".:

> Beside the sea, metallic-bright
> And sequined with the noisy light,
> Duennas slowly promenade
> Each like a patch of sudden shade,
>
> While colours like a parokeet
> Shrill loudly to the chattering heat;
> And gowns as white as innocence
> With sudden sweetness take the sense.

Those crested paladins the waves
Are sighing to their tawny slaves
The sands, where, orange-turbanned stand
Opaque black gems—the negro band ! . . .

In the last stanza quoted the poet's method of
stringing ideas like bright beads on a thread of superficial association can be observed in action.   The
real beginning of the metaphors for the sea and the
sands is in the final image of the negro band.   The
dark faces call for orange turbans, which in turn
produce something more Oriental and splendid than
the negroes—and we have paladins and slaves,
crested (which means turbanned) waves and tawny,
not black, slaves.   We have reached India, or certainly the other side of the Red Sea, to the kingdom
of Aroun el Raschid, an equivalent perhaps of the
Elizabethan's exotic " Indies " gorgeously depicted
in the tapestry at Renishaw.

Nevertheless it soon becomes apparent that the
old mood lingers, though running under golden
laughter.   Even " Minstrels " passes from whimsical-
ity to glimpses of Eternity; the queer tunes from the
band gape in the air from the far side of the boundaries of this world; but " Time is hard to kill ! "
sighs the poet.   Elsewhere Time is a drum; it beats
on like the beating of a restless heart in her poems.

Whenever the theme of a poem wanders below the
surface of appearances (until the publication of *Troy
Park*) the same weary and ironical mood supervenes,
and one is driven again to the poet's prose to discover
the source of this disillusioned pessimism behind the
sharpening wit and developing technique.   How

much of the despondency belongs to her own conscious attitude to life? There is something more positive than intellectual doubt, a nescience of the soul sincere and wide-eyed waiting behind her every experience. At this stage she is a poet without faith or hope. In sober prose she declares:

" Life is a perpetual Can-can, and underneath the rays of the stage, seas, buildings, gush from the crude, blue planes and cubes of faces as though they were fiery astral manes. This terrible gaiety is nothing but a rope ladder up which we must climb to escape from bottomless pits. But in what air and under what skies we shall find ourselves when we have climbed to the topmost rung of that ladder, I dare not guess."*

True, this was written to contrast the mentality of western civilised society with the clearer outlook brought to it by the Russian Ballet, but the gist of it is explicit or implicit in too many of the poems for this conscious criticism of life not to be rooted in the deepest emotions of the poet. It is no accident that in writing of the Russian Ballet Miss Sitwell quotes from Rimbaud's *Les Illuminations* and from Laforgue's *Les Moralités Legendaires*. If in Rimbaud she finds the refuge of artificiality, the detached restfulness of a puppet world, it is Laforgue—doomed and disillusioned Laforgue—who supplies the cynicism and ironic flippancy:

" In Petrouchka we see mirrored for us, in these clear sharp outlines and movements, all the philosophy of Laforgue, as the puppets move somnam-

* Introduction to *Children's Tales from the Russian Ballet.*

bulantly through the dark of our hearts. For this
ballet, alone among them all, shatters our glass house
about our ears and leaves us terrified, haunted by
its tragedy. The music, harsh, crackling rags of
laughter, shrieks at us like some brightly-painted
Punch and Judy show, upon grass as shrill as anger,
as dulled as hate. Sometimes it jangles thin as the
wires on which these half-human puppets move; or
a little hurdy-gurdy valse sounds hollow, with the
emptiness of the hearts of passing people, ' vivant de
cans-cans de clocher, disant : " Quel temps fera-t-il
demain," " Voici l'hiver qui vient," " Nous n'avons
pas eu de prunes cette année." ' "

" And (she says) there is one march, quick and
terrible, in which the drum-taps are nothing but the
anguished beat of the clown's heart as he makes his
endless battle against materialism. And we know
that we are watching our own tragedy."

Two noteworthy pieces, " Clowns' Luck " (in *Troy
Park*) and " Clowns' Houses (in *The Wooden
Pegasus*) would reveal clearly enough the poet in this
mood identified with the eternal clown, the fool of
God, even if a great part of her essay on the Russian
Ballet were not found versified in Canto Sixteen of
" The Sleeping Beauty." The world watching the
Ballet is the same as that

> low-hung country of the blind,—
> A sensual touch upon the heart and mind,

the world of the rural Fair. The faith of religion
cannot breathe in the narrow house of the soul

hungering for a realised and unattainable earthly
paradise. Watching the clown in Petrouchka we
" watch our own tragedy," because:

" Do we not all know that little room with the
hopeful tinsel stars and the badly-painted ancestral
portrait of God ? Have we not all battered our heads
through the flimsy paper-walls—only to find blackness ? "

This seems to be a reflection which has its root in
a personal and peculiar experience of youth in revolt
against parental and conventional authority. The
answer to this question is not at all what the poet
expected when she wrote. The majority never do
batter their heads against the walls of seeming
reality, though some are unwillingly battered
through it by circumstance; so most people are not
troubled by a knowledge of their insecurity. They
are like those symbolical country gentlemen, rooted
in *kind* earth. And of those who break down the
flimsy pretences of knowledge and refuse to accept
second-hand truth, some discover a gleam in the
dark and by its light recreate their world. Of those
others who break through " only to find blackness,"
what of those ? Few such lost souls ever tell us
ought of the terrible darkness beyond the walls of
faith and hope. The strength as well as the sensitive
instability of the poet must belong to one who, driven
past the pillars of Hercules into the wastes of the
Unknown, would cling to a broken ship's rudder and
cry out on the elemental storm with a voice still
human. Such artists in this phase of their development use a despairing energy to stretch intelligence

across the yawning void of death. Art becomes a bridge reaching from the unconscious mind to the conscious. A new sanity is salvaged from what is truly insanity; the irrational is interpreted in terms of æsthetic experience; form is fashioned out of chaos, beauty is imposed on the grotesque. The artist though concerned only with personal salvation, is like the builders of coral, contributing without premeditation to a new island of thought in the waters of spiritual nescience. Here, and only here, is the religious import of art.

Miss Sitwell has understood this experience and passed beyond it. She is no longer an unsophisticated poet, and she appears to recognise with increasing clarity her purpose and method as a poet. Drawing freely on the store of family tradition for images suggested by, rather than belonging to the historical past—especially to the seventeenth and eighteenth centuries in England she has supplemented this stage property with a vivid sensory experience of the world which is the fruit of an extremely sensitive nervous system and a mind of corresponding subtlety. In *Bucolic Comedies*, which contains some of her technically most accomplished work, the creations of her peculiarly individual imagination tend towards an inhuman artificiality, or at least to a recondite wit exercised on " still-life " pictures. Emotion becomes stifled, and when it finds a voice is shrill. Everything is sacrificed to an experimental rage in decorative effects. There is a revel of words and images, rhymes and metres, sarcasm and nonsense, humour and irony.

Miss Sitwell has indeed an extraordinarily rich

sense of humour and a love of comic effects which
she can produce with superb skill by metre and
rhythm as well as satirical statement.   There were
hints of the comic sense in " The Sleeping Beauty."
Cross Poll Troy is both laughable and slightly
pathetic; and the verses in Canto Twenty-Two expressing her dismay when Laidronette leaps out of
the fire show the poet as a virtuoso in metres lightly
producing a perfectly calculated effect.   Every accent
and every rhyme and every line-end pause counts.
This skill is displayed nearly everywhere in the
Bucolic Comedies volume, which may be likened to
the roof put upon her toy universe.

Two of the briefest pieces from the section entitled
" Façade " will represent the apex of that toy roof.
Here is No. Eleven :

> Said King Pompey, the emperor's ape,
> Shuddering black in his temporal cape
> Of dust : " The dust is everything—
> The heart to love and the voice to sing,
> Indianopolis,
> And the Acropolis,
> Also the hairy sky that we
> Take for a coverlet comfortably " . . .
> Said the Bishop
> Eating his Ketchup—
> " There still remains Eternity
> (Swelling the diocese)—
> That elephantiasis
> The flunkeyed and trumpeting Sea ! "

At first glance this might be taken for an easy

bit of comic versifying, but it would require a longish essay to translate all the philosophy of this satire on " materialism and the world." And the versifying is much more skilful than it looks. Indeed one might say that the reader who cannot feel how extremely clever this little piece is needs a course of *Bucolic Comedies* from beginning to end. My one qualification of a perfect approval would be that Miss Sitwell really ought not to have overlooked the third imperfect rhyme after " Bishop " and " Ketchup " which obviously was " Hiccough." On the other hand a Bishop who is made to rhyme with Ketchup might be considered *ipso facto* to hiccough. There is, by the way, a reference to the materialists' worship of bigness, dubbed again there " elephantiasis," in Osbert Sitwell's *Discursions on Travel, Art and Life.* It is there the steel king who replaces the bishop in the pillory; but the new satirical term for this vice of a commercial age has clearly been passed on from sister to brother.

Another " Façade " poem is an answer to Browning's cheerful song in " Pippa Passes " (might we say Verlaine's answer?) :—

> " Dame Souris trotte gris dans le noir."
>> Madame Mouse trots
>>> Grey in the black night !
>> Madame Mouse trots :
>>> Furred is the light.
>> The elephant trunks
>> Trumpet from the sea . . .
>> Grey in the black night
>> The mouse trots free.

Hoarse as a dog's bark
The heavy leaves are furled . . .
The cat's in his cradle,
All's well with the world!

Here again the satire is obvious enough without
laboured paraphrasing, and it should be fairly
obvious that the form chosen with its reminiscence
of dainty-stepping triolets and rondeaux is as suited
to the theme as the grinning irregularity of the King
Pompey and the Bishop piece. There is also a faint
flavour of the nursery-rhyme about this which leaves
naked the devastating irony of the reply to " God's
in His Heaven, All's right with the world! " Some
of the images may present a little more difficulty to
the reader, though the only one which can be
accepted as obscure is

" Hoarse as a dog's bark
The heavy leaves are furled."

It is not clear, to begin with, why the leaves, if
heavy (*i.e.*, presumably hanging in stillness) should
be " furled " except to rhyme with " world." But
since the poet says they are furled, they may be
regarded as a token that the day has departed, and
the witching hour has arrived when watch-dogs
delight to bark and bite at cats, a practice which
results in all being well with the world—for Madame
Mouse, who nevertheless keeps her ears open, and
herself in the dark, for " furred is the light." Light
spells cat. The " trumpeting sea " in the previous
piece should have prepared the reader for a fanciful

elaboration of the figure. The pause and rush of sound in

> " The elephant-trunks
> Trumpet from the sea,

is not an effect which Miss Sitwell is going to waste in deference to any owlish view that there are no elephant trunks on the sea. There are spouts of twisted water, for the sea must be rough to disturb the tiny ears of preoccupied Madame Mouse.

It will be seen that these two pieces are not at all light in theme although extremely artificial and witty compositions. The most purely comic pieces do not indeed occur in " Façade," to which the poet attached this preface, a quotation from her Introduction to the *Children's Tales from the Russian Ballet*:

" This modern world is but a thin match-board flooring spread over a shallow hell. For Dante's hell has faded, is dead. Hell is no vastness; there are no more devils who laugh or who weep—only the maimed dwarfs of this life, terrible straining mechanisms crouching in trivial sands, and laughing at the giants' crumbling ! "

CHAPTER THREE

LE PARADIS ARTIFICIEL

" The truest poetry is the most feigning."
                                        —*Shakespeare.*

" I turn with longing to the exquisite conventional
formal life of Arthur Rimbaud's heaven :—' Ces routes
bordées de grilles et de murs, contenant a peine leurs
bosquets ; et les atroces fleurs qu'on appellerait cœurs et
sœurs,—damas damnant de langueur,—possessions de
féeriques aristocraties ultra-rhenanes, Japonaises, Guar-
anies, propres encore a reçevoir la musique des anciens—
et il y a des auberges qui, pour toujours, n'ouvrent déjà
plus ;—il y a des princesses, et si tu n'es pas trop accablé,
—l'étude des astres.' "—*Edith Sitwell.*

THE word " illuminations," the title of the
strange collection of poems in *Metropolitain*
from which Miss Sitwell selected the above
passage was used deliberately by Verlaine in the
English sense, as applied to coloured and decorated
print or manuscript. This immediately suggests
something still and clear and far-away, which is
exactly the effect on the mind of *Les Illuminations*,
an effect which Miss Sitwell found in some of the
Russian ballets.

The Sitwells have all been tempted by the " exquisite, conventional, formal " in art, though Edith

Sitwell undoubtedly was the leader in the quest of an artificial heaven, and has realised it the most satisfyingly, for with her it was a fundamental need. The artificial universe of her brothers is a more purely decorative and toylike thing, though "Country Dance" in Osbert's *Out of the Flame* is close to the spirit of the witty dream poetry which she has produced by mingling emotion with elegant decoration. Here is "Country Dance":

> The Lion and the Unicorn
> Dance now together,
> There in the golden corn—
> For it is summer weather.
>
> The Lion, seen between the sheaves,
> Is more strong than fair,
> Yet he lets the singing thieves
> Rustle through his tawny hair.
>
> As he treads, the red-gold grain
> Curtsies and bows down;
> The birds tear at his ruffled mane,
> Stealing seed to feed Troy Town.
>
> For famine, in that fabled land,
> Grows, as the years pass.
> (Is it golden grain or sand
> From a broken hour-glass?)
>
> Night comes; over azure ground
> Roves an argent breeze:
> The Unicorn can still be found
> Trampling down the fleur-de-lys.

Elegant and moon-white
  As a ghost, the Unicorn
Dances for his own delight
  Under the flowering thorn.

While deep in the sleeping wood
  The Lion breathes heavily,
Though every dove in each tree coo'd
  Yet would he sleep on wearily.

          .   .   .   .   .   .

The Unicorn and Lion strong
  Dance now together
(But surely they did no wrong—
  For it was summer weather?)

In among the red-gold grain,
  Ankle-deep in the Lilies of France—
And I, for one, could scarce refrain
  From joining that heraldic dance.

This is quiet and controlled and playful, without
the morbid intensity of Baudelaire, but evocative,
for it is an almost perfect expression of child-like
phantasy. Generally purely phantastic poetry, and
its creators tend to lose touch with reality, become
absorbed in nightmares and at the mercy of ever
more eccentric impulses of temperament.   In the
quest for a mode of individual expression untrodden
by convention and unthreatened by naturalistic
banality, the poetry of sensations and symbols is
forced to cut a new channel into artificial worlds,
and too often the poets forget Keats's double-edged
dictum that " poetry should surprise by a fine excess

and not by singularity." There is a constant danger of a dissipation of the imagination in mannerisms more rigid than the prevailing artistic conventions. Only the poet with much dynamic force of personality, that is to say with a clearly predominant emotional orientation as well as energy of intellect is likely to survive in the rarified atmosphere of a toy universe filled with eccentric imagery and illuminated by a reactionary idealism. The arch-reactionary in the modern world against conventional values was Baudelaire, and it is to him that we can trace the modern cult of a sort of " still-life " in poetry, superficially resembling but far more subtle than the artificial æsthetic conventions popular in the eighteenth century. The tendency can be traced in modern painting as easily as in poetry ; there it becomes a kind of dream caricature. If a painter suddenly thinks of the tongs of a toasting-fork when looking at the roof on the platform each side of a railway-station, joined by the foot-bridge, he may depict the station in distorted perspective, with all the emphasis upon the prong-like thrust of the two straight and narrow roofs.

By ignoring the wrong-headed rant in Max Nordau's *Degeneration* one may discover some truth about Baudelaire thrown into relief in that book. Quoting *Rêve Parisien*, Nordau says of the poet :

" Such is the world he represents to himself and which fills him with enthusiasm : not an ' irregular ' plant, no sun, no stars, no movement, no noise, nothing but metal and glass, *i.e.*, something like a tin landscape from Nuremberg."

Nordau omitted to say that these visions of Baudelaire belong to the order of nightmares. They are
dreams born of fear; it is the formal beauty of art,
not the world pictured in the poems, which fills
Baudelaire with enthusiasm. The glistening solid,
noiseless world is an escape from his real world; it
is no heaven, but a simple necessity of his poetic
existence. All is cold and still. Flagstones are
mirrors of ice; falling waters are crystal curtains;
waveless waters are polished steel or burnished gold;
light and illuminated objects are flashing jewels.

" These are undoubtedly strange imaginings, anti-
natural, neighbours of hallucination and expressions
of a secret desire for unattainable novelty," wrote
Gautier;* " but, for our part, we prefer them to the
insipid simplicity of the pretended poets who, on
the threadbare canvas of the commonplace, em-
broider, with old wools faded in colour, designs of
bourgeois triviality or of foolish sentimentality;
crowns of roses, green leaves of cabbages and doves
pecking one another. Sometimes we do not fear to
attain the rare at the expense of the shocking, the
fantastic, and the exaggerated. Barbarity of language appeals to us more than platitude. Baudelaire
has this advantage: he can be bad, but he is never
common."

This is a fair comment on much of the eccentric
product of modern literature. Gautier's remarks can
be extended so that the analogy is more complete.
Baudelaire sought peace. His quest produced two
big results, a fresh release of the imagination into

* *The Life and Intimate Memoirs of Charles Baudelaire* by
Théophile Gautier, trans. by Guy Thorne.

"strange and scarce-imaginable regions of romance,"
and a new pungent satire of human life. The satirical
escape from the oppression of things as they are is
the way of Miss Sitwell's brothers more than hers.
There is pungent satire in her *Bucolic Comedies*, but
it is not essential to those playful improvisations in
metre and rhythm. Her wit, like Donne's, gets
changed into witty dream poetry.

We have seen what Osbert Sitwell can do with
" still-life " imagery when the satirical mood is in
abeyance. When Edith Sitwell avails herself of the
artificial paradise she produces a strange new eloquence shot through with the strange hues of
dream. As a realisation of artifice in poetry,
from sheer metrical virtuosity to evocative music,
Bucolic Comedies is one of the most astonishing and
revolutionary volumes of modern verse. It is not
revolutionary in Mr. Graves's sense. The philosophical or social implications of the poetic content
are merely reflections of spiritual realities in the
modern world. But work like *Bucolic Comedies* and
the obscure pieces in the *Troy Park* volume is revolutionary in its effect on poetry : it helps to shift the
prevailing conventions. An American critic discuss-
ing a current of modern interest in the Orient, hastens
to distinguish this " Orient " from the melodramatic
regions which poets from Collins to Byron visited for
opulent material. " When we fly from the obsession
of the familiar, it is growingly apt to be to the more
recondite, or precious, or quintessential, or even perverse embodiments of the strange or far," he says,
and again : " Very modern poetry has set its face
like a flint against all vastness and mystery whatso-

L

ever. These are among what it would call the
' cosmic ' qualities, and from the cosmic its very soul
revolts. That which does allure it in the East is an
amazing tininess and finesse—the delicacy, that is
to say, and the deftness, and the crystalline quality
of the verse of China and Japan. Bits of Chinoiserie
and Japanese jewels five-syllables long are our chief
modern treasure-trove "* This is a somewhat strait-
ened account of the matter, but full of suggestion.

What I have named witty dream poetry is a development of Miss Sitwell's earlier rémance, the desire
for strange beauty and recondite symbols, but without those easy echoes of sweet singers or the false
touch of melodrama. Here the dream enters into,
takes utter possession of the artificial toys, the
lacquer, the tapestry grass and trees, the periwigs,
hooped skirts and heraldic monsters ; and the puppets
of the Russian ballet. " Herodiade " moves in stilted
couplets with a faint music of a half-heard minuet.
In " Winter "

>
> Each clustered bouquet of the snows is
> Like stephanotis and white roses

And where

>
> The Countess sit and plays fantan
> Beneath the portrait of great Queen Anne,
>
> .   .   .   .   .
>
> The shuffled cards like the tail of a bird
> Unfolding its shining plumes are heard . . .

* " Convention and Revolt in Poetry " by John Livingstone Lowes.

In this remote music may be heard the preludings
of the unfaltering delicacy of the " Elegy on Dead
Fashion." The fluent phenomenal universe of nature
is seen stilled and remote in a diminishing mirror
while the still, inanimate objects are re-animated
with a vitality transferred from the world of living
things. " Winter," too, is a dream poem. While
the Countess plays cards

> The maid in her powder-closet soon
> Beneath the fire of the calm full moon
>
> Whose sparkles, rubies, sapphires spill
> For her upon the window sill
>
> Will nod her head, grown sleepy, I wis,
> As Alaciel or Semiramis,
>
> Pasiphaë or the lady Isis,
> Embalmed in the precious air like spices.

The first of the " Two Promenades Sentimentales "
is another example of the poetry of the artificial
paradise, and it has a more subtle wit and a finer
daintiness of image than " The Rape of the Lock,"
though not metrically so nearly perfect.

> Beside the smooth black lacquer sea
> You and I move aimlessly.
>
> The grass is springing pale, alone,
> Tuneless as a quartertone . . .
>
> Remote your face seems, far away
> Beneath the ghostly water, Day,
>
> That laps across you, rustling loud—
> Until you seem a muslined cloud

Beneath your fluted hat's ghost-flowers—
The little dog that runs and cowers

Black as Beelzebub, now tries
To catch the white lace butterflies . . .

But we are mute and move again
Across the wide and endless plain,

Vague as the little nachreous breeze
That plays with gilt rococo seas.

We are two ghosts to-day—each ghost
For ever wandering and lost;

No yesterday and no to-morrow
Know we—neither joy nor sorrow,

For this is the hour when like a swan
The silence floats so still and wan

That bird-songs, silver masks to hide
Strange faces now all sounds have died,

Find but one curdled sheepskin flower
Embodied in this ghostly hour . . .

It is dainty as Watteau, and evocative as a piece
of chamber music by Debussy.

The poet is to be imagined walking with a friend
over a grassy plain like the lonely heath on which
two Travellers suddenly walk out of Time to discover
those primordial Vats de la Mare told us about.*
But to touch the imagination Edith Sitwell employs
a method oppositely different from De la Mares'. An
unbroken mist of rain descends. The sea is smooth

* " The Riddle and other Stories."

and sombre and solid; the air which holds the dimmed daylight is ghostly water, an unbroken mass of fine-spun rain. And so the strange light touch of the breeze drawing closer the threads of the rain into a gleaming whiteness completes the association vaguely suggested at the beginning by the " smooth black lacquer sea." It has the gleam of mother-of-pearl on black lacquer. At once everything is plunged into the unreality of a timeless and two-dimensional world of rococo decoration. And yet the poem is not neatly artificial and uninspiring like a rococo confection, but haunted by a world un-known, for sounds and images are charged with the atmosphere of dream. Such a fusion of artifice and dream-imagery is very rare in poetry; Edith Sitwell with the " Elegy on Dead Fashion " completed her mastery of it; in *Troy Park* when this added love-liness of music is detected, as in the exquisite " Two Night Pieces," she is accomplishing the same miracle. But there is danger of mere eccentricity in quaintness when the underlying motive is not powerful enough. " Spring " begins :

> When spring begins, the maids in flocks
> Walk in soft fields, and their sheepskin locks
>
> Fall shadowless, soft as music, round
> Their jonquil eyelids, and reach the ground.
>
> Where the small fruit-buds begin to harden
> Into sweet tunes in the palace garden
>
> They peck at the fruit-buds' hairy herds
> With their lips like the gentle bills of birds.

The first two couplets evoke a picture which would make the reputation of a painter who could reproduce it in line and colour. But the poet's feeling fails to accompany her wit, when she uses the old device of likening the maiden's lips to the bills of birds. Only Mr. W. H. Davies to-day can be Elizabethan in fancy with complete success, though Professor E. N. da C. Andrade can give us the " airs."

A strange poem in the *Bucolic Comedies* volume, which has more obscurity and less forced quaintness, is " The Doll." This certainly holds difficulties for the unprepared reader. The following analysis is offered with the proviso that I am only trying to explain what the poem means to me and that some other reader may well find a more satisfying interpretation. First let us read the poem.

If cold grew visible again,
We should see bell-flowers on the plain

With shivering stalks, as white as kings
In trembling ermine. Each one rings

A little tune for vespers, matins,
Beneath, the polar sky's red satins;

(The cold is but the shivering
Of the white flower-bells as they ring.)

And Madame A . . . the elegante,
With Madame X, the elephant,

Walked down the lengthy avenue
Carrying their missals; and they knew

The point-lace hanging from the trees
Delicately laughed at these,

Knowing they'd find no angels there
With their apple-curling hair

Because the angels pulled the lapel
Of the priest's robe, left the chapel,

And with my doll and me in Heaven
Hear the nursery clock strike seven.

The angels and myself between us
We break their doll and Lady Venus

Whose curls seem petalled orange-flowers
From Heaven's tree (those perfumed showers

Fall like soft music in the mind).
Seeing my doll they are unkind

To all their toys; they break with joy
The bird-soft bricks that builded Troy—

Laugh at the thought that it could matter.
The angels' feet like bird-feet patter

Across the floor; they leave their needle
Sticking in their samplers, wheedle

Me to let them wash my daughter
Until her face is clear as water,

Her curls like bell-flowers one can see
At Easter jangling on a tree.

    .   .   .   .

But nurse is wandering on the plain,
' Midst cold grown visible again;

She looks for me, and as she walks
On toes the cold has turned to stalks

'Mid shrill steel grasses that dissemble
The cold (bell-flowers that jangle, tremble)

The angels nod their small heads, say
" It's time we were in bed, stopped play " . . .

Yet still the angels overhead
Play with my doll, though I'm in bed !

There is a double line of thought running through
the poem, threading the parallel worlds of childhood
and of the adult's dream world of desire. The very
first image might represent both the nursery window
and the real park where Madame A and Madame X
walk on the way to Chapel. Immediately afterwards
our poet shows the gulf between the conscious recti-
tude of the two adults and their suppressed happiness. " They knew " that the delicate beauty of
the snow on the trees made their stiff prayer-books
seem the tokens of an unconvincing ceremony. But
why do the angels, besides having displayed a
scarcely respectable levity at sight of the priest,

    " with my doll and me in Heaven
Hear the nursery clock strike seven ? "

In " The Sleeping Beauty " the reader will remember
that the fairy promised the princess she need not
go to bed at seven.   Seven o'clock is bedtime.   Here
it is Time's sleepy doorway to the heaven of childish
dreams.   But how do the angels and the child break
their doll the lady Venus " ?   " They," in

> " Seeing my doll they are unkind
>   To all their toys

refers to Madame A and Madame X, the representatives of adult respectability.   Their day-dreams toy
with Venus, whose curls are like the orange-blossom
at weddings.   These old maids stamp on the " bird-
soft " thoughts which are the " bricks that builded
Troy " or the earthly paradise, and there is something of the old " terrible gaiety " in the way they
" laugh at the thought that it could matter."   But
there is magic in the nursery, where the angels
patter across the floor like birds,—like children,*
like thoughts of love.   And the two old maids,
instead of pursing their lips at sight of the child's
doll, re-enter the world of childhood and play with
it.
   The last five couplets of the poem are open to
several interpretations.   I suspect that the poet with
characteristic inconsequence has suddenly discovered
a third thread of thought which hitherto has been
unconscious, the subjective " I."   Instead of Mes-
dames A . . . and X the poet herself now occupies
the adult world which is contiguous to the nursery.

---

* " The child who runs like a sweet singing bird " in " The Child
    who Saw Midas " (ii) (" Troy Park ").

Cold *has* " grown visible again," the snow has returned ; but this snow is colder than the memoried bell-flowers once seen through the nursery window ; and nurse herself has become a fateful apparition. This universal nurse comes for everyone in time and puts them securely to bed. Dreams remain :

> Yet still the angels overhead
> Play with my doll, though I'm in bed !

Some other poet has written that the flimsy fairy phantasies of the children of pre-Christian Europe have outlived the civilisations and the monuments of pagan empires.

The mood of " The Doll " clearly belongs to the poet's maturity, which is represented more consistently in the " Troy Park " volume.

The advance in technique as well as in thought marked by " Troy Park " can best be measured by comparing " The Child who Saw Midas " with " The Sleeping Beauty." " The Child who Saw Midas " is too recondite in wit to be other than difficult to read, but it is exquisitely composed and full of evocative imagery. Here it is possible only to refer the reader who would understand the mood of the poem to Miss Sitwell's " Children's Tales from the Russian Ballet," which is, like the prose autobiographical fragment, a veritable Baedaeker to her poetry. " The Pleasure Gardens "—the last poem in " Troy Park "— is also inspired by the Russian ballet, and Rimbaud.

Probably because Sacheverell Sitwell, except for some moments in his earlier lyrical pieces, is never a romantic poet of dream, his employment of artifice

is always in danger of being bald eccentricity. His
artificial paradise is a philosophical harlequinade,
half satire, half joyful tumbling among the clouds,
fountains, winds and stars. His " gentle, loving,
unicorn " and the silken bearded satyr in Fables
(" Hundred and One Harlequins ") are more natural
though fabulous than the human beings in his sister's
dream poetry.

> The gentle, loving unicorn
> Will never eat the grass—
> All bushes have too many thorns,
> Their leaves are made of brass.
> His horn is given him to take
> The soft fruit from the trees.
> " Please grasp my horn and roughly shake,
> O nymph, among those leaves;
> This pear transfixed upon my horn;
> I cannot reach "—beyond the brim;
> Clutched at; she misses; it has gone.
> " Alas ! You've got it ! " " I can't swim."

> To comb a satyr's silken beard
> Arabian travellers aspire,
> They beg, they bribe; more loved than feared
> The satyr trots to take his hire—
> Fawning, he takes from outstretched hand
> Such fruit his eyes have sometimes seen
> On swaying branches where the land
> Sighs in a soft wind and the green
> Leaves shake beneath the nightingale.
> Thus cajoled, they can reach his beard
> Where gums lie, gathered from the frail
> Flowers he feeds on, where no voice is heard.

It is his Shelleyan swiftness of natural imagery and a welling murmuring music as of cloistral fountains which condone, nay cover over with beauty his quaint " stage-property." The stage-property is not essential. His universe is external and philosophically real. That element in poetry is not his which Edith and Osbert Sitwell are able to use, an element of irresponsible pattern-making which may be almost as purely decorative if not necessarily as unemotional in inspiration as a cameo or the geometrical designs of Arabian mosaic.

CHAPTER FOUR

A Satirical Poet

And though no perfect likeness they can trace;
Yet each pretends to know the Copied Face.
These with false glosses feed their own ill-nature,
And turn to Libel, what was meant a Satire.
                                    —*William Congreve.*

" It is probable that there are no satirists in Heaven.
Probably there are no doctors either. Satire and medi-
cine are our responses to a diseased world . . . Satire
holds the medicine-glass up to human nature . . . To
write satire is an act of faith, not a luxurious exercise."
                                    Robert Lynd.

IT is not possible to read Osbert Sitwell's verse
and prose without realising this ruthless satirist's generosity of nature. He is the most fervent idealist of our three poets, but all the wit of his
acute mind became engaged in striking the stupidities
and cruelties of the world with the shafts of sarcastic
laughter. In the earlier verse he feels too sorely
and expresses his feeling too spontaneously for the
higher levels of satire. His experience of the war was
to embitter while stimulating his idealism at a time
when he was an immature artist. " How shall we
Rise to Greet the Dawn ? " the " Preface Poem " in

Argonaut and Juggernaut, answers that question
with the announcement of two purposes :

> We must create and fashion a new God—
> A God of power, of beauty, and of strength—
> Created painfully, cruelly,
> Labouring from the revulsion of men's minds.

Every word is sincere and relevant. But at first
he can voice only the revulsion of his mind :

> It is not that the money-lenders
> Ply their trade
> Within the sacred places;
> But that the old God
> Has made the Stock Exchange His Temple.

That is neither witty nor cruel. It is angry
sarcasm. He recognises the lack of sharp and
destructive wit in all honest indignation. In the
mood of the Armistice (the piece is dated November
1918) he wants to " cast down the idols of a thousand
years," and therefore, poets are to :

> " Prune the tree of language
>   Of its dead fruit," and
> " Melt up the cliches
>   Into molten metals;
>   Fashion weapons that will scald and flay," . . .
> " Curb this eternal humour and
>   Become witty."

He is innately humorous, and therefore sympathetic,
and so, as " Triple Fugue " showed, he did not suc-

ceed, fortunately, in curbing " this eternal humour,"
though he sharpened his wit. " At the House of
Mrs. Kinfoot " is witty, but it is humorous, too, and
many a reader must have laughed at Mrs. Kinfoot
with an undertone of that pardon which comes from
self-knowledge. The vitriolic touch is

> " The War was splendid, wasn't it ?
>   Oh yes, splendid, splendid,"

because all indifference to the horror of the war was
an unpardonable sin to the satirist who was made
by it. He explicitly says that before the War his
mind " was a confusion of beauty," but with the red
dawn

> " God filled my mouth
>   With the burning pebbles of hatred,
>   And choked my soul
>   With a whirlwind of fury
>   He made my tongue
>   A flaming sword
>   To cut and wither
>   The white soft edges
>   Of their anæmic souls
>   I ridiculed them,
>   I despised them,
>   I loathed them
>   . . . But they had stolen my soul away."

But a time will come when words to scorch and
flay will be his, and

> " In those days my soul shall be restored to me
>   And they shall remember,
>   They shall remember ! "

Several of the pieces in the section entitled " War
Poems " fail thus to strike with the precision of anger
gone cold, but " Sheep Song," a modern version of
a platonic dialogue, lacks nothing of the cruelty,
which the satirist has prayed for. Could anything be
fiercer than the irony of the ending to this poem?
The sheep declare that " we are the greatest sheep
in the world,

> " There are no sheep like us.
>   We come of an imperial bleat."

But they watch the blood " drip and ooze on the
walls " of the world, and their lambs fattened for
slaughter. Their eyes conceal " all the secrets of
the vacuum." They can be moved to action, for
they bleat when the head sheep bleats and

> " When he stampedes
>   —Heavy with foot-rot—
>   We gallop after him
>   Until
>   In our frenzy
>   We trip him up
>   —And a new sheep leads us."

They will not trust herdsmen again because
although these warned them not to stampede,

" Yet we were forced to do so."
 Then the black lamb asked,
 Saying ' Why did we start this glorious Gadarene
  descent ? '
 And the herd bleated angrily,
 ' We went in with clean feet,
 And we will come out with empty heads.
 We gain nothing by it,
 Therefore
 It is a noble thing to do.
 We are stampeding to end stampedes.
 We are fighting for lambs
 Who are never likely to be born.
 When once a sheep gets its blood up
 The goats will remember . . .'
 But the herdsman swooped down
 Shouting
 ' Get back to your pens there.' "

Among these sheep who anger the poet are " the
sentimental wonderless " castigated in " Green
Fly " :

  " The wonderless, the hard, the nice,
   Who scurry at a ray of light,
   Then like a flock of frightened mice,
   Career back into night."

And of these of course are Mrs. Kinfoot and Mrs.
Freudenthal. Incidentally " Sheep-Song " was not
written by a democrat. At least not one who would
be welcomed in the Labour Party. A passage in
" Rhapsode " reveals the other side to the bitter-

M

ness, sympathy with the wronged.   He addresses
those who hoped to be told that the men were happy
fighting and died with a song on their lips:

" You, my dear sir,
   You are so upset
   At being talked to in this way
   That when night
   Has coffin'd this great city
   Beneath the folds of the sun's funeral pall,
   You will have to drink a little more champagne,
   And visit a theatre or perhaps a music-hall.
   What you need (as you rightly say, my dear sir) is
   CHEERING-UP,
   There you will see vastly funny sketches
   Of your fighting countrymen,
   And they will be represented
   As those of whom you may be proud.
   For they cannot talk English properly
   Or express themselves but by swearing;
   Or perhaps they may be shown as drunk.
   But they will all appear cheerful,
   And you will be pleased;
   And as you lurch amiably home, you will laugh,
   And at each laugh
   Another countryman will be dead."

It is the mood and almost the theme of " The
Winstonburg Line."   The language is very simple,
the satire is chiefly remarkable for its personal tone
and shrewd stings; yet it comes clearly from a mind
which beyond its ready anger can see a visionary
goal.
   The " World-Hymn to Moloch " parodies a famous

hymn while satirising the worship of the God of
Battles.

> " Eternal Moloch, strong to slay,
> Do not seek to heal or save.
> Lord, it is the better way,
> Swift to send them to the grave . . .
>
> Cast on us thy crimson smile
> Moloch, lord, we pray to thee,
> Send at least one victory . . ."

But though children cry, widows weep, and the sun
" hides under heaps and hills of dead,"

> " Everywhere the dark floods rise,
> Everywhere our hearts are torn.
> Every day a new Christ dies,
> Every day a devil's born.
> Moloch, lord, we pray to thee,
> Send at least one victory."

The " World-Hymn " was written in 1917. Two
years later he wrote " The Blind Pedlar," who used
to bemoan his blinded eyes,

> " But now I thank God, and am glad
> For what I cannot see this day
> —The young men crippled, old and sad,
> With faces burnt and torn away ;
> Or those who, rich and old ;
> Have battened on the slaughter
> Whose faces, gorged with blood and gold,
> Are creased in purple laughter ! "

The satire produced by the war is seen penetrating
beyond the theme of war, and in " The Eternal

Club " it is identified with a divine anger. The old
men ask " what is it ails the young men of to-day—
To make them bitter and dissatisfied? " and the
poet's comment is

" Two thousand years ago it was the same "

The dull-minded are supposed to say

" Poor Joseph ! How he'll feel about his son ! "

That son seemed " full of life and fun " until

" Something altered him. He tried to chase
    The money-changers from the Temple door.
    White ringlets swung and tears shone in their poor
    Aged eyes. He grew so bitter and found men
    For friends as discontented—lost all count
    Of caste—denied his father, faith, and then
    He preached that dreadful Sermon on the Mount !"

" Rhapsode " dedicated to H. W. Massingham,
and " Modern Abraham " dedicated to Siegfried
Sassoon, were both written in 1917, and show clearly
the genesis of the satirist's anger against the betrayers of the ever-living Christ in Man. Humour soon
breaks in, however, and we have the delicious " Nursery Rhyme," which begins

" The dusky King of Malabar
    Is chief of Eastern Potentates ;
    Yet he wears no clothes except
    The jewels that decency dictates.

A thousand Malabaric wives
    Roam beneath green-tufted palms ;
    Revel in the vileness
    That Bishop Heber psalms."

The mock hymn soon leaves the land of the Eastern
Potentates, for " Mrs. Freudenthal, in furs," who

> " From brioche dreams to mild surprise
> Awakes; the music throbs and purrs.
> The cellist, with albino eyes,
> Rivets attention; is, in fact,
> The very climax . . .
>
> Mrs. Freudenthal day-dreams
> —Ice-spoon half-way to her nose—
> Till the girl in ochre screams,
> Hits out at the girl in rose.
>
> This is not at all the way
> To act in large and smart hotels;
> Angrily the couples sway,
> Eagerly the riot swells.
>
> Girls who cannot act with grace
> Should learn behaviour; stay at home;
> A convent is the proper place.
> Why not join the Church of Rome?
>
> A waiter nearly drops the tray
> —Twenty tea-cups in one hand.
> Now the band joins in the fray,
> Fighting for the Promised Land.
>
> Mrs. Freudenthal resents
> The scene; and slowly rustles out,
> But the orchestra relents,
> Waking from its fever bout."

An effect of irony like that in the " Nursery Rhyme " about Mrs. Freudenthal, arising from the employment of a simple hymn form for satire is noticeable in another piece, in the *Out of the Flame* volume, " English Gothic." This again is written with a playful, but more skilful pen. " English Gothic " is a curious mixture of styles, reminding the reader sometimes of Sacheverell Sitwell's incisive consonantal alliterations and tip-toeing ideas ;

> Above the valley floats a fleet
> Of white, small clouds. Like castanets
> The corn-crakes clack ; down in the street
> Old ladies air their canine pets.
>
> The bells boom out with grumbling tone
> To warn the people of the place
> That soon they'll find, before His Throne,
> Their Maker, with a frowning face."

Sometimes the quaint fantasy might be Edith Sitwell's :

> " The swans who float
> —Wings whiter than the foam of sea—
> Up the episcopal smooth moat,
> Uncurl their necks to ring for tea.
>
> At this sign, in the plump green close,
> The Deans say grace. A hair pomade
> Scents faded air. But still outside
> Stone bishops scale a stone façade."

But we very soon hear the hearty tones of our down-right satirist:

> "Wellington said Waterloo
> Was won upon the playing-fields
> Which thought might comfort clergy who
> Admire the virtue that rank yields."

And inside the cathedral:

> "Tall arches rise to imitate
> The jaws of Jonah's whale. Up flows
> The chant. Thin spinsters sibilate
> Beneath a full blown Gothic rose.
>
> Pillars surge upward, break in spray
> Upon the high and fretted roof;
> But children scream outside—betray
> The urging of a cloven hoof."

Still better is the mockery of the stilted metre of "Church Parade" (in *Argonaut and Juggernaut*) at which "nothing that's of Nature born, should seem so on the Sabbath morn." The piece can be contrasted with "Fireworks" and "The Minstrels" in Edith Sitwell's *Clowns' Houses*, both of them describing impressions of a similar sea-front, a front which is probably that in the story "Low Tide."

In "Church Parade" the sea is "harsh and blue," and

> "concertina waves unfold
> The painted shimmering sands of gold."

There is a terrace glittering hard and white

> "And china flowers, in steel-bound beds,
> Flare out in blues and flaming reds."

The throng

> "paces carefully up and down
> Above a cut-out cardboard town
>
> With prayer-book rigid in each hand,
> They look below at sea and sand.
>
> The round contentment in their eyes
> Betrays their favourite fond surmise,
>
> That all successful at a trade
> Shall tread an Eternal Church Parade,
>
> And every soul that's sleek and fat
> Shall gain a heavenly top-hat.

This is surely the scene at Newborough in "Low Tide"; and a comparison of the verse with the prose is a lesson in artistic exploitation of what has been directly observed :—

"Clasping a black-bound Prayer-Book, divided by a vivid blue or purple watered-silk marker, in a well-gloved hand, and gorgeous as the Queen of Sheba, Miss Frederica and Miss Fanny Cantrell-Cooksey would walk—though "walk" hardly describes such stately progress . . . march . . . saunter

. . . up and down, as would all the other respectable
inhabitants and worthy visitors. It was, consciously,
one of the " prettiest " sights of the town, and, what
was of more importance, an observance that helped
to keep up appearances.

" Innumerable people walked up and down, up
and down—individuals for a moment, then dove-
tailing into the crowd. Most of them were elderly
—though there were a few children—and looked
incongruous in clothes of such elaboration, as must
all people of over middle-age who adopt a minutely
decorated style. For a surfeit of decoration is no
more suitable to the elderly than a surfeit of food.
Up and down they paced, under the hard northern
sunlight, anthropoids that having massacred a
diverse regiment of beasts-of-the-field now masquer-
ade in their pitiable skins; to the latter they have
added the feathers raped from the osprey, and now
look as though decorated for some primitive, some
awful, rite. Up and down they progress, past cream-
painted houses, roofed with damp-blue slates; on
each sill is a box of red geraniums, before each house
a stretch of green, prim grass. Far below, constant
companion to their march, rolls the steely northern
sea; the prospect on the other side varies. The
cream-painted houses give way to golden lawns, the
colour of which is enhanced by an artistic green-
painted cab-shelter covered in by red tiles, a recent
inspiration of the municipal architect: then, again,
follow Gothic stone drinking troughs for beasts, and
portentous stone houses for men. Not all the people
walk. A few drive in large, open cabs, that rumble
slowly; while others, ladies of fabulous age, with

trembling blue lips and palely purple faces, with
hairy growths on the chin, and black bonnets nod-
ding on the top of their helpless heads, are being
drawn along in bath-chairs that are so many black
insects.   As they are rolled past, in a flutter of
bugles, heliotrope-velvet ribbons, and black kid
gloves, there is a trilling of jet like petrified laughter.
Each venerable image, thus trundled, would be
accompanied by a niece or daughter, pale, flat-
looking women with vague but crucified expressions,
like the female saints whose tortures are depicted
by German Primitives.   The aunts and mothers in
their bath-chairs look happy though grim (' poor old
things,' the Misses Cantrell-Cooksey would say,
rather nervously) as they clasp a Prayer Book tightly
in their gloved hands, as if it were a passport for
that equally tedious Heaven which they had prepared for themselves."

In drawing the Misses Cantrell-Cooksey, Osbert
Sitwell was working as an artist in fiction, and pre-
saging the achievement of his first novel, *Before
the Bombardment*.   His poetic satire is usually
generalised and justifies the quotation from Con-
greve, which prefaces the *Triple Fugue* collection of
stories.   These stories prepared us for the kind of
entertainment offered by the novelist of *Before the
Bombardment,* which also has Newborough characters of the same type as those in " Low Tide."
The main characters indeed, a pathetic " lady companion," and her two employers, and the leaders of
respectable society in Newborough are scarcely more
varied than the characters in " Low Tide."   The
vivid and sonorous prose of the author, and some

examples of the Sitwellian vision by which the prose
takes on certain characteristics of modern painting
and commonplace things assume unforgettable significance help to make the reader realise where he is
in the first two chapters. But until the first third
of the novel has been safely traversed, a doubt
remains as to whether the author of the brilliant
sketches in *Triple Fugue* has the power to carry off
a tale of novel-length with a plot which could be
held in a long short story. Gradually the doubt
dissolves in surprise, for his grasp of the strange and
terrible world he has conjured up is tightened with
every chapter, and what seemed a witty satire of a
social era develops into a tragic drama of pathetic
futilities. Once again the wit is happily unable to
suppress the profound humour, an almost Dickensian
sympathy with these victims of misdirected effort.
The social era satirised is that known as " Victorian," which was still putting forth, so the author
assures us, belated buds in remote fastnesses like
Newborough " before the bombardment " of the
European war brought the final disintegrating ex-
plosion. It is a pity that in his sympathy for the
" companion " he should have concluded by having
one of her persecutors blown sky-high by a shell from
a German submarine, for the reader realises that
the satirist has forgotten his rôle for the moment;
in giving way to uncontrolled personal hatred of
what that dreadful old woman represented, he makes
one feel slightly uncomfortable, as if in a theatre
while watching a performance one felt that the chief
actor has suddenly allowed his art to be submerged
in a personal distress. Nevertheless *Before the*

Bombardment is a remarkable first novel, and it
finally dispels the myth that this writer is a dilet-
tante or *petit-maitre* rather than a serious artist.

The imagery in the prose of the novel is less elabor-
ately detailed than in the *Triple Fugue* stories, but
it more frequently gleams with poetry. The images
seem indeed to bear their hall-mark of authorship;
such as " these splintering steel rollers (of the North
Sea) thudded at the town all day," and several other
images, such as green baize for leaves and lawns,
which are shared with the novelist's sister.

Some of the characters in Osbert Sitwell's satirical
verse resemble the people in his prose fiction, for the
range of his antipathies is not wide. In the verse
the figures are more generalised. Mrs. Freudenthal,
and better still, Mrs. Kinfoot (especially in the
very funny pieces " Malgré Soi " and " Paradise
Regained ") are particular instances of poetic thought
in the satire of types. " Subtlety of the Serpent "
(which opens the section " Sing Praises: Satires "
in *Out of the Flame*) is a characteristically poetic
kind of satire on human nature. The curse of the
serpent on Mankind is a mordant summary of the
vanity of " progress "; it is preceded by the serpent's
observation:

It is not only the ignorance of good or evil
That raises the monkey above the man
(Though the man knows evil and therefore prefers
    it),
But the fact that the monkey
Cannot yet disguise the good with bad words,
Or the bad with good words.

A decidedly unorthodox contribution to the theo-logical-evolutionary wrangle.

Never in his satire is the fault of human evil charged to nature. There is nothing like Leopardi's attitude in the *Ginestra*:

> Her count the foe, and against Her,
> Believing that man's race, as is the truth,
> Was fore ordained to be in league,
> Count all mankind as born confederates,
> And embrace all with unfeigned love,
> Rendering and expecting strong and ready succour
> In the changing perils and the anguishes
> Of the common warfare.

Although Osbert Sitwell's general attitude then is decidedly satirical, the visionary power of his satire belongs to the poet. It is revealed by bold general-isations that have something of Swift's insolent sar-casm, as in " The Subtlety of the Serpent "; and it is more obvious in the associations of his imagery. There is a " Nursery Rhyme " in the *Out of the Flame* volume also, entitled " The Rocking Horse," where the satire is quite playful. This piece is delightful :—

> Gentle hills hold on their lap
> Cloud-rippled meadows where tall trees sigh
> The round pool catches in her lap
> Greenness of tree and breadth of sky.

> The mottled thrush that sings, serene,
> Of English worm in English lane,
> Is left behind. We change the scene
> For jungle or for rolling plain.

I rock the children, carry them
On wooden waves that creak like me,
From Joppa to Jerusalem
Or to a far Cerulean sea,

Where flutter winds that bear the balm
And breathing of a million flowers
That nod beneath a feathery palm;
Where, dusky figures, in cool bowers

Of fretted coral, singing, swim
—Forget the missionary who wishes
To make them chant a British hymn
And hide their nakedness from fishes.

.   .   .   .   .   .

Within the limits of this stride
I can encompass any space;
Time's painted gates are open wide,
The old Gods give me their embrace.

Now off to Babylon we trot
To see the hanging gardens, where
Tree, trailing vine and mossy grot
Show proudly in the upper air

Above the shifting evening throng
Like giant galleons with full sails;
These streams have robbed their crystal song
From honey-throated nightingales.

We've watched the Roman legions pass
—The Tower of Babel, waver . . . fall;
We've stroked the wooden horse that was
The hidden breach in great Troy's wall.

Softly the rainbow Pantaloon,
Slinks down night's alley (Oh! how still is
The evening on this wide lagoon,
Where palaces like water-lilies

Float palely in the trembling peace
Of stars and little waves) sails past
Jason, who stole the golden fleece
To nail it high above his mast . . .

. . . In Toad-stool Farm we're back again;
See how the fat and dappled cow
Crouches in buttercups; come rain,
To make the green lush meadows grow!

This is closer to dream poetry than to satire, and
only finds a place here by association with the earlier
" Nursery Rhyme." The poet's advance in technique
in the *Out of the Flame* volume is not revealed by
the comparison of these two pieces.   From the
bitterest satire his mind has a way of escaping to
unforeseen images. The " War-Horse," a social type
the satirist often aims his darts at, is shown in old
age in " A Touch of Nature."   He says

They never wince, nor hurl the mirror at Truth,
Though Old Age disembowel them secretly

Throughout the day, blue shadows in the valley
Hover, crouch down, till dusk will let them rend
The last light on the hills; so wrinkles rally
To overwhelm them at their sudden end—

Which is, when you come to think about it, a very

unexpected image for the final victory of age over
the once " hard and bold," who " trained to a charm
of manner, to a smile—enamelled and embalmed by
Madame Rose " conceal the gnawing of the fear of
death.   " Giardino Publico," a satirical portrait, is
in a mocking tone but it opens:

> Petunias in mass formation,
> An angry rose, a hard carnation,
> Hot yellow grass, a yellow palm,
> Rising giraffe-like into calm
> —All these glare hotly in the sun.
> Behind are woods, *where shadows run*
> *Like water through the dripping shade*
> *That leaves and laughing wind have made.*
> *Here silence, like a silver bird,*
> *Pecks at the fruit-ripe heat* . . .

One is here moreover reminded of that communal
element in the thought of the Sitwells, for these lines
recall the garden pieces in the *Hundred and One
Harlequins* and *The Thirteenth Cæsar*, even while
they seem to carry us into the world of *The Sleeping
Beauty*.   There are indeed constant echoes of and
cross-references to Edith Sitwell's poetry in *Argonaut
and Juggernaut* and *Out of the Flame*.   " Song of
the Fawns " and " Metamorphosis," are almost
exactly paralleled in argument by " Antic Hay " (in
the *Wooden Pegasus*).   It is interesting to observe
however that Osbert Sitwell's two poems are both
moonlight scenes, while " the goat-foot satyrs " in
" Antic Hay " dance in the heat of noon.   The
source of his inspiration for the amusing " Fox

Trot," " When Solomon Met the Queen of Sheba "
(*Out of the Flame*) can easily be found in *Bucolic
Comedies,* though it lacks the superb metrical skill
and the witty bizarrerie of Edith Sitwell's *jeux
d'esprit* in this vein.

The same is true of " Bacchanalia " (*Out of the
Flame*) which opens :

Where little waves claw the golden grapes,
Springing at the terraced hills like lions,
Where pirates swagger in earrings and black-capes
And the roses and the lilies grow like dandelions,
Silenus, I regret to say, sat
On an empty, purple vat,
(And his life-long love, the Lady Venus
Had left for Olympus, shocked at Silenus)—

a complete failure.

But what is of more importance to the reader is
the satirist's individual gift for poetry.   It is
sufficiently exercised without satire to require no
elaborate proof of existence, though in his first comprehensive collection of verse, *Argonaut and Juggernaut,* for all the interesting experiments in non-
satirical poetry (like " The Silence of God " and
Cornucopia ") there is hardly a single satisfying
poem.   The reader gets at moments unexpected
shocks of delight from a phrase or an image which
rises above the general level of its setting.   There
are so many of these examples that no sensitive
reader of *Argonaut and Juggernaut* could have
doubted that a poet's original mind had produced
this variable and inconsistent verse.   " Twentieth
Century Harlequinade " opens :

N

" Fate, malign dotard, weary from his days,
    Too old for memory, yet craving pleasure,
    Now finds the night too long and bitter cold
    —Reminding him of death—the sun too hot."

He hates " the beauty of the universe," but watches
" earthly carnivals," and

" The labour, love, and laughter of our lives."

And then we have lines like these :

    From far within his æon-battered brain
    Well up those wanton, wistful images
    That first beguiled the folk of Bergamo.

The whole piece, which was published first in a
volume with the same title, and which contained
work by his sister as well, reveals the pessimism
about human existence which, as we have seen, Edith
Sitwell constantly expressed in her poetry.   It is
dated March 1916, which explains why

" The face of Fate is wet with other paint
    Than that incarnadines the human clown."

It would be unfair to make the comparison which
the subject of this poem suggests with Walter de la
Mare's " Motley " or " The Marionettes."   In 1916
Osbert Sitwell was still an artistic neophyte.   " Clown
Pondi " is a vignette, a poetic anecdote, which
promised a type of poetry he has however not given
to us, something less laconic than Edgar Lee Masters'

imaginary epitaphs and less deliberately made than Wilfred Gibson's sharp character-sketches in verse. Osbert Sitwell's inexhaustible interest in personal anecdotes and characteristic traits of individuals should certainly have resulted in a collection of " Men and Women " similar to but better than " Clown Pondi." Instead he has so far confined his efforts at characterisation to satirical stories and historical discussions like the masterly passage on King Bomba in his book on " Travel, Art and Life." The " Five Portraits and a Group " in *Out of the Flame* are pure satires. Throughout *Argonaut and Juggernaut*—an admirable title for this collection of angry satires on the war and brave but handicapped pursuit of beauty—the reader is aware of a lavish waste of ideas. What would stock a whole book of a clever verbal juggler is poured into one or two pages of patchy verse. " Night " is full of arresting suggestions, but instead of being what one feels it should have been, a remarkably fine poem, it is an interesting exercise with some unforgettable ideas :--

> The feel of one who listens in the dark,
> Listens to that which happened long ago,
> *Or what will happen after we are dead.*

and

> The awful waiting for a near event,
> Or for a crash to rend the silence deep
> Enveloping a house that always waits—
> *A house that whispers to itself and weeps.*

In " The Return of the Prodigal," a strangely moving poem notwithstanding some crudities, we have :

And all the room is full of whisperings ;
Of moving things that hope I do not heed;
And sudden gusts of wind blow cold upon
My head, lifting the heavy mantle of the air,
Revealing for an instant some vague thought
Snatched from the haunting lumberland of dreams.

In " Progress " we have beggars tramping the city,
crushed by the black shadows of stone houses and
dreaming of the breezy countryside, and the distant
time

When they could chase the jewelled butterfly
Through the green bracken-scented lanes, or sigh
For all the future held so rich and rare;
When, *though they knew it not, their baby cries*
Were lovely as the jewelled butterflies.

In " Black Mass " :

The fear of moonlight falling on a face.
The sound of sobs at night; the fear of laughter

And

Silence has ceased to be a negative,
Become a thing of substance—fills the room
And clings like ivy to the listening walls.

The melodrama of the " Black Mass " is effectively
summarised, after a catalogue of fearsome things:

These fears are gathered, press'd into a room
Vibrating with the wish to damage man;
To put a seal upon his mind and soul—
These fears are fused into a living flame.

In " Cornucopia "

" A harp sobs out its crystal syruppings,"

which is boldness of onomatopœia bordering on rashness.

But in the *Out of the Flame* volume the poet has come into his own. The title-piece does not maintain the poetic intensity unbroken in this free verse, but it comes from a genuine poet. In this poem, like riches poured out of a cornucopia, bright, gay, images, a poignant intimation of childhood, sweeping thoughts and landscapes like the vistas of old Dutch paintings, stream through the careful irregularity of the verse. Nevertheless the use made of the old simple stanzas in " Country Dance " is a finer achievement. Light as a nursery rhyme, it is a perfect artistic success; and that is not too common in poetry. And if there are profounder and more subtle poems than the " Two Garden Pieces," " Neptune in Chains " and " Fountains," that is not to say that these fail. Here is " Fountains " :—

> Proud fountains, wave your plumes,
> Spread out your phœnix-wing,
> Let the tired trees rejoice
> Beneath your blossoming
> (Tired trees you whisper low).
>
> High up, high up, above
> These green and drooping sails,
> A fluttering young wind
> Hovers and dives—but fails
> To steal a foaming feather.

Sail, like a crystal ship,
Above your sea of glass;
Then, with our quickening touch,
Transmute the things that pass
(Come down, cool wind, come down).

All humble things proclaim,
Within your magic net,
Their kinship to the Gods.
More strange and lovely yet.
All lovely things become.

Dead, sculptured stone assumes
The life from which it came;
The kingfisher is now
A moving tongue of flame,
A blue, live tongue of flame—

While birds, less proud of wing,
Crouch, in wind-ruffled shade,
Hide shyly, then pour out,
Their jealous serenade;
. . . Close now your golden wings!

This and the beautiful free-verse of " Neptune in Chains " are examples of the poet's creative power in original forms. The " Two Garden Pieces " and *Out of the Flame* alone are sufficient to arouse the liveliest anticipations of this poet's lyrical verse still to come. But with richer poetry and calmer moods, he remembers that the evil things that made him a satirist still exist. " Sunday afternoon," the last piece but one in *Out of the Flame* flagellates unmer-

cifully the mean-souled rich, lapped in " Sabbath
sentiment, well fed," who dream of Heaven as a
Bank with God as Director, ready to cast a friendly
eye on those who have gold to pay for heavenly
rank.   And the final piece in this volume is " Corpse
Day."   Opening with an idyllic picture of midsummer dusk, it then tells of

" Our Lord Jesus, the Son of Man."

leaning down from heaven and smiling to hear the
sounds of rejoicing on earth. " It was in the Christian
Continent especially that the people chanted hymns
and paens of joy."

But it seemed to Our Lord
That through the noisy cries of triumph
He could still detect
A bitter sobbing
—The continuous weeping of widows and children
Which had haunted Him for so long,
Though He saw only
The bonfires,
The arches of triumph,
The processions,
And the fireworks
That soared up
Through the darkening sky,
To fall in showers of flame
Upon the citadel of Heaven.
As a rocket burst,
There fell from it,
Screaming in horror,

Hundreds of men
Twisted into the likeness of animals
—Writhing men
Without feet,
Without legs,
Without arms,
Without faces . . .
The earth-cities still rejoiced.
Old, fat men leant out to cheer
From bone-built palaces.
Gold flowed like blood
Through the streets;
Crowds became drunk
On liquor distilled from corpses.
And peering down
The Son of Man looked into the world;
He saw
That within the churches and the temples
His image had been set up;
But, from time to time,
Through twenty centuries,
The priests had touched up the countenance
So as to make war more easy
Or intimidate the people—
Until now the face
Had become the face of Moloch!
The people did not notice
The change
. . . But Jesus wept!

It is a strange perversity of judgment which
declares a satirist like this to be irreligious or callous.

CHAPTER FIVE

PROSE SATIRE AND URBANITY

I wear my pen as other do their sword
To each affronting sot I meet, the word
Is *satisfaction* : straight to thrusts I go,
And pointed satire runs him through and through.
                                        —*John Oldham.*

For travel is like a drug that permeates the mind with
an indefinite but unusual tinge, stimulating and releas-
ing, imparting a greater significance than they possess
to the things that interest and amuse it.—*Osbert Sitwell.*

SOMETHING that belongs to the spirit of the
author of *Heroes and Hero Worship* is in the
Sitwell brothers. Carlyle was a hero-wor-
shipper with a purpose; the hero was to him the
great enemy of stupidity and dullness. The Sitwells
reserve their keenest admiration for those individuals
whose eminence is due to magnificent and lavish
achievement, and their keenest curiosity for supreme
examples of meanness and dullness in vice. The two
characters who receive the most careful attention
and some of the best prose in the sparkling *Discursions on Travel, Art and Life* are King Bomba of
Naples and Sicily, and Gabriele D'Annunzio. The
author's interest in Luca Giordano and other baroque
artists is tinged with admiration for their terrific

energy, versatility and prolific output, and one feels
that he allows eulogy of these virtues to fill the room
which a severer criticism of the quality of such work
ought to occupy.

The Sitwells' interest in the autocrat cannot arise
from a love of autocrats in general; they have—and
for the same reasons as Shelley—a Shelleyan jealousy
of external authority.   Their interest then is due
rather to a poetic appreciation, which most of us can
share, for the extravagant.   Extravagance is a relief
from monotony.   Either circumstances or individual
genius can cause a human being to resemble a
creation of art in being impossibly great or grotesque.
Describing the degeneracy of the Bourbon Kings of
Spain and Naples in *Southern Baroque Art* Sacheverell Sitwell is no more friendly to the theories of
absolute rule and divine right which produced them
than his brother in the *Discursions*.   They both have
a profound respect for the dignity of man as he may
be and a scorn of what in degeneracy he may become.
A frequent motive of their travelling across epochs
and civilisations is the escape from the dangerous
levelling process and the standardisation of modern
civilisation, satirised in *Triple Fugue*.   They are
æsthetic Vikings seeking " the rare and unattainable
brightness " which like a mirage hovers over the
tracts of history and in the works that have outlived
the societies which produced them.

There is more praise than satire in the *Discursions*
of Osbert Sitwell, but his collection of stories entitled
Triple Fugue is quite sufficient to maintain his reputation as a satirist of meanness and stupidity.   As a
social satirist he seems to have been trying his wings

in verse before launching out into fiction. The title-piece of the *Triple Fugue* collection, which occupies a third of the book, is the most definitely conceived as social satire. The poet's vivid perceptions and mastery of words are frequently in evidence, but the explicit *Foreword* begins by stressing the writer's purpose to satirise the scientific, political and social tendencies which seem to him to-day to threaten individuality in a machine-run civilisation. Although he makes a roaring farce out of the idea of " the group soul," he is in deadly earnest. He is bent on showing that for all the " progress " of civilisation, society promises to go on degenerating morally and intellectually while retaining the stupidities, the cheapness of sentiment, the petty greeds and the inhumanity which offer now such targets to his satire. At the beginning of this essay, for it is as much a Wellsian essay as a story, the author supposes himself looking backward at the present generation, much as Mr. Wells did across a much wider imaginary interval in *The Dream*. An example of his ability to hit off a complicated social phenomenon in a few strokes is the paragraph in which he examines the consequences to western European societies of the presence in their midst of the Jews. In a page he says as much (that is to the point) as Mr. Hilaire Belloc once said in a whole book. He reaches his argument by first approaching what he is most familiar with, the effect on artistic taste of the fact that " in this world the prevailing and unexciting vice is that of mimicry." In ascribing this vice pre-eminently to the Jews who are forced continually to adapt themselves to the changing environment first

of a new country and then of the social stratas to
which they climb, Mr. Sitwell is saying no more than
many Jewish critics of Jews have said; but for a
non-Jew to say it in a satirical phantasy requires a
certain amount of moral courage. Here is the briefer
paragraph which follows the general statement of
the case:

"The world they have influenced for the last
quarter of a century is, then, perhaps a little more
intelligent, but one with far less character, than
before the corruption began; more cosmopolitan,
more like the world of pleasure in every other capital
—in New York and Paris, Berlin and Rome. But
it has become the 'right thing again to manifest
a faint interest in music, poetry, portrait-painting,
above all in house-decoration; and books, even if
their pages are still uncut, lie once more on the
drawing-room tables."

It will be apparent from this that the satirist's
concern is with those Jews who are always trying
to look like something other than what they are, and
whose use of their money is an expression of the
snobbery of imitation. One could pick holes in the
argument here and elsewhere, but there is no need
to over-stress the author's qualifications as a sociologist.* To criticise him as a sociologist would perhaps be a tribute to his seriousness, but it would
amount to a misdirection of attention. *Triple Fugue*
is the work of an amusing satirist: its values are self-
contained and poetic. Any Jewish reader of this

* His limitations as a social philosopher are obvious in " After the
Bombardment."

fantastic satire would probably thank the author for the entire absence of the patronising or apologetic tone which so absurdly pervades much criticism. *Triple Fugue* is at any rate a brilliant promise in a first collection of prose stories.

As a story " Low Tide " is the most successful; the reader never doubts the reality of those pathetic and lonely creatures the Misses Frederica and Fanny Cantrell-Cooksey, though the climax of the story, as it is in every one of the pieces in *Triple Fugue*, except " His Ship Comes Home," is the weakest part of it. The author of " Low Tide " is a kind-hearted satirist. There is no kind feeling in " Friendship's Due." All the characters—Ferdinand McCulloch, Arthur Savage Beardsall, T. W. Frendly, Mrs. Stilpepper and Miss Ellen Durban are objects of contempt. McCulloch was a mountebank who came from Belfast to an eighteen-ninetyish London in which there was a " mingled atmosphere of a wet Sunday afternoon on the Irish Lakes and Greek passion." Ferdinand's " clique " was a mutual admiration society, except that the poor and energetic Cockney journalist Frendly's part was to admire rather than be admired. He is the only character who reveals one worthy motive for his actions. " His simple mind was intensely impressed with the genius of his two companions, and he reserved all his energy for the preaching of their gospel." As the portraits of the chief characters are savagely filled in stroke by stroke one realises the mixture of impersonal satire and a very offensively personal attack. Manners have been refined since the eighteenth century and the author cannot vie with the brutality of the *Dunciad*, but his cruelty (alas, to what small ends he has here turned the gift he prayed for once!) is scarcely less than poor, twisted little Alexander Pope's.

It is much easier to enjoy the ferocious wit of the piece called " His Ship Comes Home." The sketch of Arthur Bertram deserves to rank with Goldsmith's portrait of the more pathetic Beau Tibbs. Whether Bertram was drawn from a living model or is entirely fictitious, he is a thoroughly unpleasant fellow, and his world is an unpleasant world. The theme is altogether more worthy of the poet whose mouth was filled " with the burning pebbles of hatred " and swore

" In those days my soul shall be restored to me
   And they shall remember,
   They shall remember!

Quite as obnoxious to the satirist as Arthur Augustus Bertram's supremacy of moral meanness are the vanity and affectation which belong to him, and we realise that these are the author's pet aversions, and may go far to explain his severity with literary côteries, which of course are composed of an infinite number of individual affectations and interests that gradually crystallise into conventions. Throughout his satirical work, in verse as in prose, he is a relentless hunter of every conceivable pettiness of insincerity. Another feature of " His Ship Comes Home " is characteristic. The satire of the individual is surrounded with a sort of aura belonging to his environment. His environment provides a satirical picture of " society " as it was understood in the mid-Vic-

torian era. With one vindictive sweep of the brush
the satirist touches with damning caricature the
character of Bertram and " the great outcrop of rich
people created automatically by the diversion of
trade to this country from France and Germany during the war of 1870." Except perhaps " The Greet-
ing," a story revealing the influence of Henry James,
and possibly also of Walter de la Mare, all the pieces
in *Triple Fugue* remind us that the author is no mean
historian, following the phases of " society " at
different levels and epochs with an intuitive sense of
perspective. This is the one important feature of the
Discursions on Travel, Art and Life which belongs
to the satirist.

The *Discursions* are however distinct. They share
much subject matter with *Southern Baroque Art*,
though for richness of poetic content they cannot vie
with those four essays by Sacheverell Sitwell. But
unlike the *Southern Baroque Art* essays the *Discursions* are carefully written, with one or two lapses
only, and contain no unnecessary difficulties for the
reader. They offer pleasing evidence of the versatility and restless variability of an author almost
over-richly endowed with vivid impressions and
volatile ideas. In these fascinating papers Osbert
Sitwell is revealed an urbane as well as humorous
essayist. He carries lightly and gracefully a considerable knowledge of men and places, of social and
artistic epochs; and there are times when his prose,
while retaining very skilfully its unstudied air,
becomes an artistic medium hardly distinguishable
from poetry. It is then resonant, finely rhythmical,
and freighted with rich imagery which, like that of

Out of the Flame invades and occupies the reader's mind. The discursiveness which in his brother's book often becomes incoherence and breaks up too much the flow of thought, is here a most pleasing feature of the traveller's diary, and one feels that his preface is justified in offering to those who cannot afford to travel something of the stimulating experiences of the author. There is a pleasant self-revelation in the opening:—

" It is with yet more than his usual diffidence that the author begs to present these ' Discursions ' to the public. But since volumes of travel are his favourite books, and travelling rather than golf or hunting, his chosen form of exercise and sport, he will be perfectly satisfied if they communicate some of the pleasure himself has experienced to the gentle reader. Nor, in his opinion, is it enough to describe the things seen; for one of the chief virtues of travel is that it enables the mind to voyage more easily, even, than the body, to move backward and forward through time as well as in space."

Satire comes in only occasionally, and is generally excellent and amusing, for it is directed against all kinds of Philistinism, in royalty, in politics, in millionairism and in æsthetics. Like *Southern Baroque Art*, the book is divided into four parts— (1) Southern Italy; (2) Cities of the Phœnix; (3) Fiume and D'Annunzio; (4) Teutonic Variations. Sacheverell Sitwell's counterpart to the " Teutonic Variations " will not be found in *Southern Baroque Art* but, amplified beyond recognition, in certain sections of his study of architecture and other arts under the Holy Roman Empire. Otherwise the brothers cover very similar ground in *Discursions* and *Baroque Art*. The descriptions of Lecce, for instance, and of certain monasteries like the Certosa di Padula, in the *Discursions*, appear in Sacheverell's book embedded in historical atmosphere and a mass of imagery and myth which they have suggested to the poet. These mental Vikings went on their raids together.

In progressing through the *Discursions* one soon comes to feel that the geographical divisions are incidental, and that the author's mind is a traveller greater than his body. It discovers more variety in ranging through time than in ranging through Europe, and the unexpected contrasts, comparisons and conclusions it gathers from schools of art, social epochs, and obsolete and modern institutions form the pattern which lend a unifying personality to the variety of contents in the book. A fair specimen of the rapidity of his mental travelling and the kinematographic prose which carries the reader with him is at the end of the section on Lecce, which, he says, " has a thousand beautiful buildings and no reputation. It has therefore never indulged in the intricacies of Venetian or Chinese Gothic, or in any variant or sport of the Restaurant-Car architecture. It even dares to entertain Signor Marinetti, for perhaps it knows what Venice will learn too late, that Waring and Gillow's and self-conscious Little-Art-Shops-for-Peasant Pottery are a greater menace to beauty than all the futurist poets and painters and musicians in the universe. Lecce has never been self-

o

conscious; the lovely florid style of the early six-
teenth century refined itself gradually into the simple
shepherdess lines of 1760, and then slowly changed
into the plainly-built simple houses of to-day."

He refers to Norman Douglas's "Old Calabria"
for an account of the Flying Monk, San Giuseppe di
Copertino, one of the horde of miracle-workers and
saints produced in Southern Italy in the late seventeenth and early eighteenth centuries. Then comes
the concluding passage :—

"After the piazza della Prefettura, the finest
piazza in the town is that outside the Cathedral, an
imposing though not particularly exciting example
of sixteenth-century work. The square is an exceed-
ingly large one, full of palaces. The Seminario, the
chief building in it, rivals the prefettura, and is the
work of Cino, pupil of Zimbalo, who built it about
1705. Here also is the Archbishop's palace, a delightful arcaded building of the middle of the same century, less rich but equally elegant. The whole
square has only one opening, where it tapers to a
very graceful gateway opposite the Cathedral façade.

"It was our good fortune to see this great square
illuminated on the night of Good Friday. In the
fanatic atmosphere of Southern Italy the Church
dares to move with the times, and a lavish use had
been made of electric light. By the side of the
Cathedral a large plaster grotto, brilliantly lit,
showed the various scenes of Our Lord's life. All the
palaces and houses were decorated with lines and
garlands of light. Trumpets brayed mournfully in
the distance, and from out the dark blue canal of

the street floated a procession of strange figures, displayed by the flames of the torches they carried; for the wide square, still empty, though in a few minutes it would become crowded, seemed in the dusk like a stretch of blue water. On came the procession, curling like a dragon, with mournful cries, wailing, and the brazen tongue of a trumpet, while high above were held up the illuminated sacred images and relics. All the figures in the procession were masked, figures from some ballet by Callot, or from a drawing of the Inquisition by Della Bella or Goya. Some were dressed in flowing black with wide black hats, their eyes gleaming through the two slits in the long black cloth that fell over their faces. Some were decked out in light blue and pink—a sort of skirt of blue, and coat of pink—while large red hats, like those of a cardinal, completed the costume; others again wore robes of silver and purple. After them followed an army of children, singing in time to the slow waltz, which by some odd chance had been chosen for the occasion by the Municipal Band which wound up the whole procession. The children sang in the peculiarly nasal, shrill meaningless voice of the South. The darkness had increased; it was night. The fixed garlands and festoons of lights now fully displayed the intricacies of the architecture; while the torches, moving through the air, threw distorted shadows on to wall and pavement, gave false value to the stone carving, touched for a moment door or window, gilded a stone rose or triton, or threw a flickering patch of light like a halo upon some human face. The crowd was not very quiet; and framed by a wandering flood of light in a narrowing swirl of mer-

maids, roses and cupids, the sullen bearded face of a
monk peered down at the procession as it slowly
filed round the farther corner of the square and out
again into the engulfing darkness."

Prose like this has all the merits and some of the
limitations of impressionist art. Objects, memories,
light and shade, stand out momentarily in sharp
revelation before merging into the streaming phan-
tasmagoria through which the author is producing
an atmosphere that is partly a subjective creation.
One is tempted to continue the quotation for another
page, into the opening of the section entitled King
Bomba, which follows the account of Lecce. The
story of that relic of Divine Right affords the author
a good opportunity of satirising royalty as represented by the House of Naples. His account may
not be impartial, but it is very lively and full of
unexpected information. We are, however, more
concerned now with his prose as an artistic medium
and accordingly re-read the first three paragraphs
in the section on King Bomba :—

" When the flamingo-tinted rays of the early sun
lay light as feathers along the ledges and on the sharp
angles of church and palace, I was already walking
down the empty streets. The Palazzo della Prefettura was still drenched from the night's mists, and
the feathers of the sunlight could almost be seen
brushing the stone, drying the wet cupids, and wring-
ing the dew out of the huge roses, or striving to rid
thicket and mysterious grove of their lingering darkness. The eagles on the church next door were most

clearly preening their golden scales, and the lions were shaking their manes free of the dew, while, as if in echo to their deep rasping voices, the folding thunder of shop-shutters, drawn up, sounded out from the main thoroughfares. This was accompanied by continual whisking, sudden floating fragments of Neapolitan song, and the rattle of hurrying feet, though the broad way, in which I stood looking up at the palace, was itself still full of the silence of earlier hours.

" The monk's face, set off by the exquisite carving of the Seminario windows, had certainly looked incongruous on the evening before, but it was certain that these much lovelier windows had often served as a foil and frame for a yet more unsuitable physiognomy."

This last sentence is an execrable ending to an eloquent passage. The next paragraph is a change in *tempo*, and introduces twenty-seven pages of mingled history, biography, memoirs, itinerary and art criticism around the repulsive figure of Bomba, King of the Two Sicilies. This is how the author affects the transition :—

" Built originally as a convent, this palace had been turned into a royal residence by Murat, and remained such until after the unification of Italy, when it was converted into a museum. For some reason or other it became quite a favourite visiting-place for King Bomba (Ferdinand II), playing a part in his life, as well as in his death."

Such a discursive method allows the greatest possible freedom to the mental traveller. Osbert Sitwell by his employment of it stamps it as almost a new form of essay, a prose narrative, which is the story of a geographical mind-wandering from tract to tract of interesting and unexpected relevances of memory. In *After the Bombardment* the method is used in an ostensible fiction. It is indeed his peculiar characteristic although both Edith and Sacheverell Sitwell at times produce similar effects, Edith in verse and Sacheverell generally in prose, especially in *Southern Baroque Art*. Before attempting to contrast this extraordinary book with the *Discursions*, however, let us follow the latter a little further, where the author is in his most discursive and perhaps also in his most interesting vein (the two conditions are not found simultaneously in his brother's prose).

The third section of Part I, " La Certosa di Padula," is a good piece of Sitwellian high-speed travelling. But although the going is fast there are moments when, as if he has taken us up in a plane, the speed leaves ample leisure for the eye to take in wide views or, with the aid of field-glasses (the author's vivid memory of unexpected details) to examine the curious and the beautiful closely. This chapter begins with notes on two of the three monasteries in the Naples district, Monte Cassino (which " has other claims to distinction besides its learning for the town beneath supplies itinerant musicians of the barrel-organ to every town in Europe ") and Monte Vergine* (where " in the summer, it is still possible to see thirty or forty thousand people climbing up the steep cliffs on their hands and knees).

---

* The subject of Sacheverell Sitwell's poem " The Winter Walk."

Unfortunately we visited it at the wrong season of the year . . ." but our traveller hastens to the third, the " most lovely in situation, though less impressive in size than its brothers," La Cava.

" To this day one can see how such a religious house evolved, for the building is fitted into caves and grottoes in the natural rock, and one can imagine the anchorite in hair-shirt, with gaunt body and long beard, first encrevicing himself here as an insect seeks refuge under a stone."

He pauses to admire the Norman cloisters, related to Saracenic architecture, the picture gallery and the illuminated missals in the library. He retells the story he heard there while admiring some illuminated missals of the eleventh or twelfth century, how an archivist in about 1860 went from La Cava (which had become a convent and is now a public school) to the village to buy some cheese.

" He chose a piece of his favourite ' Mozzarella,' and it was handed to him wrapped up in a sheet of an early illuminated missal. Inquiring where it had come from, he learnt that the farmer wrapped up all his eggs, cheese, and butter in these papers, which he had found lying about in the library of the empty Certosa di Padula. The archivist was able to buy the two remaining cartloads, and these exquisite fragments, as fine as anything of their kind in Italy, now repose in the library at La Cava."

Even this extraordinary accident, however, did not focus attention on Padula, which was not declared a national monument until a few years ago, says the author, and the observation leads him to contemplate the leisureliness of the traveller before the Steel Age dawned in Europe. " Up to 1830 any traveller who succeeded in getting so far as Naples would be sure to persevere, venturing through the beautiful but dangerous landscape—a landscape swarming with brigands as well as with the minor plagues of the South to inspect the famous Certosa di Padula, as certainly as he would visit Pompeii, Pæstum, and the other classical ruins in the Neapolitan kingdom."

But the " Steel Age " has set the satirist on the track of the steel king. " He visits Pæstum, about forty miles from Padula, in his steel torpedo car, draws a hasty comparison between Greece and the grandeur that is Chicago, and charges home again— at eighty miles an hour—to Naples. Steel Kings trained to the worship of elephantiasis, should prefer vastness to proportion, Padula to Pæstum : but Pæstum is a Paying Concern, and Delivers the Goods."

This observation leads to the reflection that as the human eye judges size roughly by the standard of the human figure, photographs of the Paying Concern " are carefully circulated, with the doll-like temples rising up immense, a child or a dwarf in the foreground . . ." The continuation of the sentence is amusingly characteristic : " much as one of the more manikin-like of European kings is continually photographed striking his breast in a Louis XIV manner, with a dwarf placed in the offing. This gives scale."

He then dashes in again at the steel king, whose tastes in art, *via* the Greek, lead with breathless speed to " our own cenotaph," which " is not a triumph of good or of bad taste, but simply a triumph

of no taste at all,"—a very shrewd and unexpected
hit.

Follow some notes on "good taste" and the
history of the old monastery, including reference to
Massena, Murat, Nelson, brigands, lazzaroni, and
Ferdinand IV, "afterwards—his only paradox—
Ferdinand I. This monarch was the 'Re Nasone,'
so called because of the full Bourbon development of
his profile, and grandfather of our former hero,
Bomba." To describe the King and his brutal parti-
sans of the time, William Beckford; Madame
Giglioli; Hugh Elliot, a British Ambassador, and a
journal of 1820 by Lady Morgan are interestingly
quoted.

Follow notes on Murat's reign in Naples, a description of the landscape passed on the author's journey
to Padula, and a quotation from a guide-book,
published in 1853, concerning the murder by brigands
of an Englishman and his wife on the road to Eboli,
which is passed on the way to Padula. Then more
description and reminiscence of literature and history :

"From Eboli onward, the journey becomes in-
"creasingly beautiful; the valleys are full of asphodel
"and marigold, narcissus and jonquil spring up from
"the level lawns of grass on each side of the narrow
"streams, and over all these float the magenta or
"rose-pink blossoms of Judas and Upas-Trees. The
"fantastic landscape, of enormous dimensions, is
"dominated by Monte Alburno, that mountain
"beloved of Virgil, the cracked and riven outline of
"which shows like a broken knife-edge against the

" vibrating blue of the sky. It is not possible to
" imagine the other side of this giant mountain, for
" it seems as if that nearest to us had been cut in
" cardboard and painted to resemble a hill, so that
" the other side would be hollow, unpainted and
" dusty, a shelter perhaps for theatrical ogres or
" stage thunder. The long summit looks as though
" pieces had been cut out of it by a child with a pair
" of scissors, but the bare granite surface is coolly
" radiant as ice on this hot day, showing every colour
" embraced in the predominant blue or purple of its
" shadows. Far down below sings that Greek stream,
" the Tanager, and to echo it lies the lovely Valle di
" Diano, a volcanic valley with the usual array of
" craters and hot streams, and rivers that run under
" ground for a mile or two. Through the haze that
" hangs over this vast view, small hills rise up so
" regular in shape that they appear to be blue
" pyramids."

The brilliance of the flowers then brings to the
author's mind the contrast of the dreary old quarrel
of the French and English being fought out again
in that landscape; the ruined houses calling to mind
earthquakes; a few inhabitants are seen; then the
towns become more frequent, " and then, suddenly
a great gateway, unattached to any road, appears
out of the plain, and beyond it an enormous, low
building, vast as a town, swelling out of the vegeta-
tion round it, as if it, too, were part of the soil. Here
in this distant, unvisited, poverty-stricken plain,
unwept by the world, with only a slight mournful
keening from Baedeker, is a monument of the first

order, the discovery of a building as romantic and
remote as any that would be encountered in the
central forests of Brazil."

If the reader continues with the traveller he will
agree that the satirist of unleisurely steel-kings is
not altogther unjustified in his reproaches. The same
feeling results from accompanying him to Bayreuth,
in the last section of the book. The admixture of
satire in "Fiume and D'Annunzio" (a wild and
extravagant genius who of course is made a hero)
smothers altogther the topographical itinerary and
changes the character of the writing into that of a
controversial political and artistic biography, but
even here the author's irrepressible fun finds a
pleasant interlude. Speaking of the pleasant contrast
with England of France and Italy in that a poet
has no shame in avowing his profession among the
Latins (an observation arising out of the fact that
d'Annunzio the politician was also a poet) Osbert
Sitwell suddenly remembers a visit to a chiropodist
in Venice. Asked his profession, and reassured by a
signed photograph of d'Annunzio on the wall, he
pulled himself together and answered boldly "Poet."
"And I too," replied the chiropodist flourishing his
razor and thumping his chest. While the English
poet's foot lay neglected the chiropodist-poet
declaimed poems in the Venetian vernacular. Two
problems then oppressed Osbert Sitwell. Ought he
to chant some of his own poems, and how many?
And the approaching hard necessity of injuring this
poetic fraternisation with ugly questions " as to the
cost of these material labours," supposing the operation to his foot ever completed. Unfortunately he

does not tell us how he solved the first problem; perhaps he funked reciting in return. As to the other, the chiropodist was an artist and understood. " No payment would he accept from a brother-poet —only a present, given of free-will."

Many passages in the book, unlike the description of Lecce, are not examples of prose artistry. They reveal a quick negligence which often overworks words like " beautiful," " wonderful," " splendid " and hastens on without having captured the just phrase, the accurate sentence or the satisfying rhythm, relying on intuition and the poet's luck for occasional felicities. Sometimes this freedom in using language occurs in a striking passage, like that in a fine account of the visit to the island city of Gallipoli, where the author describes the din of the bells for the Easter procession of Maundy Thursday. " The reverberations sank down and seemed to strike the hard cobbles of the streets," he says, capturing one of his momentary felicities; then, " there was as much sound in each street as there is water in a canal, so that each man standing there was soaked through with it, drowned with it," extends the figure to the verge of the appropriate in a manner typical of his brother's style. But next comes a rush right over the verge of the sublime: " The whole town was inundated, as if the blue water had upreared itself into a venomous wall, and all the houses were sinking beneath the fierce rush and swirling eddies."* On second thoughts, however, one finds that the writer somehow most surprisingly makes this metaphor of a metaphor, this piling of verbal Pelion on verbal

* " In the Heel of Italy," p. 87 et seq.

Ossa a happy escape of the mind into an unforgettable memory.   He has already told us that the
streets end as cul-de-sacs of blue sea, and " venomous " is, one decides after hesitation, a proof that
the writer is a poet.   The translation of sound waves
into an image of water is a device which he is fond
of.   It occurs several times in *Before the Bombardment*.   For instance, in Chapter One, where the
German house-maid " creaked blunderingly " out of
her room after getting up in the morning : " she was
wading through the familiar stillness, a silence in-
fringed by a thousand crepuscular crepitations, of
the hotel-corridors.   As she moved, these minute,
crackling vibrations were lost in the cascades of
sound which her clumsy feet unloosed to dash up
against tiled walls."   The first part of this chapter,
which bears the same title, too, is a detailed prose
sketch of the theme of Edith Sitwell's poem,
" Reveille," about " Jane."   But Newborough,
which occupies so much of the novel, is a fictive
Scarborough, which means once more that the Sitwells are drawing on a common store of raw material.

CHAPTER SIX

HARLEQUIN SHELLEY

What tree, what shade, what spring, whàt paradise . . .
—*George Peele.*

As is the garden such is the gardener.
—" Proverbs."

Here at the fountain's sliding foot,
Or at some fruit tree's mossy root,
Casting the body's vest aside
My soul into the boughs does glide :
There like a bird, it sits and sings,
There whets and claps its silver wings,
And, till prepared for longer flight,
Waves in its plumes the various light.
Andrew Marvell.

THE difference between Sacheverell Sitwell's
style and that of his brother and sister is
remarkable, and most obvious in his lyrical
poems. His genius is incompatible with the " artificial paradise " of Rimbaud which has attracted
them. The point is elusive enough to justify stressing because his fondness for fabulous creatures and
the translation occasionally into eccentric imagery
of a subtle sensory impression blurs this radical distinction between the poet who is temperamentally

classical and those who are, for all their satirical
wit, romantic. There is nothing of the unreality of
a toy universe in Sacheverell Sitwell's ironic thought
or in the rapid flux of his natural imagery.   His
predominantly classical mood and his reverence for
certain fine poets must not however persuade us that
the deliberate gesture with which he will write a
" Variation on a Theme by Alexander Pope " or "An
Adaptation from John Milton " is anything more
than a gesture. An artist can always induce a given
frame of mind much as the actor enters into a part
without being identified with it, and the reader may
feel in several of these " variations " and " adapta-
tions " a kind of sensitive critical approach to something essentially belonging to the original, but the
resulting poem is art unmistakably belonging to the
present :

> Now all the branches lift their arms
> And the great Sun pours down his balms,
> The leaves bud out, and wink their eyes
> Gently lest a frost surprise.
>
> Full is each river to the brim
> Running so fast, its glass is dim
> Those rocks that burn in summer sun
> Bow down to let the waters run.
>
> All snows are melted from the hills
> And fledgling birds now try their bills,
> Or preen themselves in leaves' soft shade,
> Dreaming of the flights they've made.

The gardener, stumbling, heavy shod,
Prints dew as though a bird had trod
By boughs that only want green sails
To start off down the panting gales.

Now do the Indian birds appear,
False summer, for they fly in fear
Floating to this cooler clime
Where through the leaves they sound their chime.

Far down in the myrtle grove
Wander the youths who died of love;
And the hero's armed shade
Glitters down the gloomy glade.

The virtue of this is individual; the poem is
classical in the sense that Gray's " Elegy in a Country
Churchyard " is classical, because it not only em-
bodies an external reality in the images but these
are so co-ordinated as to express a premeditated
attitude and manner.   The attempt to recall the
Augustan manner in diction adds nothing of importance to the poetry; the best lines indeed are the
least like Pope, the poet whose name is taken in vain.
Certainly " panting gales," " myrtle grove," and
" gloomy glade " would not have appeased Pope,
who said of his own pastorals, " if they have any
merit, it is to be attributed to some good old authors,
whose works, as I had leisure to study, so, I hope,
I have not wanted care to imitate."   Still less like
the modern artificial paradise of Rimbaud's *Les
Illuminations* are the satires and the descriptions,
which include the prose of *Southern Baroque Art* as

well as fluent, and sometimes facile verse like the
longer " Variations," and " Doctor Donne and Gargantua," " The Thirteenth Cæsar," " March past at
the Pyramids," " The Neptune Hotel."

Sacheverell Sitwell's art, beginning with the little
volume *The People's Palace* is more consistent in
its development than that of his brother and sister.
The poetic method in *The People's Palace* is no
different from the method in *The Thirteenth Cæsar*,
though a continuous technical refinement can be
traced. " Pindar," in the early volume, presents a
train of pleasing imagery loosely strung on a fabulous
invention of the poet's. It is deliberately written on
a literary argument, as " Bolsover Castle " was
written on an historical background, and the " Variations on Themes out of Zarathustra " were written
with the motive indicated by the title. " Pindar "
is less verbose than the last of these, and less picturesque than " Bolsover Castle," but from the premeditated text the poet's ideas bubble up with the
seeming carelessness of a sparkling fountain. It is
prefaced, too, by an explanatory note : " There are
two legends of Pindar. One tells how when he died
when he was asleep in a wood whilst quite a baby,
a swarm of bees settled on his lips. The other
describes how Pan stole Pindar's song, and sang it
on the mountains. In this poem these two incongruous elements have been combined. It is on the
same principle that bad Greek wine is improved by
the addition of rancid honey." Not so modest as
the Preface to " Endymion," and it must be confessed that the " incongruous elements " do not com-
bine with any very satisfying result. The pleasure

P

given by the poet is in the presentation of images, generally in movement, a characteristic which, with myth-making, he shares with Shelley.   In *The People's Palace*, he is feeling his way through a newly-discovered forest of thought and feeling; he is, with an extraordinary intellectual clarity testing the instruments which shall garner the harvests of his teeming brain.   " Lil-Tai-Pe " is a relic of a passing enthusiasm for Chinese (translated) poetry. It is not in the least Chinese.   He goes to the South seas for novelty, and in " Tahiti " brings back a mythological image for the sun, which is perhaps the best thing in the piece :—

Far off, the sun, caught spider-like
In its cloud-web, is seething down the sea
And churns the waves, spatters them with blood.
Despairingly it waves red tentacles, clutching
Fiercely each wool-white wave-crest, then splutters
    out.

" Barrel-Organs : (1) Prelude (2) Feathered Hat " reveals the influence of pieces in Miss Sitwell's *Wooden Pegasus*.   It contains poetry in pleasing but irrelevant passages, which show that the scheme of this piece was alien to the poet's mood.   Here is one such passage :

" The moon, young light-haired shepherd
    Has but to lead away his star-fed flocks
    The wool-white foaming breakers of the sea,
    Then pasture them again :—
    And when he rests behind those thyme-clad hills,
        the clouds,

To see the homing stars, striped honey-bees,
And shuns the sun-god's ravenous embrace,—
Without a sight of him, the dragon-writhing foam
To the gentle piping of his wind-stopped flute
Draws back again."

What is remarkable in these early pieces is the
avoidance of familiar echoes in metre and imagery.
And the very positive attitude of mind is indicated
by the readiness to draw new myths out of ancient
symbols.   One might have expected the youthful
Shelley to see the moon as a " young light-haired
shepherd."

"The Mayor of Murcia," in five divisions, is
rambling and rhetorical, with occasional gleams of
the true gold.   It promises the powerful rapidity as
well as the discontinuity of thought to be found in
the later philosophical satires.   When the Mayor has
finished the " speech " the reader is moved only to
an intense sympathy with his audience, a sympathy
which even the poet seems to recognise as warranted :

> The swirling smoke of words
> Had blinded every citizen
> To sober hard reality

When he continues :

Great thoughts, those striding bridges
Athwart the crystal chasms of our dreams,
Seemed like accomplished facts
And on the prancing horses of ambition
Each conscience leaps the river
That runs between the thought and fact accom-
    plished,

the poet has once more unconsciously made a pertinent comment on his own work. The one remarkable exception to the failure of the *form* is the fourth Part, entitled " The Festa," and this is a descriptive passage which might have been a sketch for some of the picturesque passages in the prose of *Southern Baroque*. Marinetti's method of sending serried rank on rank of ideas and images charging upon the reader is cleverly adopted to describe the town's holiday gala mood; but the influence of the Futurist movement on the immature poet seems to have been a not unmixed blessing, since it resulted in so much verse and so little satisfying achievement.

In 1922, four years after the publication of *The People's Palace*, *The Hundred and One Harlequins* rushed upon a dazzled and somewhat resentful world. The title-piece, a group of eleven " selections " mixes fairly equally the poet's good qualities and faults, both being subdued here to an average. In each of these eleven pieces (they cannot truly be called poems) is a quaint glimpse of reality obtained from some unexpected angle of vision. The content of the vignettes is a kind of amused surprise at human existence which continually gives way to wonder at the beauty of natural phenomena. We find here the images of water, wind, cloud, foliage and light coming in as inevitably as nouns and adjectives would come into any ordinary character sketches. But these " Harlequins " are not really character-sketches; they are fragments of a poet's view of life which seem to have been poured out in rapid conversation. The verse-form, like the style, is of the loosest. Laforgue, in his passion for a method of expressing

the " tel quel de la vie " could hardly have wished
for anything more supple in style.   Here are numbers
One, Two and Three of the " Harlequins " :—

I

A Pro's Landlady

Mrs. Serapion knocks upon the door,
The sun has risen from his couch upon the floor,
" Mr. Grimaldi ! seven o'clock ! "
Above the foam of the sea he shows,
And Harlequin jumps from his bed of snows,
While Mrs. Serapion warns the block.
He walks to the window where a tree grows in,
Stirring the leaves that are green and thin.
He shaves. He washes. And he combs his hair.

II

At Breakfast

" A glass of milk as white as your hand
The foam of seas that lie on the land,
Their grass runs swift in the wind like a wave ;
A cup of this foam :—and then I crave
Snow-bread that the hills have ground their gold
    to ! "
        The cheap shepherdess replied,
        Her words still-born—dead drowned by the roar.

A railway engine ran across the field
Galloping like a swift horse down the rails,
As it came quicker the window-panes rattled,
The roof shook side to side; all its beams trembled,
Thundering hoofs were upon us—glass chariots.*

III

READING THE PAPER

The second train he boarded with a paper,
He hides behind it from his fellows,
This bird-mask lets him know the news,
He sees, like they do, from the air,
There they ride, each person in the carriage,
Each of them steering his cloud through the air.
All that goes on in the world they gather.
A visor to guard, and a mask to protect them.
Now, with their speed the white mane flows loose.

Now it is obvious that these pieces have the merit
of vividness, and a condensation which would be
wholly admirable but for the resistance it offers to
ready understanding.   Obscurity is a fault in the
most profound poem; it is not necessary, though it
seems deliberate, in these semi-satirical vignettes.

* It is probable that the " Memoirs of Joseph Grimaldi " (which
Dickens edited) are one source of these " Harlequins," and
No. Two seems to contain a reminiscence of the print in the Burney
Collection of Theatrical Portraits showing Guiseppe Grimaldi,
Joseph's father (who was the founder of the new school of English
pantomime which appeared at Drury Lane, Sadler's Wells, and
Astley's in the second half of the 18th century).   The print shows
Guiseppe at the breakfast table with Mrs. Brooker, who was
Joseph's mother.

The condensation in Number Two dislocates the reader's attention by describing the effect in the breakfast room of the noise of a passing train outside, before explaining what " the roar " is all about. Another more formidable mental gymnastic feat is required immediately afterwards to realise the startling poetry of

> Thundering hoofs were upon us—glass chariots.

This is cubist vision in verse metaphors telescoped into one another; not merely a confusion of visional planes, but a transference of the movement of the roaring train to the shaken houses, the heavy pounding calling up hoofs—charging horses—chariots. The inmates of the vibrating room turn their gaze to the rattling windows—glass—hence glass chariots. Mr. Grimaldi when he gets into the next of these charging trains on his way to town is converted into a birdlike mental traveller (a Perseus ?) ranging the whole world spread over the news columns of his paper. So all of the passengers; and the carriage is " a visor to guard them," and their papers each a " bird-like mask," and past them flies the white mane of steam from the engine. The sense of speed excites further images in the poet's mind and so Pegasus fairly breaks loose in No. Four:

IN THE TRAIN

In crystal chariots drawn by unicorns,
As did old Fortunatus in his day:
I can shine in loud streets with honour,
Grip the gold reins and go just where I will:

Ride from the town beneath an arch
Whose bricks like honeycombs shall store my name.
Beside the river we will gallop.
My rattling wheels outpace the drifting float
Of leaves that whirl among the river's eddies
As fell strong towns that glittered as my foes;—
Down to where it mingles with the sea
Fanning new freshness to the foaming waves.
Just there my unicorns sniff in the salt,
Worry the water with white trembling feet,
Whinny their pleasure, and turn back again.

The imagery here is probably a recollection of the
railway which runs from Chesterfield to Sheffield and
just by Eckington approaches the Rother and also
runs parallel for some distance with a canal, along
the banks of which the poet as a child went on many
a ramble. It is also like a youthful memory of the
train journey to Oxford, where the line comes near
to the river. Even the delight in gloriously extravagant imagery seems a symbol of the joy of the returning undergraduate's self-conscious mental growth.
This poet's imagination had pinions which would
have taken him anywhere; he was not made by the
lucky opportunities of constantly visiting the bright
Mediterranean. When the facts are commonplace he
will analyse and recombine their elements. The sooty
bricks of the tunnel become honeycombs storing
memories of the iron steed, and the spurts of steam
go wandering away down to the railside water like
white unicorns (he might as well have said horses,
or antelopes, or zebras, except that unicorns are
unicorns, and white!). The hovering, sinking, drift-

ing steam is beautifully captured in the last two
lines. This mind-wandering is not unfruitful. One
pursues with pleasure the flying imagery through
these Harlequinades of poetry, compelled constantly
to skip about with all the agility possible. In Number Five Grimaldi is being measured at the tailor's;
Grimaldi is far away. He does not hear the tailor
say

> " Forgive the liberty, bend your elbow.
> Where do you want the outside pocket ? "

He is trying to think what God said "when he ordered
birds." The last two lines of Grimaldi's conclusion
as to what God said read rather like an ingenious
acrostic. "On the Telephone," Number Six is almost
incomprehensible. Grimaldi sits in a telephone box.
The noise of the wires he hears are like " jangling
sledges." This suggests a lady's carriage—and when
someone's voice (can it have been the telephone
operator's by any chance ?) " rang loud in the
pauses " of the jangling, it becomes the voice of
Madame Hanska ! So follows " the man who wrote
novels and had such queer manners " (Balzac and
Madame Hanska's story in ten words) and specula-
tions as to what he, who " liked a fierce polonaise "
would have thought of " the noise down these cold
wires." Music, like speed, is an irresistible lure to
the poet's mind : tinkling pagodas, glass bells, travelling pierrot minstrels, singers on the Rialto, and back
home again to the telephone which

> " carries
> The fur-footed dance of a person he marries,"

which conclusion may refer to Balzac or to Grimaldi, or (but this is less likely) it may be as inconsequent as some of the rhymes in Edith Sitwell's *Façade*. Number Seven is like a mixture of the Dug-Outs' Club in Scarborough with its staring bay-windows and old gentlemen gazing through telescopes, and some remembered print of a portrait. The harlequinade here becomes decidedly inconsequent. There are some characteristic images in Number Eleven, " From a Hill Top " like that of the falling river gliding, like slow music, through gold plains. So, just so, one may see the Arve, muddy in flood from melting snows, pouring in curved sheets over the periodical barriers which break its flow as it skirts Geneva; in the bright sun, viewed from a hill on the outskirts of the town the brown water is a broad ribbon of gold. There is no coherence or reason in " From a Hill Top," other than a free association of ideas. Probably the Showman decided to put one more Harlequin on, in order to make Eleven. Eleven in Roman numerals is 10 and 1; and 10 and 1 without separation makes all the excuse, I suspect, which he has to offer for entitling these " selections," and the volume in which they occur, *The Hundred and One Harlequins*. Mr. Arnold Bennett, who asked where were the other ninety Harlequins, please note.

Before we leave *The Hundred and One Harlequins*, it is interesting to recall those strange prose and free verse poems, the " Métiers Divins" and " Le Bourg" of Jean de Bosschère.* There is in these symbolical little pictures of the commonplace a more profound

* A selection from " Le Bourg," translated, was published by Elkin Mathews in 1916, under the title " Twelve Occupations."

mysticism, less poetry and an equal obscurity at
times; it is not improbable that Sacheverell Sitwell
owes something to de Bosschère's work, for the
Flemish poet-artist is a true Harlequin, and his
method of setting out from a mirror-maker at work
to black magic, from a clock-maker to the time-is-
money social tyranny and the fear of the old man
beholding the end of time; or from the Mask-Maker
to Dionysus, is very similar to that of the Sitwellian
harlequinade.   There is, moreover, an austere, rather
cold, ironic detachment in de Bosschère, which can
be felt in the satirical discursions of the younger
poet, who displays none of his brother's generous
fervour of anger.   Except for the difference of form
" Ulysses Batit son Lit " in " Portes Fermées "
might easily be a " Variation " in *The Hundred and
One Harlequins* volume.

The air of deliberation noticeable in the poet's
choice of themes is as evident in *The Thirteenth
Cæsar* as in *The Hundred and One Harlequins*, and
the contents of the more mature volume fall into
a similar division of mainly-lyrical and mainly-
satirical verse.   The ten " Serenades," the " Italian
Air," " Fables," and the three " Variations on a
Theme by George Peele," in the *Hundred and One
Harlequins* correspond roughly with the twenty-five
poems grouped under the heading *Hortus Conclusus*,
and the " Two Water Songs "; " New Water
Music "; " The Fisherman "; " Wind as Husbandman "; " Gardener Trimming Hedges "; parts of the
" Santander Quartet "; the " Two Mirror Poems ";
" The Winter Walk "; " Bolsover Castle," and parts
of " Actor Rehearsing " and " The Neptune Hotel."

By " lyrical " is intended not only the more musical verse and more delightful imagery but what is largely the cause of the distinction, a disinterestedness of motive, a purely playful activity of the mind, instead of the ambitious and scornful satire of human nature, in making which the poet's tendency to produce a " swirling smoke of words " accomplishes itself with fatal ease.

,When his mind goes flying across the phenomenal universe, gathering up rare marvels of beauty, weaving them into glorious singing-robes with which to invest some flying form of thought, this poet at his best has few living equals.   Images of incomparable delicacy float on the wind of song; rhythms subtly beautiful move under the swift current of ideas, displaying them in perfection like the skilled hands of an Oriental artist-merchant showing off the opulence of precious silks.

> Sigh soft, sigh softly,
> rain-thrilled leaves,
> Let not your careless hands
> stem the gold wind
> Let not your greensleeves
> swim in its breath,
> as water flowing;
> lest your thin hands
> make gurgle down the crystal hills
> the gaudy sun's pavilions
> whence he distils those showered scents
> whose virtue all true turtles croon
> beneath their swaying palaces.

Sing low, then, turtles,
　Sigh soft, swift wind,
　　and, fountains, cease your flutings,
　　Melulla, now,
　　　Lean on your balcony ! look down !
　　　My strings shall sing.

This is the first of the lovely " Serenades." Number
Four opens :

I see no breath upon the window's water,
hear no feet below the shining trees;
must I never let the music slacken,
fold its wings away, sink on my knees ?

Here is the very trembling of rapture in which the
poet sings his serenades, and when he sings so who
shall deny him the rank of greatness ? Often he
sings so, and with a rare delicacy of metrical control ;
sometimes explicitly as the lover :

Low wind, soft light, and the crumbling waves
Lay down their fleeces at the mouth of caves ;
the lion sands become clouds and beds,
Windows in the foam, cool roof for our heads.
Here are new seconds in a moment's bliss
to add a paradise to our kiss.
The unicorns gallop over the sand
To give the bird songs into my hand,
they spread their wings and move their tongues,
the leaves are lute-strings to their lungs,
the clouds dissolve and shower-down, sharp,
rain that the wind plucks as a harp ;

the music bridges the shallow stream
that cuts reality from this dream,
to cross it, listen with keen ears;
this voice that sings shall ease your fears.

Or, as in the " Italian Air," which although too long
for the internal unity, has lovely things scattered like
bright diamonds of dew all over it.   Here are the
opening stanzas.

> In among the apple trees
> and on their echoing golden roofs,
> a singing shower rides on the breeze,
> and prints the grass with crystal hoofs.
>
> The sighing music faints and fails
> among the far-off feathered boughs,
> the birds fold up their painted sails;
> but voices sound, until they rouse
>
> the sleeping birds and silent leaves;
> and now a harp once more resounds,
> to utter what her heart believes
> and what her trembling sense confounds.

This Phœnix of song, lighting the air with fire and
dew, serenades lovely things whose loveliness dulled
senses do not catch—sunlit foliage, lucent water,
plastic and elastic wind, the infinite variations of
tapestried light and shadow.   So much of his raptur-
ous singing is, as in *Hortus Conclusus*, that of a
garden bird.   Even the gardener shares in the per-
vading beauty; he is akin to the wind, an active and

beneficent agent, influencing the ceaseless changes
in the forms of things, and partaking of the life of
nature. But what a song is this for a Gardener :—

> " Wind come run to help me,
>   Flash your wings, I see you clearly."
> I waited till he stretched them wide
> Down sailing through the sparkling tide;
> Now he helps me floating here.
>
> At my side he rides above
> Wherever on my work I rove,
> If at a tree's foot stooping low
> He sways the branches to and fro,
> In green shade waiting.
>
> When I fear the staring sun
> By my ears I feel him run,
> He can make me all the shadow
> To hide in while I walk the meadow,
> By cool air quickened.
>
> Lawn and hill are just the same,
> Cool and happy at his name,
> The hanging wood which is his home
> Rings with bird-songs while we roam,
> Together working.
>
> While I nurse and prune, he sows
> Deft at the labour that he knows,
> The seed-pods with his plumes to touch,
> Not too soft, nor overmuch,
> With wide wings scattering.

So does the seed float down the air
While loudly shines the sun's gold hair,
And in and out the strands there fly
The floating birds who call and cry,
Their harvest reaping.

The seed, like grains of gold, they take
And for their airy roofs they make,
Where for their store they heap it high
And all the leaves and branches nigh
Ring while they glisten.

Most the wind has scattered wide
Like yellow sand for air's strong tide,
Here is my harvest that I wait,
The sunny waves run here to mate,
With the gold sand lying.

Come, wind, make me quick a shade,
For, like a bee, I rob and raid,
The offspring of this love to snare
And take their increase for my share,
In hot sun reaping.

Here as in much of his garden poetry, if he chose
to use the title " Variation on a Theme by Marvell,"
we would yield assent with some conviction, remembering the high-water mark of lyrical poetry in the
age that was a stagnant preparation for the August-
ans. Sacheverell Sitwell's work provides the richest
collection of purely garden poetry in the same bird-
voice in English literature.   Over and over again
ranging through the pleached alleys, the far bright
vistas, the green glooms, the cloudy palaces of these

poems the reader's mind is borne away by a magic
that seems as open and simple as the magic of a
sunny day. In " Shadow " is not any grisly darkness
but the purple shades and ever moving forms of
wind-stirred foliage and sailing cloud, and the mind
becomes a playmate of nature in her summer mood.
" The Dancer " is the playing fountain, turning the
liquid air into wine and creating images of the sun.
The Kingfisher, too, is here (under one of those curious titles : " Variation on a Theme by Marlowe ").
In this mood, what has the poet to do with " variations on themes " ? The two lines quoted from " The
Jew of Malta," oh, let us take them as excuse; let
us pretend excuse is required for

Where is my halcyon ? Is it hid in leaves ?
Does it run in the corn between the yellow sheaves ?
Does light like heavy myrrh cloy its wings
Flying from the sun's heart while it sings ?

And yet it must be confessed that by some unac-
countable magic, some mysterious alchemy known
only to himself, Mr. Sitwell has, without losing his
originality, brought Marlowe to life again. Not only
" The Jew of Malta," from which he quotes, but
Marlowe's other plays remind us that the modern
poet has been rambling through the shimmering
precincts of this genius. From *Lust's Dominion* :—

Chime out your softest strains of harmony
And on delicious Music's silken wings
Send ravishing delight to my love's ears ;
That he may be enamour'd of your tunes . . .

Q

Verses and imagery like these were surely not un-
familiar to the poet of the " Serenades." There are
several passages in *Tamburlaine* which may have
inspired that early exercise " The Mayor of Murcia,"
and have assisted the satirical manner of the " Zarathustra " variations—a sort of extravagant irrespon-
sibility of statement. In *Edward the Second* it is
easy to find lines as suggestive as the following of
a source of inspiration for lyrical imagery which we
have come to regard as Sitwellian:

> And in the day, when he shall walk abroad,
> Like sylvan nymphs my pages shall be clad;
> My men, like satyrs grazing on the lawns,
> Shall with their goat-feet dance the antic hay.
> Sometimes a lovely boy in Dian's shape,
> With hair that gilds the water as it glides.

The less Italianate Peele is also interesting to compare with Sacheverell Sitwell in lyrical mood. *David
and Bethsabe*, from which the modern poet was able
to quote so " Sitwellian " a couplet as

> God in the whizzing of a pleasant wind
> Shall march upon the tops of mulberry trees

has certainly another element felt in his own verse.
Bethsabe's song is very suggestive:—

> Hot sun, cool fire, temper'd with sweet air,
> Black shade, fair nurse, shadow my white hair.
> Shine sun, burn fire, breathe air and ease me;
> Black shade, fair nurse, shroud me and please me;
> Shadow, my sweet nurse, keep me from burning,
> Make not my glad cause, cause of mourning.

Let not my beauty's fire
Inflame unstaid desire,
Nor pierce any bright eye
That wandereth lightly.

And the speech given to Bethsabe after the song
is full of glimmering images of clear water and leaf-
barred sunlight.   It appears that the young poet
in reading the Elizabethans eagerly fastened on two
types of imagery which occur with a peculiar
brilliance in renaissance poetry.   First, the simpler,
general, pictures of " nature," springs, fountains,
trees, sunlight, which came to renewed life out of
their chrysalids, the ancient classical divinities, and
the dryads, fauns, satyrs, nymphs.   Secondly,
peculiarly Elizabethan, fantastic, images, like unicorns, and a weird collection of magical furniture,
in which crystal and amber and musical instruments
are an important part.   There is another indication
of an individuality of imagination shaping itself in
the fact that the clearest approach to seventeenth
century poetry is to the half-magical garden imagery
of Marvell.   Mr. Sacheverell Sitwell retains the Elizabethan freedom of myth-making while adding to it
the modern vividness of detail in picturing natural
objects.   Not a little of the myth-making in the
lyrical poems of this poet is paralleled in his prose,
especially in *Southern Baroque Art*.   The following
are representative examples of his imagery in prose :

" The ship sailed into shore like a horse galloping
over the fields."
" His lowest notes were like the roaring of flames

imprisoned deep down inside the earth, and in the highest register his voice was a wind playing among the lolling bells of green leaves on every bough."

" In another moment she would have travelled far enough over the blue plain to show far down the horizon, with no hull, but only her sails and rigging like a few white flower petals blown by the wind into a spider's web."

The greater part of *Southern Baroque Art* is myth-making which belongs to lyrical poetry as much as to criticism. *All Summer in a Day* is also rich in fantastic imagery, which is used with great success to represent memories of childhood. In the *Thirteenth Cæsar* as in the " Variations " in the *Hundred and One Harlequins* volume, the poet shows himself to be a master of metre. No better lyrics in free verse have been written than the best of his. " The Cherry Tree " is an exquisite little love poem which disposes of all sweeping arguments against irregular unrhymed verse as a vehicle of vital and evocative poetry. Such poems, in which the accustomed patterns and chimes of regular metre are discarded, afford the surest test of a poet's authenticity, for rhymes and old metres may awaken pleasing associations to veil any failure in the essential poetry. But all degrees of so-called " regularity " in verse are alike to Mr. Sitwell in the lyrical mood. Sometimes in the same piece, with perfect propriety, the irregular verses run into a breaking wave, a regular couplet such as

> Let light out of the black coal break
> And shadows on the four walls shake

in " Shadow."   Or, as in " Fortune," the irregularity
of the verse is a response to rhythmic changes which
seem like happy accidents :

> Grass, that green fire is lit
> And trees are aflame :
> If we sing out loud will echo call our name ?—
> Echo—the answer to our heart's desire,
> Telling us we live with tongue of fire :
> Tread the sliding shade, then, and try your voice !
> I stood below the shadowed boughs
> And sang out loud
> The birds, soft and crooning, did I rouse.
> The leaves shook, and shook again
> As struck by rain,
> But every time the boughs were lifted
> The shadow leaves altered,
> And when I tried to follow them
> My footsteps faltered . . .

But if one turns to " New Water Music," it
becomes obvious that the poet cannot avoid monotony and incoherence in writing free-verse at length.
In all these longer pieces that are not satirical many
lovely images float or flame up, but the lack of any
continuous rhythm and the absence of a co-ordinating harmony causes a more or less wholesale dis-
integration.   The poems break up like over-blown
flowers into separate clusters of petals.   As their
length is less, so, like " Wind as Husbandman " and
" Gardener Trimming Hedges," they approach to
coherent unity.   It is remarkable also how the occasional rhymes and assonances in the latter strengthen

the continuity of the poem by merely suggesting a
pattern. The poet appears to have realised his failure
in the free verse form for a prolonged lyrical or
philosophical poem, and so in " The Satander
Quartet in a Programme of Spanish Music," an
ambitious, and generally successful long poem, he
has not only made twelve divisions, but employs all
varieties of verse, rhymed and unrhymed, regular
and irregular.   One might say that the various
sections are separate poem, but he must be credited
with having produced a whole here worth more than
the sum of the parts : it is a true sequence, and does
impress the mind like a " programme of music."
Certain other long pieces in this volume are at least
extremely interesting experiments.   " Actor Rehearsing " is very like a new form for the dramatic monologue.   " The Winter Walk," which is far too long
for such formless reflections in free-verse, has the
vividness of imagery which is so dearly purchased
at the cost of unity.   The note which prefaces this
poem reminds us that much of the poet's serenading
is in prose born in Italy and Spain.   The same view
of the monastery on the steep hill to which the
beggars climb for alms is described in his brother's
Discursions on Travel, Art and Life.

CHAPTER SEVEN

DR. DONNE AND GARGANTUA

"Never, never, never make a simple statement. It has no effect. One must always have analogies, which make another world. Through the glass effect, which is what I want."—*T. E. Hulme.*

"Purposed laughter is the expression of the will to kill emotion . . . It is also the sign of a revolt against the oppression of emotion by minds that hunger for relief, a need of human nature well known to the showman."—*M. Willson Disher.*

"Pity is opposed to the tonic passions which enhance the energy of the feeling of life."—*Friedrich Nietzsche.*

A CONSIDERABLE quantity of Sacheverell Sitwell's satirical work is a failure regarded either as art or as intellectual synthesis, notwithstanding frequent gleams of irrelevant poetry. These rambling and formless discursions often seem to derive an initial impulse from pictures, though they are not so poetic as the prose of *Southern Baroque Art,* which is ostensibly "A Study of Painting, Architecture and Music in Italy and Spain of the 17th and 18th Centuries." This pictorial inspiration is felt sometimes when the poet is content to do without satire or philosophy, as in "The Italian

247

Air," " The Fisherman " ; the " Extract from ' Bird-Actor '," the last piece in *Hortus Conclusus*; and nearly all the pieces in the " Santander Quartet." " Et in Arcadia, Omnes "—a melancholy failure by reason of its terrific verbosity and the misuse of the sarcasm which only Osbert Sitwell can effectively employ—actually suggests in the title a pictorial derivation. Goethe used it as a motto for his *Travels in Italy* and this or " Et in Arcadia, Ego " was often used by Italian painters for their pictures. The latter was used at least by the French painter Poussin on the famous " Bergers d'Arcadie " in the Louvre.

To make good use of a limited amount of space, an examination of the most important of the longer pieces is better than a description of the failures. As regards these, one has only to note the incoherence of thought, the formlessness, the prolixity, and the wretched attempts to be funny in " The Hochzeit of Hercules," " The March Past at the Pyramids," and (without the jokes, these 350 lines, despite the frequent glow of true gold, being beyond any joke) " The Neptune Hotel." But *The Thirteenth Cæsar* (" Thirteenth " presumably means unlucky), the " Variations on Themes out of Zarathustra," and " Doctor Donne and Gargantua " reveal the poet's attitude to human existence. These pieces alone are therefore sufficiently important to justify a detailed consideration of their content. The ironic detachment from emotion which would become oppressive, which brings Sacheverell Sitwell into touch with certain modern French poets from Laforgue to Cocteau, and with the Flemish de Bosschère, is here elaborated in a manner more original than eccentric. The waste of words, the mere talkativeness which ruins much of his work, is not entirely absent from these pieces, but the vision in them is clear and the thought tangible.

The " Two Variations on Themes out of Zarathustra " own by the title a debt to Nietzsche. Nietzsche was a philosopher-poet, for the presentation and the association of his ideas are worth more than his rational system, such as it is. The scheme of " Zarathustra," ideas delivered in speeches by an imaginary hero to imaginary audiences, is reflected in parts of many of Sacheverell Sitwell's longer poems, in the early " The Mayor of Murcia " as well as the later " Dr. Donne and Gargantua," the other element, the *manner*, being reminiscent of Marlowe.* The hero or prophet impersonates a dominant idea, and the reception of his teaching symbolises some attitude of human nature towards that idea. This is a modernised version of the myth-making method of Shelley's " Prometheus Unbound." Fresh views of eternal verities can in this way be presented imaginatively, so that generalisations can be expressed concretely and in language far more expressive than that of the truly scientific philosopher. It is probable, notwithstanding certain dogmatic assumptions of Mr. I. A. Richards, that only by poetry can language express new perceptions of abstract truth. Without incarnation in imagery and music, ratiocination is apt to become sterile dialectic, by means of which anything can be proved according to the rules of the game, and nothing illuminated by what alone can be called vision, a re-combination of the elements of

* See p. 242, above.

experience comprising within itself the vitality of an organism. All that is not poetry in philosophy is purely scientific discovery* or else dialectical ingenuity. Nietzsche's Eternal Recurrence was not science and certainly was not born of ingenuity for he constantly, as in *Thus Spake Zarathustra*, implicity opposes it. His Eternal Recurrence comes into *Thus Spake Zarathustra* as a kind of after-thought, in direct contradiction of the scope of will in reaching upward to the *Superman*. Thus Eternal Recurrence is a tremendous idea which lives as poetry, by a sort of divine right derived from the manner of its birth. The Superman, too, is an imaginary hero, as poetic in conception as the idea of human perfectibility which Shelley took from Godwin and transformed into a sort of Spinozian Eternity. Both may eventually prove valid as philosophical and scientific facts, but it is to be feared that they must remain purely poetic ideas for some considerable time yet. Mr. Bertrand Russell thinks that in the next stage of our civilising progress the eugenics which Nietzsche saw as the road to the superman may become a fresh instrument by which rulers can control the ruled. The ideal aimed at when the all-powerful government of that day gives the individuals of its choice not titles but exemption from sterilisation will presumably be the production of super-Prime Ministers, super-Judges, super Business Magnates, super Wire-Pullers.

From this gloomy prospect we must return to

* This term being taken to comprise any rearrangement of ideas into a system which covers our knowledge of reality more closely than previous systems. But poetry always implicitly anticipates what philosophy makes explicit.

" Laughing Lions Will Come " and " Parade Virtues
for a Dying Gladiator " to find a scarcely brighter
outlook, for these pieces are indeed " variations ";
they contain no hint of the faith which Zarathustra
left his mountains to preach to mankind. According
to Sacheverell Sitwell, Zarathustra, failing to gain by
other means the attention of the people intent upon
amusement, races madly backwards and forwards
through the town until a bewildered crowd caught
in a kind of tarantella craziness is running as madly
as he. Then

>   He ran into a house
>   And climbed the shaking stairs.
>   Out from a window on a roof he stepped
>   While the people ran up stairways
>   Like a flood inside a well;
>   Down a drain-pipe on the ground again
>   He heard the tumbling ceilings
>   And the roofs fall in.
>   Whilst the survivors took the road again
>   Zarathustra ran out from a gate once more
>   Till he reached the burning sand,
>   And fell back breathless,
>   Blind from the dust
>   And dead with running.
>   Clouds of dust still rose from the town,
>   Blurred murmurs
>   And the tread of hundreds running.

It is astonishingly like a Harold Lloyd film. But
what are the reflections of this prophet of the Superman ?

>   " I won attention by my ruse."

In " Parade Virtues for a Dying Gladiator " a
similar idea is elaborated.   The world which in
" Laughing Lions " resembles a vast circus, where
the people are a shallow-minded mob intent on
shallow amusements, is the amphitheatre where
these doomed gladiators give their performance.
They are the prophets and the Kings, sublime or
false, who have captured the attention of mankind,
and vainly striven, with noble or ignoble motives,
to fill the role of an Almighty God or to do his work
for him.   They are doomed all to the same fate of
being replaced in the popular affection by the gladiator whose turn follows theirs.   Their rostrum is a
scaffold.

> The scaffold stands and totters in the wind,
> a cage for the light—a platform through the clouds :
> remark—a scaffold and a scaffolding,
> a terrace for death—and bars for young birds.

" And bars for young birds " !   The pinnacles of
individual " greatness " crumble like the monuments
of material powers, and are used by the creatures
of nature for their own unconscious and deep-rooted
purposes . . . Nietzche for all his disgust with the
world was never so completely pessimistic.   Considering the betrayed prophets of humanity, as if he
were one of the vast crowds of spectators around the
amphitheatre, God, or the poet, speaks (in very
idiomatic English presenting a strange contrast to
the measured dignity of the speech of the protagonists
in *Paradise Lost*) :—

It seemed to me if my turn should come,
that I would not take the sand, scour out,
and clear the threshold of the Statue dust;
any more than build with the dead, mute, stone;
that I would not snap the fallen swords,
or sharpen their points to help me,
neither slay the old, or build the new religion,
neither beg the streets, or live on an altar.
Parade these virtues, dying gladiators!
Beware of the final finishing copestone.
Hang many masks from your belt,
but the last one awkwardly stops your disguise,
until you break the string, to take the bead—
And tumble the walls of your Paradise.
If you cage your growing trees,
no birds will float through them and sing;
if there are walls, you cannot watch
the fields that slope down till they hold the sea.
Between yourself and the waves there lie
all that divides and walls you in.
A Paradise is dangerous to hunt through
for the rare tigers among the tropical trees;
if you had never attempted this,
you had never been lying wounded now.

The culmination of pessimism is in the conclusion
where the last of the gladiators appears to gain for
himself a more enduring fame than his predecessors
by smart trickery.

"Dr. Donne and Gargantua" is also rather
Nietzchean in its method of impersonation. The
first Canto appeared in *The Hundred and One Harlequins* volume; the second Canto in *The Thirteenth*

Cæsar. Once more the gist of the satire is the futility of all efforts to be like God. Dr. Donne is an impersonation of intellectual (here including spiritual) ambition, and Gargantua is of course the fleshly and wordly successful. A third character is the Almighty, who speaks throughout in the first person. He does not interfere in the action, though as the author of all life He is responsible for the existence of the two protagonists. Such a God clearly is compatible with the free will of the individual, but since the story does not reach a conclusion in Canto Two, it is not possible to say whether the poet regards the freedom of choosing one of many different roads a blessing or a curse, and in any case the poet's opinion on the question does not affect the poetic value of the piece; what matters is how he incarnates living ideas.

As the poem develops Dr. Donne and Gargantua are seen to be antagonists, each in competition with the Almighty; both

> laid a wager, neither won,
> Yet neither underwent the yoke.
> Gargantua said he would contrive
> to get a mandrake root with child.
> Dr. Donne had said he'd strive
> to snare a meteor, wet and wild.

The first Canto is prefaced by a quotation of John Donne, whose inharmonious soul may have suggested itself to the later poet as symbolic of the conflict between spirit and flesh :—

> " Run and catch a falling star,
>   Get with child a mandrake root."

We very soon find the motile imagination of the poet at work. The abstract idea of the poem is developed by a series of cross-country runs on the part of Dr. Donne, Gargantua and God, all three of whom rival the energy of Sacheverell Sitwell's Zarathustra. In the pursuit of their aims Dr. Donne and Gargantua are sometimes in front of and sometimes behind the Almighty, who in spite of their freedom to go whither they will is never very far away from them. No one, at any moment of their life can be very far from birth or death. We are tethered by a rope of time. In Canto One the tricky character of Gargantua, child of Satan, is revealed. He knows that God will not openly interfere with his actions, and that if he is punished it can be only by his own folly, not by direct divine action. God is represented as falling asleep during the chase after Gargantua. He awakens and says

> Fatal weakness, to let slip
> the firm control I exercise,
> for should I sleep, then should Gargantua.
> He only speaks when I'm away,
> and only acts when I'm asleep.

There is a sardonic humour in the next passage, where God describes the mischief Gargantua was up to while He slept. Failing to do more than infuriate the mob by the announcement of his mystical mission, Gargantua is pursued, God (or Death) nearly catching up with him. But

I saw Gargantua far along a street,
open a door, and run inside the house.
Unluckily for all concerned
my hero made himself at home,
professed affection for the daughter,
locking her, and himself, upstairs.
Well he must look after himself,
and I left him, jumped the wall, swam the ditch,
ran, right deep into a wood, and slept.

Next morning—how absurd it seems
that I should share their little day—
I started off, at sunrise, for the West;
but not before I'd climbed a tree
and listened for Gargantua's voice
to crack the stillness and the earthen bowl.
In vain.

The Almighty's attention turns to Dr. Donne

who counts the glittering stars.
He numbered more than the biggest lapful,
forgot his counting, and drifted into sleep.

While the spirit is overcome like this,

" not far away Gargantua slumbers,
fondling the girl he kidnapped, who enjoyed his
violence.

The next episode is Gargantua's usurpation of the
place of God. He founds a religion. The girl is to
be represented as his daughter as well as his wife.

" The child of your parents with an added grace,
    my holy paternity is also yours :
    if their conception, it was my idea.
    You shall be my priestess ; they shall pray to you.

God watches all but cannot interfere.

The irony grows deeper. Gargantua in his glory actually " tempts a meteor with his lance to drop on them." This symbolical lance " that challenged topmost stars, stood, the pinnacle of this temple " —a temple obviously of a cult which did not frown upon the flesh. But the crusading spirit captures something that Dr. Donne is after, something more disinterested, less material than the world and the flesh, so

> Donne could see
> the meteor dancing in cold space
> above Gargantua's boastful head.
> He saw it and he started off
> and ran to bask beneath its light.

Canto Two of this extraordinary myth begins with reminiscences of a madrigal by Roberto Greene :

The swans whose pens as white as ivory,
Eclipsing fair Endymion's silver love,
Floating like snow down by the banks of Po,
Ne'er tuned their notes, like Leda once forlorn,
With more despairing sorts of madrigals,
Than I, whom wanton love hath with his gad
Pricked to the Court of deep and restless thoughts.

This is worked into the texture of Canto Two as a folk-tune might be used in the movement of a symphony. The story reopens at Rabelais' Abbey

R

of Thelema, which thus becomes an image of the
" Court of deep and restless thought," for even the
people of Thelema, by reason of their seclusion, must
have been confronted by unexpected aspects of truth,
if only as memories of former liberty. Most of this
Canto is engaged with Gargantua's speech to the
inmates of Thelema against true religion, telling them
to follow him, who will make the human race immortal, and with the fresh plans of Gargantua and Donne
for co-operation to achieve their aims. Gargantua
says he will persuade the ladies of the Abbey to show
him the herb garden when the light has grown dim,
and there he will look for the mandrake while he
stoops to pick up the falling apples, giving them the
ripest as a gift.

After supper they accompany the Knights and
Ladies on a river-trip; Donne is star-gazing,

Checking up his count lest one should fall;
He might as well be counting in the flowering fields,
For the gold heads grow as fast as he can move.
Gargantua, on another barge, preached his mission,
Telling them the mystery of the mandrake root !

Gargantua concludes by asking to be allowed to
search the garden for the mandrake root. He does
not find this ancient emblem of Aphrodite though
the janitors help him in his search.

" there came the moonlight and it fell through the
      leaves
Lighting on Melulla as she stood there still and quiet.

Gargantua was watching her, as at a window,
And when he saw the air so silver and so cool
That played around her body till it gleamed afar
He ran to Melulla and held her in his arms.

The last words of the Almighty, who is the narrator,
are :
Where is now the mandrake ? Like the meteor, lost.
The silver cord is loosed. The golden bowl, broken.

The reader will not need to be reminded that Melulla
is invoked in the " Serenades," and this echo is the
personal element in a philosophical satire. " Dr.
Donne and Gargantua " is the story of a universal
conflict experienced by the poet himself. The Third
Canto may resolve the conflict but clearly, so far, the
human being is doomed to failure left to his own
devices, as a general truth, while the personal
emotion behind the myth is probably an outcome of
the conflict between love, which is sacrifice, and art,
which is, in the artist, egoism. The theme of Donne's
song from which the poet takes his text, is also instructive. It is an aspect of the eternal theme of
Adonis and Venus, the male's well founded distrust
of the female.

It is noteworthy that Sacheverell Sitwell finds an
important influence in the poet of the avid intellect,
who reacted against contemporary thought and
plunged into scholastic and classical philosophy.
Donne was eager to make use of contemporary
scientific knowledge, but he made a mediæval use of
it ; his co-ordinating principle was that science must
serve theology, or rather mysticism. His poem on
" the progresse of a deathlesse soule " is as adven-

turous intellectually as Lucretius, and nobody could re-read it without being aware of the modern poet's debt to " Metempsychosis," which Donne himself described as a " sullen writ."

The Thirteenth Cæsar, like the Zarathustra variations, expresses a contempt for the ways of the modern world. The first section appears to have been suggested by the taste for rifling tombs of the ancient Egyptians. " Cæsar " is therefore a symbolic term for great autocrats. The cheapness of the mob manners of modern civilisation, which is the butt of the poet's most corrosive contempt, is set in relief by the curiosity of archæologists who confront the present with the past. The first of the five sections of this piece, which is mostly in angry staccato prose, though chopped into lines resembling free verse, is a comment upon " The Opening of the Tomb." It begins :

'Tis a pity they are ashes !
Could we but find their bodies,
Opening the porphyry to see those sores within it,
We'd unroll the league-long bandages
And rub their bones with salt :
We'd see if they have life yet—if their sores are open
And as the lids—those locked jaws—still ;
We'd prise and lever open,
We'll treat them to a trumpet blast :—
They'll know those brazen tongues once more.

The mind of the present comments conversationally, rather like a tourist, upon the quaint idea the old Pharoahs had of being buried with a loaf or a chicken,

Something to give them confidence, for them to pin
    their faith upon,
Like a cache on an Arctic shore, an oasis in green ice,
Or the rails we clench our hands on in the dentist's
    chair.
But the Cæsars proved themselves more progressive;
they had foraged on those frontiers of death and
knew the fields beyond.   They would be burnt, not
buried, so that now

   If you but blow on them their dust escapes you.

" Have we better notion of what next will happen ? "
asks the poet.   The Cæsars travelled light.

It seems that since the Cæsars we are back again,
Tombed and boxed for travelling with large writ
    labels;
But this shall not be always :—
For ever since Democracy was born among us,
(From the foam of the French whirlpool the new
    Venus rose)
As the people get more numerous, what's left grows
    smaller :
We can take still less away with us, and leave less
    mark :
Though, of course, the sheep have sheep dogs
And the loudest bark they most obey.

The last two lines are not closely connected with the
preceding ones but they serve to remind us how
similar to the mood of this was the much more
effective " Sheep-Song " in Osbert Sitwell's *Argonaut
and Juggernaut*.   The disdainful softness of the voice
in the following is characteristic only of Sacheverell :

Well, now we are at his bedside,
Dust, or ashes, little matters
As long as this was Cæsar;
Though his ashes, when I think of it are not so good
For there is no actual drama:
They're more dead, in fact, than bones:
They've not got so much story, as the newspapers
   would say:
All the same we must be satisfied.

He must wake up at the trumpet's sound
So his memory, as it forms again, will show just how
   he stands.

He'll know that he is safe with us,
That not much has altered.
We'll welcome him among us as an honoured guest:
I think he'll find his niche all right, and be his best.

   Which shows that the irony is not confined to the
present.   The second section " At the Bedside "
brings the reader back to the opened tomb.

The mere act of talking blew those ashes in our faces.

This dust that was Pharoah or Cæsar hung in a
column on the wind, still for a moment

As though the winds held back from it and would
   not wave their wings,
Lest these ashes from that old flame raked
Grow cool and are scattered by the soft breath of
   feathers.

Everyone waits for a voice to " speak the soul out
of this emptiness."   All were waiting, with hats off
for the flashlight.

Cæsar's dust, trembling column, can be clearly seen
To the right of the photograph
To the left the famous company
Gathered here to greet him, and to see him wake.

Cæsar is made to say a few words before relapsing
to the loved peace of his coffin. Apparently the poet
has forgotten that he has just told us the Cæsars
preferred urns to coffins. Yet the words Cæsar is
made to mutter in " clipped Latin " are of the camp
and the circus of Rome, not of Egypt. The reader
who is not exhausted tackles next the third and
longest section, " As of Old." The course of history
from Greek hero-chiefs to the feudal autocrats who
came after the Cæsars is surveyed in a sarcastic mood
as a preliminary to " this last century " when

> " we came to knock the idols down
>   and quickly put up others ! "

We came to the Roman rule of Napoleon. He was
the first man " to make a study of the public " :

To find out what they wanted
And to make his wants their own,
By subtle persuasion, and by vaunting of his patriot-
    ism,
Shouting his own virtues till others had to copy them.
The art of proclamation he invented for his purposes,
And to this end alone it is better that a crowd can read,
For then, as they gather round to read the printed
    placard
No longer is it magic that he works among them,
But they are all in his confidence
And he becomes their spokesman.

By this alchemy, what was autocracy became democracy, and the eyes of the people were like the horse's, obedient to its master " because it sees him twice his size."   So the Cæsars make the people " bow ten times before the idols that we carve for them," and declare that they

. . . shall shiver like young leaves at the mention of
    their enemies;
If we start a fire, they'll watch it
And their breath will fan the flames.
The trumpets blown for us, to shout our honour,
Will sound so shrill to them, they'll hear no others,
They will ride in our triumph, willing captives to our
        stratagem,
Snared by steely mirror, and glass armour bright to
    look at.

From this follows inevitably Section Four.   " They are Still With Us."   " Our Modern Sort of Cæsars " use popular education as an instrument to play on.
    " Teach them to read," they say, " and we will educate them."

Memory they want, too, but only back to yesterday;
And their future but a week ahead,
White clouds or black, about their head,
Which at each week-end, they will net and drag
    towards them,
Safe for another seven days, and one more week of
    learning.
Those glorious paladins, the peers of penny papers,
Those Cæsars of our chivalry, our modern splendid
    despots,

Must keep their public gaping with a wish for knowledge
And this meat for their appeties should have a taste ·
of salt,
Its blood must be bitter with a sting that whets their
want for it:
Like the hunter whose pleasure is the pain he goes
to,
The cold wind that baffles him, and sharp sighing
rain.

The passage grows more mordant. " Last Will and
Testament," the final section, gives a reader his first
inkling of the fact that all the foregoing is supposed
to be the Testament of the latest of the Cæsars, " a
peer of penny papers "; " these words are a lifetime
of experience." But his final words ramble so wildly
that one feels it would require more effort to disen-
tangle their meaning than their meaning is worth.

Satire like this implies a positive attitude and a
strong grasp of the neglected ideal. It is less poetic
than Osbert Sitwell's satire, but it is intellectually
more comprehensive. The truth is that Sacheverell
Sitwell has not yet come into his own as a philosophical poet. His satire is like a preliminary clearing
of lumber while he is getting his bearings. What he
will do with the rich material owned by his intellect
has yet to be shown. " Dr. Donne and Gargantua "
is a high promise. Meanwhile the value of his work
is not to be estimated by that of his inartistic satirical
philosophisings, interesting though these are as indication of his intellectual outlook.

CHAPTER EIGHT

BAROQUE AND CLASSICAL

"What was not valid from the beginning cannot become so by the lapse of time."—(A principle of Roman law).

"We talk of creation as a past thing. But the truth is, creation is eternal. Creation never ceases."—*P. S. Menzies.*

THE *Discursions* leave no doubt that Rococo and Baroque are to the Sitwells interesting and neglected subjects which appeal deeply to old loyalties in them, and in treating which they can exercise an original outlook and impart "an unusual tinge" to their work. The element of critical detachment from the subject is explicit in the Introduction to *Southern Baroque Art*, where Sacheverell Sitwell says of the matters he is dealing with : "there is hardly a fresco noted or a building described which has not become blackened by the smoke of adverse criticism, for our elderly critics were bred to hate these manifestations, just as many people born in Dickens' day still deny the humour and the force from which they themselves date. One of my objects has been to dispel these smoke clouds in the belief that there has been no age in history that is not worth examination, and that in the par-

266

ticular period I have chosen there are many qualities to be praised of which there is a total lack in our generation, for self-confidence and fluency are, surely, two qualties which no one could deny even to Luca Giordano. It has also been my intention to establish a definite short-circuit, by extolling practically the only kind of art that is not yet tarnished with a too extravagant admiration, thus completing the round and leaving our own generation free to follow out their own ideas."

And, finally, he says : " Let no reader imagine that because this book deals with a particular period and school, the writer prefers the works of this date to those of any other. So far is this from being the case that a book on Venetian sixteenth-century art, that culmination of the civilisation of Europe, would have been the lightest labour to his enthusiasm." If the book had justified this proclamation of the writer's critical standpoint it would have been a masterpiece of criticism.

The very titles of the four sections of *Southern Baroque Art: A Study of Painting, Architecture and Music in Italy and Spain of the 17th and 18th centuries* prepare us for the difference between this classical poet's method of objective evocation of appropriate atmospheres to serve a descriptive purpose and his brother's Perseus-like journeys. Motility of imagination has already been attributed to Sacheverell Sitwell particularly, and if his method of presenting ideas is compared with Osbert's, the distinction will be found to hold good. Osbert Sitwell's mental travelling indicates a freedom of association rather than the motile imagination. He sees things

almost as statically as Edith Sitwell, but his thought
is naturally almost as disjointed as hers. Philosophical conceptions are not his, but when he releases
his mind to pursue the associations of ideas clustering
around a few dominant interests and emotions the
result is delightful. Not so with Sacheverell Sitwell,
who rarely can visualise an image as a static and
disparate object to be replaced kaleidoscopically in
bright sequence by others. His thought is naturally
continuous and finds readiest expression by following
up the movement of things. The consequences of a
futuristic freedom of association of images in his work
is generally, as we have seen in his verse and as we
are about to see in his prose, a shattering of the
coherence of thought. The unfortunate effect of
running after every fresh image and idea suggested
not merely by the object contemplated but by other
images is reflected in the looseness of his syntax and
the loss of the sense of direction without which it is
impossible to preserve the internal unity of a passage
in verse or in prose. These remarks will seem ungrateful when one considers the richness of the content of *Southern Baroque Art*; but the author of
what should have been a fine work of art instead
of an overwhelming book, offers proof on every few
pages that such criticism is justified. Merely on the
score of negligence—due perhaps to over-much of
that " self-confidence and fluency " he praises in
Giordano—he convicts himself too often of being a
bad artist as well as a critic without perspective.
Words are placed or used wrongly (as one does in
careless conversation). He will write : " As this was
a victory of equal importance to those which ended

in the expulsion of the Moors." Idiom becomes a perfect nuisance in the magical realms he opens up. "So that you could see"; "I think that we have . now summarised"; "It requires only another week"; "as I have said"; "I mention these artists immediately in this connection," and half a dozen lines later, "Zarcillo, I mention." Repetition when a slight rearrangement of the material would have preserved symmetry, is frequent. On one page: "they guard their houses and surround the objects of their worship with lattices of marble, glittering and delicate like falling water frozen before it tumbles to the ground . . ." and on the next page: "For example, the marble screens and lattices already mentioned seem to be made of frozen spray . . ." He allows sentences to sprawl. The vivid thought does not justify afflicting the reader with the following, for the prime virtues of prose are symmetry and clarity and expressive music.

"Sometimes, with the excitement of the chase, with the heavy, rocking swiftness and the unerring course between the huge forest trees, the whole army of waves, of which you were at once, a part and a whole, would spring forward, until the castle from which you were watching the game would seem as if flying swiftly above the rushing waves below, and you were thrown onward, speeding with your own volition, at the pace of the racing body, until you were ready to drop back again into the saddle and go slower now your quarry was certain."

This, no doubt, is a deliberate device, cleverly employed, not a piece of carelessness; but too often his sentences are a wild confusion of co-ordinate and

subordinate clauses involving a plethora of relatives,
demonstratives and conjunctions. All these obstacles
to the reader's understanding are the more damaging
on account of the wealth of imagery and information
which the poet is presenting. His ideas tumble over
one another in glittering cascades. The first section
opens characteristically :—

" Six o'clock in the morning, and already the heat
of Naples was such that it required confidence to
believe in any hours of darkness. Most of the houses
were still latticing the light with their barred shutters.
They were skimming a soft music off the stillness,
and as, one by one, the windows were thrown back,
so that the shutters threw their shadow on the wall,
the very strings of this fluttering music were visible,
lying there as plain as anything for skilled fingers.
Opposite the Church of San Domenico, in the middle
of the square, there sprang forth a foaming, bubbling
geyser, blowing out its lava like fine glass. With
marble and tufa it suggested equally and simultaneously a fountain playing with molten malleable
stone, and a very quivering temporary tressel. The
one was leaping desperately against the sky, which
had lowered a cloud as cymbal for the fountain to
beat upon, and the other was manifestly a hasty
affair, a platform to preach from, or a pulpit high
above the surging crowd."

A closer view of the fountain shows the author that
the figure of St. Dominic is actually upheld by the
jetting water, the saint is " standing like a lodestar

between the hot heavens and the noisy populace, his only support the shaking petals of water." He leaves this square, comes to another, and enters the Gesu Nuova Church in which is a fresco by Solimena.

I do not understand how a sensitive critic like Henry McBride can say* of this method of inducing a mood : " My sense of frustration began not only with the first chapter, but with the very first words." It is true, as Mr. McBride complains, that the reading is often difficult, but the difficulty is caused by careless writing, not by these ingenious improvisations of imagery; and although baroque itself is not subtle, there seems no reason why the prose which is a poetic criticism of baroque should lack subtlety. Where the author does fail critically by pouring out his lavish praise indiscriminately, when carried away by poetic association, it is true he will ignore critical standard and rhapsodise where merciful silence would at least be more decent. But his language is a feast for the mind. He will picture Solimena, for instance, working on the fresco of the Expulsion of Heliodorus from the Temple. He turns into dramatic imagery the progress of the painting. Divinities arrive on clouds before the reader's eye; some Virtues have appeared, half-way to earth; the Temple is a-building. Mortals enter the picture. And below all this activity of the industrious painter lies the church shimmering with light. " It had the air of slowly sailing, like a ship, among those spaces that fire fell on to out of the

* In " The Dial," October 1925.

clouds." The painter works at a staircase, "with steep steps like the channel of a waterfall." This figure would satisfy the most picturesque of prose writers, except the author of *Southern Baroque*, whose mind is now captured by the waterfall (what does it matter if Solimena is scarcely worthy of this fantastical rhapsody?). The staircase, he tells us, was built for surging crowds. So, "like a cascade it would collect all the colours of the spectrum, without the fabulous help of a rainbow." A rainbow of course suggests rain. So, "Intermittent music, that rose from falling rain to the thud of waves, now throbbed with a softer heart-beat in its intervals— a musician or two in broad-striped clothes played his guitar. The rush of the waterfall was even now cooling the hot marbles and sifting the stifled air in the church. This staircase, with its steep and breathless flights as yet unpeopled, seemed already to run with flashing water."

But the most notable characteristic of this poet's prose is the consistently classical attitude of mind it reveals. Although the information, the argument, is attenuated and sometimes broken up by these divagations into poetic imagery, the vision never loses sight of the subject of the whole book, which is Baroque Art as seen by Sacheverell Sitwell. A romantic, let us say Mr. G. K. Chesterton, would have forgotten entirely the critical purpose of an essayist writing about a school of art. He would be riding a hobby-horse belonging to the crusades from the moment that he came across St. Dominic "standing like a lodestar between the hot heavens and the noisy populace." Sacheverell Sitwell's only hobby

horse from the beginning of " The Serenade at
Caserta " to the conclusion of the fourth essay,
" Mexico," is the one he had mounted directly after
or before writing the Introduction, in which he
professes not to have a special preference for baroque.
Considering the immense poetic energy expended in
the 270 pages of this amazing book, one is only too
ready to forgive (although not excusing) the numerous and unnecessary flaws in the writing as well as
in the criticism. Even when these faults are a serious
interference with the coherent sequence of the fascinating argument, they are so often vices full of their
own poetic virtue that the more one reads the more
is one tempted to condone them. An example of
this occurs in the first essay, soon after we have left
Solimena and the church of Gesu Nuova. In three
and a half pages the writer has passed over a wild
confusion of imagery inspired by the church, a water-
side recalling Venice; back again, to the summer
palace of the Doges; a wonderful canal between
colonnades,· with a population of statues. More
visionary landscape, bringing one back to Vesuvius,
and a contrast between its sparse use in Neapolitan
art and the omnipresence of Fujiyama in Japanese
art. How the artists of Naples and Tokio resemble
as well as differ from each other, and then, " to
value all this," a visit to the Certosa of Bagheria.
A vivid description of the town of Bagheria in a
festive mood, recalling the description in the *Discursions* of the procession at Lecce, but inferior as
description, for Sacheverell Sitwell is not a good
descriptive writer, paradoxical as this may sound.
He gathers only the impressions which will assist his

s

critical task of evoking the spirit of Baroque in a deliberately extravagant manner.

Just outside Bagheria he brings you to " the wizard-world of Prince Palagonia." The Villa Palagonia is one of those cases in which his poetry can disport itself and cast aside thoughts of the long, long journey to be accomplished yet. And it takes advantage of the opportunity. First we are conquered by the vivid and numerous details gathered with so much erudition as well as sensitive appreciation of their value, details about the eccentric Prince as well as his Villa. Besides spears, among other things he collected were horns. " He was anxious and willing to buy for great sums of money, antlers of any rare animals. They hung in immense profusion in his villa. He must and would have every extant specimen of antler. Some of the walls seemed hung with dry snapping twigs, ready for firewood." There, one feels, the author might have left Prince Palagonia's horns. The suggestion of their profusion in " dry snapping twigs " is ample. But no ! " The quantity of them drowned the fine aspect of these many-pointed spears given to their ancestors, perhaps, long ago, as a protection against pterodactyls, and the huge winged and beaked air monsters." Will this trip to a pre-Eolithic age dispose of the horns ? No. " Perhaps Prince Palagonia feared some such steel-winged aggressor, for he is reported to have kept his wife in undue seclusion, and to have created the world of stucco and stone monsters to frighten her before childbirth. Many of them he caused to be copied from the fanciful Central Africans described by Diodorus Siculus. Almost a majority of the dwarfs, more to hypnotise and distract attention than to while away their own time, were playing on every variety of musical instrument." If you fancy that stone dwarfs and musical instruments have led the author away at last from the horns, you are mistaken. "Besides these two, Prince Palagonia had a third formalised, and most objectively crystallised, preference—for mirrors." "Mirrors?" you ask, "but we have escaped from the horns!" Not at all. "With music to disarm and mesmerise, and horns to press against beating wings to spoil their heroic clanging, he liked to case the walls with mirror, that no expression and no gesture could escape unobserved. The ball-room is roofed and walled with mirror."

This dissatisfaction with one illuminative figure, this continual quest after the extravagant and surprising and magnificent is due in part to the author's conception of the most effective way to evoke a baroque atmosphere. But it indicates also an innate delight in extravagance and splendour. One feels that notwithstanding the air he puts on in his preface, of deliberation in choosing such a subject, baroque with its theatrical grandeurs and adventurous experiments in novel effects offered a theme congenial to the poet of half the verse in *The Hundred and One Harlequins* and *The Thirteenth Cæsar*. Almost certainly he would have experienced great difficulty in writing so poetically had he undertaken the task of writing about the gentlemanly architecture of Wren, or the noble harmonies of the ancient Greek.

When the theme lends itself to the fervent embraces of imagination, his prose becomes an orgy.

Farinelli's singing of the same four songs every night
to the King of Spain to cure him of his madness is
the story of Part III, " The King and the Nightingale." He pours 25,000 words into this huge prose
poem, which is mostly a series of scintillating rhapsodies intended as a verbal counterpart to the
miraculous bravura of Farinelli's singing. The theme
contains the extravagance of baroque in its most
lyrical vein. The reader's mind is captured at the
very opening of the essay. No hesitation, no variety
of subsidiary themes leading through sixty crowded
pages towards the title-theme, as in the " Serenade
at Caserta "; no preliminary sketch of the plot of
this historical interlude. The critic and the poet are
one, and the poet is lyrical, not didactic or so rarely
didactic that the mind becomes a ship flying wildly
past a strange landscape on the spate of words.
Exhilarating to the soul, but bewildering to the
mind.

" This story, and all its action, is laid in one of
those rare worlds where the children play with young
nightingales as elsewhere with a kitten, and where
a cruel child would pull off the nightingale's wings
instead of tormenting a fly. All through the night
there is a dripping, gurgling music that drifts in at
every window like the spray from a tilt of waves,
and its soft cadences lay an easy road into uncon-
sciousness. Each morning this faint music has an
extraordinary renewal, as if a choir of full voices
were added to it, for the fountains dash up wildly
into the air as soon as the water reaches their pipes,
and for a few minutes they tune up and practise

their throats before they are ready to take their places in the measured music. So sound is their wind that they contrive to keep up their singing all day, never letting its volume die down, however fiercely the midday sun may scald them; but just before dark the water is cut off from the top of the cascade, and one by one the water-voices die away, till their last breath has gone out and they are silent; and now the continuous soft accompaniment of dripping, gurgling music can be heard again, as if it were at the same time the background and the vital heart-beat of this small secret star. So steady is it, and so unchanging, that you cannot hear below its stir, the throbbing and the whirring of the bigger world as it revolves underneath our feet."

All this, and much more, is but a preliminary to the King's insomnia and the nostalgia of his mind, which is then explained in language of a welcome directness, leading to the critical moment when Philip V must either die of his melancholia or be saved by a miracle. There is another long passage, about 1800 words, of imaginative evocation, describing the King's sleeplessness, and then a helpful account of the Court politics and the motives which induced Elizabeth, Philip's Queen, to make a great effort to save her husband. Everything had failed except music. She would buy the finest musical technique obtainable.

" By now, observant eyes can see the mechanical nightingale flapping in the sky on its way to sing to the King and cure his madness, and while it arrives, growing from a speck to a black glossy bird, we will describe the career and the adventures of the magician."

The " career and the adventures " of this rare bird are then introduced into a discursive and highly interesting sketch of the royal architecture and musical entertainments in Vienna in the early part of the eighteenth century. In the following passage we see the essayist undergoing a characteristic metamorphosis as he moves forward into the poet-critic :—

" That was the age of music in which stringed instruments were still written for in proper fashion, and as they never have been again since the death of Mozart. The composers of these pageants were not afraid of extending a long virgilian campagna for the mind to wander across like the shadow of a cloud, and after the fashion of Gluck, one of their latest pupils, the Elysian fields may, of a sudden, be seen sparkling at a window's level, down the perspective of a colonnade, as if they were the transitory and airborn annexe to the palace, a hanging garden anchored here for the occasion. As the music drifts on the boundaries of Elysium roll farther away, until its extent is indefinitely prolonged in every direction. It seems like the proof of the immortal condition into which the music has conveyed you that the way you choose at random out of this limitless paradise towards something with a more living and durable fertility should lead you, after long journeying, to the seashore, where those of a like mind with you are setting off in the dawn wind. The long balustrades of the palace that juts over the water are lined with rows of orange-trees* in ports, and the hundreds of flaming mouths of the fruit among their dark leaves glow like the artillery of rockets which are let loose into the air to summon help from the far side of the water when there is danger."

And so on, into one magical vista after another.

A description then follows of " the heroes in whose company Farinelli lived his illusive secondary life upon the stage." And another significant glimpse of the range of accumulated observation behind this historical discursion—" They will not seem strange, let me say at once, to anyone who has looked at engravings (particularly the *Jerusalemme Liberata* the author adds in an interesting footnote), " or who has seen at Greenwich the portrait of James II, as Neptune in command of the English fleet ! "

The astonishing skill and femininity of the castrato's singing (for these human nightingales were castrated in youth, which explains the tone of the first sentence of the essay) is compared to a strange insect's day-long performance in praise of its summer life. The lavishly extravagant artificiality of the musical entertainments is presented as the background for Farinelli's star turns. Hogarth's and Amigoni's portraits of the prodigy are made use of to give him substance in this fluid prose, and a typical scene is described when he sings before the Emperor Charles. Marvellously realistic scenery, recalling the early Greek painting for which the artist was especially praised

*Just like the balustrades in the " Indian " tapestries at Renishaw !

if the birds came to peck his two-dimensional bunches of grapes. At Venice, a magical world of architecture; wood painted with trees, statues, façades, windows, colonnades and balconies, forming and disintegrating under the hands of Bibbiena's scene shifters almost as quickly as a scene in the theatre is changed for the next act. " City succeeded city with an increase in splendour that ran in proportion to the distance travelled. It was obvious that the moment must come when the objective of these travels had been reached and where the music, that had up till now been eclipsed by the fascination of the journey, must come out in a fine climax of grandeur." From a window or balcony in the centre of one of these magnificent toys a leading singer would answer the serenade sung below.   It was veritably a kind of super-grand opera, and the author shows us the whole mechanism, not forgetting the Bolognese adepts in this strange art of fake architecture. The scene being staged, we are made spectators and auditors. The dramatic presentation of the event is extremely skilful; but the temptation to quote again must be resisted.

It is clear now that the author has never lost sight of his critical purpose, which has frequently ignored æsthetic standards. The wealth of imagery and the varieties of rhythm he has expended on his subject in so far as they have been poetic have been classical poetry. The knowledge which has been the excuse for the poetry has never been overwhelmed by the flood of divine egotism which issues from the soul of a romantic poet and as Goethe put it, goes out into the external world, coiling around external objects and identifying them with the poet's own emotions. He is consistently developing the same theme. The author indeed has the happy idea of transcribing a lengthy list of items from a programme of fireworks given recently at a spa in the north of England (one suspects Scarborough, and remembers Edith Sitwell's poem " Fireworks "). It reads so like the catalogue of the effects of a virtuoso that the quotation of it serves well to show the trend of Farinelli's art. For the benefit of any reader who is sceptical, another programme is quoted immediately afterwards, the programme of a performance " by some one of Farinelli's tribe." It is that of Paganini's very last concert, given at Covent Garden on the 3rd August, 1832. We are compelled to agree that " these two programmes read in a strangely similar manner." They both represent the cultivation of skill at the expense of every other consideration. Farinelli was to renounce this false ideal. We are soon to be told how and why, but only after another extravaganza in prose, a · brilliant mixture of just comment and illustrative fantasy. It is the Emperor himself who while congratulating the singer advises him to renounce all the marvellous virtuosity he had spent the first part of his life in gaining. It amounted to a proposal to exchange artificial sunlight, the product of enormous ingenuity, for natural sunlight, and this gives our author an opportunity for some illuminating criticism not only of Farinelli's singing, but of the school of art it was born from.

The reader who does not know *Southern Baroque Art* will begin to appreciate now the richness and staggering quantity of its contents (there cannot be

less than 100,000 words in it), for we are only half
way through " The King and the Nightingale " essay,
which occupies just over a fourth of the whole book.

Having observed how the author seems to play
variations on his theme, mingling with the central
thread of history and description the improvisations
born of his imagination, we have an opportunity at
this point of seeing another element in his method.

When he has done with Farinelli in Venice, he
says : " if we take an evening where Farinelli was
not singing, we may study him better in his absence,
by contrast with his rivals." It is an attempt to
maintain the dramatic illusion of a story by means of
a conceit. " For example," he continues, " one
winter in Madrid, Charles III engaged the singers
Egiziello and Carafelli to appear in the Opera *Achille
e Sciro* of Pergolesi. To keep this contract, Carafelli
journeyed the whole way to Madrid from Poland,
and Egiziello travelled from Portugal."

These two geographical facts serve the same logical
purpose as the conceit. Carafelli's location gives the
writer an excuse for an interesting account of Polish
manners and art, and the historical events which
produced them. Similarly because Egiziello was at
Lisbon when he received his call to Madrid, we get
an account of Portugal's extravagant king, Joao V,
and the vast Palace-Monastery of Mafra which he
had built with the ambition of rivalling the Escurial.
The interest of the builder of Fonthill Abbey rein-
forces the author's and our interest in this masterpiece (or monstrosity, according to taste) of the
Portuguese empire. Among the surviving relics of
that royal magnificence are the state carriages. They

are, says the author, " like the most elaborate crystal chariots ever designed by the Elizabethan poets to be drawn by unicorns along the level golden sands · of a river bank . . . They still glitter, although long since empty of their load, and stand there with sparkling wheels, still and silent, each like a great sea-shell which is only waiting for the waves to reach it, when the sea-god will come back to his home again, and, released by the waves, the shell will sail out once more to sea, riding easily over the white-crested hills." Splendid nonsense.

There follows a fine account of the typically Portuguese baroque, contrasted with the Spanish, and reasons for granting to the Churriguerresque architecture the meed of praise that is long overdue. But " this is the starting-point of our travels deep into the interior of Spain once more."

Farinelli, who has meanwhile conquered England as he conquered Italy and Vienna, is about to be sent for by the Spanish Queen, and all over Spain workmen are putting up buildings in a style " now so dead and unappreciated," which " had exactly the same virtuoso qualities of rapidity and brilliance that caused Farinelli to be acclaimed as a hero and a genius by his audiences. And it is not to Farinelli alone that this architecture is a parallel, but it affords a clue also to the minds of Paganini and Lizst and, seeing one of its best examples for the first time, you might fancy yourself present at the first performance of the Fandango Spagnuolo, or the Hungarian Rhapsodies."

An incident in Strindberg's " Inferno " is described in order to bring in an appropriate illustra-

tion of the effect on the mind produced by the
Paganini-Lizst Campanella. This is an introduction
to another long virtuoso passage in which the poet
is trying to conjure up something almost inexpress-
ible in words, the advance in Farinelli's art, the new
element of permanence which by hard practice and
study the singer has added to the former brilliant
rapidity. Entirely admirable is the ingenuity and
the imagination of the writer who is trying to produce
in words an effect which shall give, in the manner of
poetry, concrete illustration of the idea belonging
to another art. If one cannot keep separate from
admiration of the skill a doubt as to the æsthetic
justification of such a method, this amounts only to
saying that the fine imagination expended on baroque
is not sufficiently watchful where the critic's own
medium of communication is concerned. The fresh
descant upon Farinelli for instance, forces the essayist
to repeat himself. He has to go back to those
builders who were, he told us earlier, busy in Spain
while the great singer was unconsciously preparing
himself for his life-work at the Spanish Court. Some
intricate facts are unwound from Spanish history
during the discursion on architecture. But the
history, although it sometimes throws some light on
baroque, or perhaps one should say, develops the
poetic theme, adds much to the difficulty of reading
the essay as a consecutive whole. There are interesting details of the life of Charles III and his mental
condition which imperceptibly merge into a fresh
account of Philip's. Indeed one goes on reading
about Philip under the impression that the subject
is still Charles. This is due to another example of

the writer's carelessness, in using the same personal pronoun in consecutive sentences for different subjects.

The preceding divagations of the essay suggest now to the author another device to preserve the tottering fabric of the main theme. Like a repeated passage in a symphony, or a refrain in a poem, he describes once more in a similar vein, the awakening of the king by the nightingales, and the invasion of the king's chamber by the golden hosts of the morning sun, which occupied several pages at the beginning of the essay. But this time the account of the king's insomnia is to lead directly to one more eloquent passage of interpretative prose describing how Farinelli, who has come from England at the Queen's bidding, is smuggled into the room next to Philip's bedroom, and begins singing to the sleepless and melancholy-mad king.

" Les Indes Galantes " and " Mexico," the other two essays in *Southern Baroque Art,* must be left alone because this little work has to deal with three poets and the peculiarities of their work. There is little to choose between any of the four essays in respect of the superficial faults and the radical virtues noted already. " The King and the Nightingale " has been selected here for extended examination because it is the least complex in theme. The same fountain-bursts of prose sparkle in the other essays along avenues of argument that sweep paths through great areas of research, or gleam amid bewildering patches of shapeless forest, where the mind goes hither and thither along paths leading nowhere before it strikes some central avenue again.

Having reached the end of the story of " The King and the Nightingale " we may observe that the author maintains the dramatic illusion even across the gulf between Farinelli and Mexico.   Part IV opens :

" Our Conquistadores are upon the point of starting. The masts are flapping under every conceivable piece of bunting and the whole ship is held back on its cable only with difficulty. Don Antonio Gonsalez is in command once more, with his old charge Luca Giordano on board, and the latter's pupil, Solimena. They are bound for Mexico."

The advancement of the central theme by an incident like the journey to Mexico of the two baroque artists is of course a method congenial to the author, who never misses an opportunity and frequently creates one of describing styles and even sensations (like the tonal scale of Farinelli's singing) in terms of movement.

Careful as he is to weave a contemporary background for the objects of his criticism, the critic of *Southern Baroque Art* fails our expectation in what we may call the pre-history of his subject. Continually he goes back over the route of his criticism to trace the baroque from Italy, and especially from Naples and Sicily, and yet he makes nothing of the significant resemblances in many striking features of South Italian, Sicilian and Spanish baroque and the Asiatic (Moorish, Arabian and Byzantine) manifestations of the artistic impulse. It is hardly sufficient in so full a study of the subject to account for such magniloquent architecture, for instance, as the Seminario, the Church of S. Croce, and the Prefettura at

Lecce, the Church of S. Chiari at Naples, the Certosa of Padula, not to speak of the Spanish and Portuguese variations, as due to the adventurous originality of the chief artists and the " emotion and superstitution of the large town populations of, say, Bologna or Naples." And " the fervour and the hysteria, with all its pagan accompaniments of an un-Christian import." If " pagan " refers only to pre-Christian Rome and Greece the critic has ignored the Arabian and Hebraic elements in the soul of Europe after the collapse of the Holy Roman Empire, and yet these are the elements which produced the distinctively Gothic age, of which baroque is properly an off-shoot.

The account, in the last essay, of Mexican music, which is ascribed to the Creoles, and the descriptions in " Les Indes Galantes " of Spanish music reveal an interest that goes beyond the baroque and which, if one may judge by the content of certain poems, is shared by all three Sitwells. But it is imperative to resist the strong temptation Sacheverell Sitwell offers to go wandering with him into other regions of magnificence. One must throw a word of praise in the direction of " Les Indes Galantes " for the vividly presented generalisations in the account of the foreign influences on Spanish art, especially the transfer from the Flemish to the Italian; and also the illuminating distinction drawn out of the St. Maurice, between the style of El Greco and the realism of Caravaggio, which actually triumphed. In many such passages we are given an opportunity of realising the potential existence of a great critic.

In reading *Southern Baroque Art* we have been

excited, we have been irritated, we have been treated
to a feast of reason and a flow of soul, and we have
been exhausted. But above all, we have been en-
thralled. No work of creative interpretation (I
hesitate to call it criticism) written in English since
Walter Pater's *Renaissance* (half a century ago) is
more clearly marked with the stamp of original power
and vital permanence. Had Sacheverell Sitwell been
as good an artist and as judicious a critic as Pater
he would have stepped with this one book above the
head of the Oxford recluse and have found his
immortal place among the greatest critics in
European literature. But if he does not show more
respect to his medium and his reader, the prose he
leaves behind him will become a neglected quarry
from which later critics will dig out treasures of the
mind to build into their new façades on the ancient
culture.

This staggering essay has persuaded me into allot-
ting so much space to it that *All Summer in a Day*
can hardly receive adequate treatment here. The
preceding pages were written before the publication
of *All Summer in a Day*, which is not only a finer
work of art, but is sufficiently conclusive evidence
in support of the contention that *Southern Baroque
Art* is the work of a classically minded poet, in spite
of all its extravagances.

*All Summer in a Day: an autobiographical Fan-
tasia* established Sacheverell Sitwell as a master of
prose. The carelessness which marred *Baroque* is
replaced by a fresh classic grace of manner. The
potent charm of the memory-burdened rhythms and
the beauty of the images by which he illuminates

those early experiences of childhood which began to accumulate from the dawn of self-consciousness can only be guessed from reading the earlier volume. Mr. Sitwell seems to have instinctively adapted his medium to its very different task. In the preface he asks us to bear in mind the sub-title, *an Autobiographical Fantasia*, " and such is the spirit in which it should be read." Reading it so, one perceives how similar it is essentially to the essay on baroque, which might well have been called a " fantasia " instead of a criticism. But here the sound of the words is remote; the images are more in keeping with the childish mode of seeing things, and the flexibility of the prose is well adapted here to the task of carrying trains of ideas, one pursuing the other, as memories do, forming loops of thought which return like imperfect boomerangs at a point a little in advance of the starting place. The reader is impressed once more by the really amazing richness of material thrown out by the writer, although he declares : " I have chosen but one or two ghosts from my cupboard, brightly glittering ones by preference, whom I have dangled in the light for a few moments before I put them back in their dark corner."

The character of Part One, " Summer in a Day " (Part Two is entitled " Summer in a Night ") is defined more nearly in the next sentences of the Preface : " Some day, perhaps, I may open both cupboard-doors, dusting and brushing at least a few of the ghosts, before it is time to put them away. Here, in these pages, it has been naturally the oldest and most ragged that have required attention, lest

T

they came to pieces and were useless, and so I have
stretched into distant corners to see what I could
bring to light.

"It is noticeable how very little most people can
remember who have not had their memory specially
trained, or, if you like, distorted, by drawing or
writing. 'Oh! your uncle remembered Lord Byron.
What could he tell you about him?' 'He had very
curly hair and used to limp.' Or—'So you often
used to meet Oscar Wilde. What was he like?' 'He
was very fat, he was wearing one of those green
carnations, and he spoke in a loud, affected tone.'
And this is about all."

Oral and visual memory, the seen and the heard,
direct or indirect, providing such scanty material,
need the important supplementary content of art,
especially of painting and literature. The principle
guiding the author of *All Summer in a Day* is simply
that the accumulation of human knowledge, the preservation of the past, is absolutely dependent upon
the loyalty of the individual to his own past. Realising the evanescent character of this past, Mr. Sitwell
stretches as far back as he can reach, to net as much
of the spoil of childhood as possible before it sinks
irrecoverably in the abyss. He tries to start from
the very birth of self-consciousness. It is unlikely
that he succeeds; but he is able to hit upon an
experience typical of that moment, which has many
repercussions in the developing consciousness of the
child. "Time had halted by my side for a second,"
he says, "and I became suddenly drenched and wet
for ever more in the waters of memory . . . I was

filled, of a sudden, with this double-consciousness, both realising the moment and wondering how long I should be able to remember it, for these scenes of early childhood which one recalls with so minute a vision on the rare occasions that they come swimming to the surface seem to set up an anniversary each time they appear, which, like your birthday, leaves you older every time it fades back."

The two brothers and their sister had been on an expedition across the misty fields of North Derbyshire for blackberries; when they returned, the youngest went up to his room, which looked out of the bleak north side of ancient Renishaw Hall, for every day he had to lie down to sleep before lunch. He is ready to come downstairs again, and the sound of his feet on the wooden space between the edge of the carpet and the door throws him dramatically into yesterday, when he did precisely the same thing. He suddenly realises that to put his hand on the door-handle and to step on the wooden boards will bring to birth a new yesterday and cast away the old one. From this point he follows the bidding of memory to call up some of the people who bulked so large in his childish vision, and he contrives to evoke about each of them a self-consistent little world. The Miss Morgan will be no stranger to readers of his sister's poetry and his brother's fiction; there are many scenes which are like sketches, from a different angle, of the scenes depicted in *Before the Bombardment*. That retired old soldier who was his tutor, with whom we are now almost as familiar as the Sitwells, he names Colonel Fantock, following the example of his sister in the *Troy Park* volume. One suspects that in bestowing names on people the order of priority should be Osbert, Edith and Sacheverell. There is a profound sympathy for the inner being of the characters resurrected by these memories and fantasies; Colonel Fantock is especially vivid and real in these pages, and the pettiest of the old man's affectations only serve to make the reader love him.

The nature of the second part of this lengthy " autobiographical fantasia " is also foreshadowed in the Preface, though unconsciously perhaps. After his remarks about oral and visual memory, he observes how few are the ghosts of the past who are still able to attract our busy gaze for a moment. " Posterity " is a fickle and indiscriminate goddess, and has few worshippers. " When we say that William Blake or Luca Signorelli are safe in the verdict of posterity, we mean that a few people of discerning minds are continually shouting about them. That is all the noise there is; and, for the rest, the great masses of humanity are silent—not in tolerance but in ignorance."

We know how varied, and close to the vast sphere of human life outside the small circle of æsthetic interests, had been the early experiences contributing to this artist's education, otherwise the preceding observation might cause a momentary surprise. But he tells us in the first chapter that during his childhood his world did not know " clever people," by which he means " persons invested with some amount of personality, living in an atmosphere distilled by their own words and actions," a fact for which he is strangely ungrateful, since it has given roots to his reason and a broad view to his imagination.

What is indicated in the Preface as to the nature of Part Two, is the sense of the aristocracy of intellect, in which the artist is a leader. Since fame is in the keeping of a little clan surrounded by the vast majority of human beings, and fame is the survival of certain values immensely important, "with regard, then, to one's private mythology, for in this way one might describe the arsenal of memory, those who know anything of interest had better say it . . ."

This manifesto is by no means a defence of what is usually meant by memoirs; it is, in reality, a restatement of the function of the poet as a hero, a torchbearer. The occasion of an autobiographical fantasia is merely an inviting opportunity for such a manifesto. For one might argue that all verbal creativeness is a kind of autobiographical fantasia. The author of this beautiful book has merely found a path towards illumination by following the flashes and flickers of memory. "Summer in a Night," although treated to a separate title, is not a sudden break with the first part, but marks the growing admixture of critical observation with the recreation of memory. The most interesting, at any rate the most important, psychological characteristic which emerges once more is the breadth of view, the firmly homely roots of an adventurous mind which is tracing the ingredients of poetry in the common life of men, and the ever-changing " choice of spectres " which, from one side, is the process of the individual intelligence feeding upon experience. Incidentally, to anticipate the argument of a later chapter, the writer of *All in a Summer Day* has definitely passed out of the mood of the clowning spirit in modern poetry.

CHAPTER NINE

POETIC IMAGERY:
AN ANALYSIS

" Le dandysme introduit le calme antique au sein des agitations modernes."—*Barbey d'Aurevilly.*

" Le métier d'écrire est un métier; mais le style n'est pas une science."—*F. Flaubert.*

" Nothing is more dangerous to reason than the flights of the imagination, and nothing has been the occasion of more mistakes among the philosophers."—*Hume.*

" Tous les rapports dont le style est composé sont autant de verités aussi utiles et peut-être plus précieuses pour l'esprit humaine que celles qui peuvent faire le fond du sujet."—*Buffon.*

" The measure of a man's obscurity to his earliest readers may prove the measure of his interest to posterity."—*Osbert Burdett.*

" The artistic man . . . according to the complexion of his feelings imparts a colour from his own mind to the literal record of his experiences and to the imaginary constructions which he builds upon them."—*Sir Sidney Colvin.*

CERTAIN peculiarities in Sitwellian imagery hardly need mention. They have been the occasion of some controversy among the critics who, generally, have shown a disposition to find in them either an illustration of the theory of

" free association " or a sad example of the limitations of artifice, of the box of toys method. Without
ignoring either point of view, I want to relate Sitwellian imagery to what is typical of to-day and also
reach some conclusion about its relation to what is
typical of undying poetry.

When Moissan, the great French chemist, set
himself to make diamonds synthetically, he took
carbon and dissolved it in molten iron at a temper-
ature thirty-seven times as great as the boiling-point
of water. He plunged the molten mass into cold
water, and the cold outer crust of the iron carbon
mass contained a liquid core of hot iron carbon
exerting tremendous pressure as it cooled. From
the results of heat and pressure a little diamond
crystallised out, a crystal of carbon exactly the same
as the diamonds found in the earth's crust and
produced by the same forces. In the creative
imagination nature is transmuted by a process
resembling in its main phases the experiment of
the synthetic chemist. The heat corresponds to
unexpended emotion; the iron is the imagery, and
the diamond is the finished product—poem, picture,
musical composition. If the artist works without
the heat he will also lack the requisite pressure, but
by the employment of the imitative imagination he
can produce an attractive crystal, of glass instead of
diamond. The simile breaks down when our work
of art is—as most art must always be—something
between pure diamond and glass imitation.

Poetic imagery constantly tends to become more
glass than diamond because similar images are used
over and over again in similar patterns by the poets,

and as poetry accumulates into tradition the scope
of the imitative imagination is increased and its
activity is facilitated. The consequence is an increased
production of work that is described, more or less
politely, as " derivative " and which may vary in
quality from inferior diamond to the cheapest glass.
Unfortunately there is always a receptive public for
imitations of masterpieces. " Unfortunately " only
because there is a corresponding indifference or
hostility to original creations.   Familiarity with
diamonds enables the expert to detect not merely
the difference between true and imitation stones but
degrees of quality in true stones.   There are far finer
nuances of quality in works of the imagination than
in diamonds, and although scientific standards are
helpful in criticism a purely scientific judgment without sensitive intuition is more dangerous than a
purely instinctive and untaught judgment. The first
duty of the conscientious reader therefore is to be
alert, which implies the acquirement of standards,
certainly, but also necessitates attention to individual
reactions set up by a poem.

The content of the work of the three Sitwells is
not so complicated that it cannot be roughly summarised in a few sentences after what has been
remarked in preceding chapters. They have justified
Miss Sitwell's claim in *Poetry and Criticism* that the
typically modern poet records " the common movements of life," though their record is often extremely
symbolic in method.   Queer, quaint characters,
pathetic either in their self-importance or their loneliness, and exploiters and exploited in modern society
—these throng Edith Sitwell's poems and Osbert

Sitwell's satires and stories: aunts, nurses, grandmothers, old maids, servant girls, children, clowns,
pierrots, politicians, bishops, poets, old roués, and
comfortably rich materialists, appear often with a
breathing individuality which interferes with their
puppet-rank as types and symbols. Sacheverell
Sitwell, who does not need and knows not how to
work puppets, makes his criticism of life now a golden
tongued praise and now an ironic comment. All his
finest imagery is praise.

A characteristic of the imagery used by all three
Sitwells is found in painting, particularly in painting
since Picasso. That is a kind of truthful exaggeration, producing the effect of subtle caricature, but
of course with nuances of meaning not available to
the mere caricaturist. It is, except in some of
Sacheverell Sitwell's poetry, quite unlike the exaggeration of the Elizabethans, which was usually a
glorified fustian. It is rather a means of using
ancient imagery without obeying ancient associations
induced by classic myths, fossilised dreams, conventional moods such as the elegaic, and habitual forms
such as familiar rhymes. In Edith Sitwell's verse
this exaggeration often occurs in a series of vivid
images strung together by " free association," one
image calling up another without the control of the
reason. So she writes of the three sailors who met
" Queen Circe, the farmer's wife at the Fair " (by
the way, how caustic is that appellation!) that they

" came from the parrot-plumed sea."

There is a popular association between parrot and

the man who brings the exotic bird from over-seas, and we may pause to remark that if this poet religiously avoids old poetic associations, with a sound instinct she welcomes old vulgar ones. But there is another association arising out of the image just quoted.

"We come," said they, "from the Indian seas,
All bright as a parrot's feathers, and these

Break on gold sands of the perfumed isles
Where the fruit is soft as a siren's smiles . . .

A string of opulent images is called up by the exotic plumage, its irridescent startling green and blue, which was used first only as an exaggerated and vivid image of the tropic sea.

Osbert Sitwell's poetic exaggeration is usually in prose, and does not differ from his sister's except that there is less freedom of association, more continuity of thought. In Sacheverell Sitwell's work the poetic exaggeration is used with a more deliberate purpose still, and differs from that of Edith and Osbert Sitwell generally in type as well as employment. He says, for example, of the Gardener whom he "must snare . . . with a stretch of notes . . ."

His wide hat cooler than a whole tree's shade
Like the snow cap on a mountain shelters him . . .

The image is less direct than Edith Sitwell's purely sensory impression. It is a more conscious exaggeration designed to produce an expressive caricature in the mind. The caricature is in perfect harmony with the theme—a modern pastoral of a country house gardener—and the poet is not tempted to follow the associations of the " snow cap on the mountain." When again he makes out of a serenading song a " ladder of notes " climbing to a window, as he does in both prose and verse, this too is a fresh use of ancient images and also a recall of the best of the witty conceits in seventeenth century poetry; which of course means Donne. It is not however due to " free association " but a process of building up a metaphysical conception with the child's fresh imagination.

Another characteristic of these poets is the reduction which their imagery frequently effects in the dynamic potentiality of certain ancient symbols like sea, stars, sky, fire, in order to throw into relief a quaint or curious idea or some intrinsically lighter, less suggestive image; and this again reminds us of Donne. With Sacheverell Sitwell, it is hardly necessary to remark, this immolation of tradition is a sacrifice to the curious thought. So in an unforgettable though fanciful simile he writes (" The Poet and the Mirror ") :

Deep as the deepest sea, unruffled, never cut by wind,
This mirror is the water where I write my name,
Eating earth up inch by inch
As the tides do, tilting at us out of the salt sea.
I stand before this mirror and I walk away,
While my image, like the dying tide, ebbs before its
    change :

It walks out of the mirror as though I climbed out
  of the water
But yet it never ruffles and I hear no lapping waves :
These waters like the Dead Sea
Keep us floating though we cannot swim.

The reduction of potent images in Edith Sitwell's
verse produces quaintness, decoration and description rather than curious thought.   She is metaphysical only by implication, as a child is, of course.

The sky was of cinnamon

is excuse enough, in her scheme for

Stars were like cloves,

and if you don't like it, better not go on reading or
you will almost invariably forget to protest.   For
instance, after learning that the stars were like cloves,
why be surprised that

The wind cherubinical
Fawning and finical,
Faintly inimical
Wears silken gloves ?

It is part of a decorative and playful pattern in
Façade, where of course rhythm and sound are not
less important than image.
Osbert Sitwell is, on the whole, an exception.   He
does sometimes half obey this Sitwellian convention,
to write, in prose, of " ballooning balconies " and,

in verse, of a " rainbow Pantaloon that slinks down
night's alley "; but his most characteristic imagery
in poetry follows imitatively the established canon
of the poets, that to gain force you should compare
the smaller with the greater, the near with the
remote.   Hence his verse is hospitable to the old
stock in trade, well-dusted, of the poets:

> palaces like water-lilies
> Float palely in the trembling peace
> Of stars and little waves . . .

and

> Night's grape-stained waves
> Cool his aching body.
> The song of the nightingale
> Falls round him
> Like the froth of little waves . . .

Where he approaches most frequently the reduction-
method is in images which compare the far with the
near and produce a stereoscopic clarity of description,
as in *Out of the Flame*:

> One can see beyond
> Into far valleys,
> That seem at first
> To be open blue flowers
> Scattered here and there on the mountains.

He comes still nearer to Edith Sitwell's quaint min-
uteness of image when, in the prose of *Discursions*
he describes blue looming mountains as like scenery
of cardboard for a toy theatre.

Quoting Blake that in this age the five senses are

the chief inlets of soul, Miss Sitwell in *Poetry and Criticism* proceeds to proclaim a theory of sense-confusion in poetry very similar to that of Rimbaud's "derangement of all the senses."* If the speech of one sense is insufficient to convey his meaning the poet, she declares, uses the language of another. "He knows, too, that every sight, touch, sound, smell of the world we live in has its meaning; and it is the poet's duty to interpret those meanings . . ." Here is a challenge to criticism which cannot be ignored, and it may serve as the occasion for examining a Sitwellian peculiarity especially found in the work of Edith Sitwell. In *Poetry and Criticism* she tries to illustrate her argument by an interesting analysis of "Aubade," a poem in *Bucolic Comedies*. The interest of her analysis is immense to a critic; for one thing, she is obviously more concerned with her theory than in doing justice to the poem. "Aubade" begins (and of course immediately reminds us of the Cinderella-like theme running through the "Sleeping Beauty"):

> Jane, Jane,
> Tall as a crane,
> The morning light creaks down again.
>
> Comb your cockscomb-ragged hair;
> Jane, Jane, come down the stair.
>
> Each dull blunt wooden stalactite
> Of rain creaks, hardened by the light,
>
> Sounding like an overtone
> From some lonely world unknown.

* Quoted in Section One, Chapter 6.

She writes of this :

"*The morning light creaks down again.* The author said ' creaks ' because, in a very early dawn, after rain, the light has a curious uncertain quality, as though it does not run quite smoothly. Also, it falls in hard cubes, squares, and triangles, which, again, give one the impression of a creaking sound, because of the association with wood. *Each dull, blunt wooden stalactite of rain creaks, hardened by the light.* In the early dawn, long raindrops are transformed by the light, until they have the light's own quality of hardness; also they have the dull and blunt and tasteless quality of wood; as they move in the wind, they seem to creak; *Sounding like an overtone from some lonely world unknown.*"

Instead of continuing the quotation it will be more helpful to examining closely these first nine lines of the poem in the light of the poet's own analysis.

It will be apparent that she does not mention the most poetic suggestion in her use of the word "creak." Surely this is the association of the cold dawn light and the creak of the attic stairs the sleepy servant girl descends to light the fire. Jane would simultaneously be aware of the familiar creaking of the stairs and the day's reveille. The sense-confusion is no more than condensed statement. The poet again fails to do justice to her own metaphors in

> Each dull, blunt wooden stalactite
> Of rain creaks, hardened by the light,

which gains force from our memory of glistening twigs of bare, creaking trees in the rain. Such imagery is not different in kind from Wordsworth's " trampling waves," or Keats's " rustled air " in

> " Just at the self-same beat of Time's wide wings
>   Hyperion slid into the rustled air."

Each strengthens and extends the original idea. There is nothing new in such telescoping of statement though it certainly is an escape from effete poetry which toys with Tennysonian heirlooms.

But obviously the poet is not trying to associate other images with *light* and *rain* by using the word *creak*, because she goes on to say of *Sounding like an overtone from some lonely world unknown,* " though it seems to us as though we heard them sensorily, yet the sound is unheard in reality ; it has the quality of an overtone from some unknown and mysterious world." But does this halting paraphrase reveal any poetry in the couplet quoted? Does it not rather show that this couplet is a prose statement, and an unconvincing one? What is " the quality of an overtone from some unknown and mysterious world ? " The poet does not make it real in our imagination ; her statement lacks the categorical finality of poetic unreason. But here the fault is in the poem rather than in the idea behind it. It is true that sense-impressions are full of rumours of some other world, and when Poe writes " and the shadow of that perfect bliss is the sunlight of ours " the rumour strikes us as truth.

" Aubade," however, is not the only or even the

best example of sense-confusion, and the question is by no means settled when this poem has been examined. Many striking Sitwellian images really express · audile or visual sensations in terms of tactile sensations, or audile in terms of visual and motile. Sacheverell Sitwell constantly expresses audile sensations in terms of movement, as in his account of Farinelli's singing, or visual in terms of audile, as when he says the barred shutters of the Neapolitan houses at dawn, in latticing the sunlight, "were skimming a soft music off the stillness, and as, one by one, the windows were thrown back . . . the shutters threw their shadows on the wall, the very strings of this fluttering music were visible, lying there as plain as anything for skilled fingers"; which is poetry in prose. Edith Sitwell, whose verse is always crowded with suggestive images, favours tactile and visual terms, and constantly translates these into one another, besides expressing audile sensations in either. She nearly always makes music visible. Wind when it is violent and clouds when driven by the wind are furry and bear-like. Wind too becomes "pig-snouted," an image partly tactile (thrusting against) and partly audile (grunting) as well as visual. Fire also, as we have seen, because of its heat and the animal associations of heat, is furry and purrs. Sunlight, soft and warm and bright, is gold brocade, the tactile being turned into the visual; while curded milk or ruffled clouds as muslin reverses this, the visual being expressed by a tactile image, because it is the feel of muslin (and also the sound of the word) rather than its appearance which calls forth the image.

U

How does imagery of this kind arise, and what is its value to poetry? Does the sensitiveness it indicates belong to the creative imagination? Some help may be afforded by the psychologist. The question may be put in different terms. Is such imagery the fruit of a refinement of the senses, which thus enable the mind to perceive correspondences not apparent to the normal individual, or is the eccentric angle of vision an indication of emotional experiences peculiar to the poets who possess it? To anticipate the conclusion, I should declare neither question sufficiently subtle. Emotional complexes, as asserted in the discussion of poetic clowning, must to some degree influence the mind's mode of perceiving, that is of experiencing life. But if a peculiar type of imagery appears in poetry with a constant frequency, the theory of emotional conflict alone will probably be inadequate to explain it. Against the adequacy of this theory too is the belief of an increasing number of people that we are reaching a stage of consciousness which is characterised by a greater sensitiveness to external impressions. It is a fallacy that the senses of the savage are more acute or refined than those of the modern civilised individual. With the possible exception of smell the savage is sensually inferior to us.* It is claimed to-day that a sign of the new stage in human consciousness is the ability of people to be aware of colours and sounds more acutely and subtly and also to hear music in colour and see colour in music. It is difficult to arrive at any satisfactory conclusion about this claim, for it may arise from hallucination and auto-suggestion.

* I have the authority of Sir Arthur Keith for this statement.

But from this alleged experience of many people it is only a step further to experience, with Edith Sitwell, the inter-communication or confusion of all the senses in perception. The hero in Arthur Machen's *Hill of Dreams* declares that " literature is the sensuous art of causing exquisite impressions by means of words," but his fate, like the experiences of a similar real theorist—Huysmans—lent no support to a belief in the empirical or artistic value of such sensations. If we grant, with Rimbaud, that sense-mixing may be a means of poetic creation, a way of discovering fresh relations, there remains the psychological problem of its sanity or morbidity. It is hardly necessary to say that Baudelaire's mind (and it was Baudelaire's practice which inspired Rimbaud's theory) was morbid to an extraordinary degree. This does not detract from the value to us of Baudelaire's poetry,* but it makes theories based upon it unsound for poets without Baudelaire's abnormal experiences.

The scientific view of abnormal susceptibility to sense impressions of any kind is that it indicates an emotional tension resulting from what is called a complex. It is a great pity† that so many able literary critics are content to sneer at psychology (instead of criticising it) while the average person's idea of a " complex " is that it means a desire to commit adultery or incest. Only a perfect saint, supposing his existence, could experience complete

---

* Because our response to it expresses our own mind, not Baudelaire's. We can perceive nothing that does not latently exist in the mind.

† Though not surprising, in view of the pig-headed assurance of many " psychological " determinists.

harmony of all his desires. Every failure to find
satisfaction of one's wishes leaves a residue of unexpended emotion. If the unsatisfied hunger is intense
(and because sex is so powerful and universal an
impulse, sex takes a big part in the discords of the
personality) and this intense need remains unsatisfied, a morbid mental condition may result. There
are of course all degrees of morbidity. The retired
tradesman who cannot argue about socialism without
losing his temper has a " sore spot," or a morbid
area in his mind. He is especially liable to " see
Red."

A heightened nervous sensitiveness is a psychological intolerance of perceptual experience. The
cause of that intolerance may vary as infinitely as
the motives of human conduct vary. The intolerance
begets a desire to escape into the world of phantasy.
The wish for escape induces a conflict with reality,
with " materialism and the world " in the case of the
typical dreamer. This wish for escape can be
sublimated into ideal strivings or imaginative recon-
struction of the phenomenal universe. Although sex
impulses take a large share in these conflicts, perhaps
the longing for peace is more fundamental. It is,
speaking scientifically, a desire for reunion with the
mother or the oblivion of death. This desire is
opposed by the instinctive feelings of self-assertion
and preservation, and may produce in poetry an
alternation of dream imagery and fierce satire, as
one or the other tendency is ascendent. Such conflicts could not occur if the individual were sensitive
to objects and could exhaust emotion in them, from
which we may understand how a poet can be a

disinterested artist and yet hunger for fame.* Fame offers him a satisfaction in the external world, which helps to set flowing the current of his soul. If he finds so much satisfaction in the rewards of the world that these relieve all emotional tension in him, he is no longer what is called "inspired." The "sensitiveness" of the poet is really an intolerance of certain objects and a desire for phantasy substitutes. So when women speak of a woman as sensitive, they say "poor thing," and "oh, dear me, poor thing," in a sort of mock derisive tone and manner. They mean that the actual is not good enough for her; she is really *insensitive* to it, and sensitive to the non-actual—the moon of childhood. Hence the artist's ideal, "the rare and unattainable brightness." The pursuit of phantasy is in psychological terms a regression to infantile thought. The word "infantile" must not be read in any derogative sense. Regression is a remembrance, a regretful remembrance of "the clouds of glory." A scientific recognition of the processes of the dreamer's mentality cannot dispose of whatever reality may inhere in those "clouds of glory" trailing across the skies of art any more than the scientific theory of evolution could dispose of "God" and the experience offered by religion. The psychoanalyst is concerned with the diagnosis of morbid mentality; his analyses have no bearing other than philosophical on the æsthetic experience, and leaves our sense of beauty only deepened by understanding.

* As a matter of fact, the artist is only a sensitive representative of human nature, which never does exhaust emotion for long in the external world. Very likely even a cow has touches of " divine discontent."

Sense-confusion is a special phase of regression. It may of course indicate in a poet's work a deliberately cultivated eccentricity instead of regressive thought. An element of both may be present (as in much of the Sitwell's imagery of this kind) but the deliberate eccentricity alone could not make poetry out of the sense-confusion. The mind of the child mixes up sensory impressions more easily than the mind of the adult because it is comparatively undeveloped and rudimentary in its perceptions. Development is a process of differentiation and discrimination between the senses. An intellectual and highly skilled poet like Meredith is conspicuous for the normality of his sense perceptions and affords a good approach to the study of sensation in poetry. The emotional value in his imagery seems almost equally divided between the five senses. The result is that people may read into such lines as

" Lo, where the eyelashes of night are raised
  Yet lowly over morning's pure grey eyes "

the experience which their own proclivity guides them to. One will smell the scent of the sea and behold the faint grey dawn. A motile-minded person will see the eyelid, a vast curtain going up, rolling back like a big level cloud and showing a brighter silver grey beneath. A tactile and audile mind will seem to feel the silkiness of soft shining light suggested by " eyelashes," and hear the whisper of the breeze in the trees. When poets tend to use one or two senses most they will be best appreciated by readers with a similar mentality. Robert Graves has shown

us* why he enjoys the tactile Keats more than the
motile Shelley. But images with less variety than
Meredith's may appeal to various senses by the power
of suggestion in the thought and the exciting influence of the verbal music. Gordon Bottomley is a
modern poet predominantly tactile who has written
a beautiful poem in praise of the sense of touch, but
it is easy to feel the tactile quality in his very rhythms
when there is no tactile image. In a line like Shakespeare's,

" How sweet the moonlight sleeps upon this bank "

an infinite variety of impressions may be called up
because of the indefiniteness of the images and the
suggestiveness of the words and thought. *Sweet—
moonlight—sleeps upon—bank*; five out of eight
words open vistas of associations and all the vistas
move out from the motive of two lovers. But this
is not imagery of sense-confusion. Its relation to the
imagery which comes of sense-confusion is like that
between immature and mature thought. The
imagery of sense-confusion is a rejection of the dis-
criminations made by an adult conscious mind. It
is a pursuit of the phantastic heaven of childhood
along the very thought-processes of the child. An
infant's world is a sensory continuum, and the child
in developing passes through the phase of sense-confusion represented in this kind of Sitwellian imagery.
We may regard sense-confusion in poetic imagery
therefore as a legitimate device for capturing the
imagination by phantasy, but with a narrower appeal

* In " Poetic Unreason."

than the more musical imagery of the poet of dream
who makes every potent word evoke the exact perception it symbolises logically.   The most convincing
answer to Miss Sitwell's essay on *Poetry and Criticism*
is that when her verse most securely captures the
irrefutable and final beauty, the " derangement of
the senses " is least evident in her imagery.   Just
a few isolated marvels will do for examples :—

> *The saturnine cold laughter of the water.*
> *Beneath the Asian darkness of smooth trees.*
> *O thou art veiled with tears like some sad river.*
> *Like Ethiopia ever jewelled bright.*
> *We are one now with the lonely wise.*
> *The goat-foot satyr waves were sighing strangely*
> *Of unseen beauty.*

In a piece like " The Child Who Saw Midas "* the
poet can be observed lifting the childish imagination
into poetry, so that what is an individual memory,
such as our amused recollection of queer childish
thoughts, at moments becomes charged with light :—

> The goat-foot satyr waves were sighing strangely
> Of unseen beauty ; at the hot sand's edge
> Anchored by waters like the sound of flutes
> Our nurses sat ; it seemed, I thought, they listened.
> And they were black with shade, and so we named
> Them Asia, Africa, and still they seem
> Each like a continent with flowers and fruits
> Unknown to us ; in the hot noon they glistened
> With wild dew crying of some long-still dream.

* *Troy Park.*

Every clause opens up a new vista, but all of them together blend in a marvellous picture of the child's feeling about the sights and sounds and people in its little world at a given moment. The poet's insight brings out of the mind's dark cupboard something charged with meaning for everybody who can remember childhood. And the passage uses, in a temperate manner, the imagery of sense-translation as well as the normal metaphor. " Water like the sound of flutes " is an elided statement, and equals water sounding like flutes first of all; but by the rearrangement of the sentence the poet is able to suggest also the further meaning in the preceding sentence, that the appearance of the little breaking waves call up an image of goat-footed satyrs, and this leads subterraneously to the idea of the pipes of Pan (the poem opens with a reference to Spring); hence the calling tune of the waves is a complement of the suggestion of their appearance. " The Child Who Saw Midas " contains many evocative images, but most of them lack the continuity of thought in the passage quoted. Miss Sitwell's *Elegy on Dead Fashion* indicates that she has reached the stage where incoherence of statement does not seem necessary to the evocative power of imagery. If the Elegy represents a conviction about technique, we have only to read it as a development of the art in *The Sleeping Beauty* to become eager with anticipation of what she has yet to give us in poetry.

CHAPTER TEN

THE CLOWNING SPIRIT IN MODERN POETRY

" And this laughter of reason refreshed is floriferous."
—*George Meredith*.

" The mingling of the sublime and the ridiculous was an unchanging human need. Long after his tradition had been broken, the clown was still required to find surroundings of emotional significance. That is the idea of pantomime. That is how Perrault and our own nursery tales came to be jumbled together with the ' commedia dell' arte,' music-hall turns, topical allusion, stoutly filled fleshings, sentimental ballads, mechanical devices, patriotic tableaux and advertisements. And that again is how the importance of clowns and pantomime has been hid."—*M. Willson Disher*.

" La question du bien et du mal demeure un chaos indebrouiable pour ceux qui cherchent de bonne foi; c'est un j'eu d'esprit pour ceux qui disputent; ils sont des forçats qui jouent avec leurs chaines."—*Voltaire*.

" If amusement is a recompense secured by laughter from broken expectations and hopes, artistic comedy may triumphantly enjoy a broken beauty.—*J. C. Gregory*.

IN Chapter Eight, Part One, an attempt has been made to find the source of the poetic *paradis artificiel*, the toy world of conceits and images selected to create an illusion of divorce from the world of common experience. This illusion is a con-

314

stant need of poets because the experience of an
" other-world " of reality is inseparable from human
life. It may be possible to find in the *paradis artificiel*
more significance than has yet been indicated. Our
preliminary enquiry began, for the sake of conven-
ience, with Baudelaire as the creator of a new point
of view and a fresh stage-property. He was seconded
by Rimbaud, whose artificial paradise was consciously built up as a harbour from reality, though
afterwards he turned round and scoffed at it. Rimbaud's greatest need was a refuge from the dionysian
fury, which in some individuals always and in the
crowd at particular times, threatens to overwhelm
both the orderliness of civilisation and the austere
rapture of beauty. The flower of experience is rooted
in primeval mud. But the Laforgue of the *Moralités
Légendaires* is the most instructive example of the
new spirit in modern poetry, a spirit which seized
the fresh stage-property and the increased flexibility
of expression for its own purpose. Laforgue, although
a forerunner of Futurism, was a scrupulous artist,
because like Rimbaud and like Baudelaire, he found
in art something more than a means of self-
expression, a refuge from the commonplace and a
discipline of if not an escape from the emotions
generated by tortured sensibilities. The revolt
against the classical tradition towards the end of
last century made poetry the vehicle of a new world
of thought and feeling which included the *fin de siècle*
mood and a great deal more. In striving to reproduce
the *tel quel de la vie* the poets disclosed a fear of
emotion and an envious dislike of faith. Envious,
because faith was a road to peace, and above all they

hungered for the peace which their passionate intelligence rejected. The colloquialisms, neologisms, slang and technical terms imported into the diction of the poets served generally to embody their cynical revaluations of life, often, as with Laforgue, in a Hamlet-like mood of painful flippancy. They were clowning.

> Encore un des mes pierrots mort;
> Mort d'un chronique orphelinisme;
> C'etait un cœur plein de dandysme
> Lunaire, en un drole de corps . . .

James Huneker says of Laforgue:

" This young Hamlet, who doubted the constancy of his mother the moon, was a very buffoon; I am the new buffoon of dusty eternities, might have been his declaration; a buffoon making subtle somersaults in the metaphysical blue. He was a metaphysician complicated by a poet . . . He promenaded his incertitudes." And: " This Pierrot lunaire, this buffoon of new and dusty eternities . . . sings the sorrows and complaints of a world peopled by fantastic souls, clowns, somnambulists, satyrs, poets, harlots, dainty girls, Cheret posters, pierrots, kings of psychopathic tastes, blithe birds, and sad-coloured cemeteries."*

In the lyrical, subjective mood the poets laughed at themselves; when they externalised emotion they laughed with the same bitterness at the world. To produce a new, hard, cruel laughter at the stupidities and sins of the world was the task which Marinetti once urged upon the music halls. Twenty years later

* " Ivory Apes and Peacocks: The Buffoon of the New Eternities."

he might have assigned the task to the "movies," that glorious opportunity shamefully lost. But all the time this function was being performed by poets, · painters, and musicians.

The outbreak of the European war seemed at first to cause a revival of faith in the poets, but as that last overwhelming irony of "progress" loomed ever larger anything like heroics in verse began to read like a final text on futility. The new mood could not be adequately expressed by the poets who were soldiers, and those who were not soldiers were, generally, unable to feel the emotional conflict. Some of the soldier poets turned away from the horror to sing desperately of birds and green fields, of ivied churches and winding rivers of home. Others, like Siegfried Sassoon and Osbert Sitwell, turned in a rage upon the sentimental and the profiteers. Intolerable disgust with the betrayers, intolerable pity and love for those whose sacrifice was vain, intolerable disillusionment in the face of triumphant greed in the exploiters and noble folly in the exploited—how should poets caught in that maelstrom blow soul animating strains? As we proceeded, after winning the war, to win the peace, was it not natural that many of the most intelligent and sensitive of the younger poets resorted to satire, bitter satire mocking at themselves as well as the world? Read Laforgue's *Hamlet*, or even his "Solo de Lune" since this is in verse, and then read T. S. Eliot's *The Waste Land*. The difference in the two hardly measures the increased dimensions of the tragic irony of the fact that the spiritual chaos has grown wilder. The mood, mingled disillusionment, diffidence, cynicism, flippancy, and recurring hints

of some *Ultima Thule* of the spirit, is the same,
Robert Graves in an interesting analysis of *The Waste
Land** based on the poet's notes finds in this poem
the following threads : A semi-mystic ethnological
theory of the " Holy Grail "; a clairvoyante's prog-
nostication from a Tarot pack of cards; the wish for
death that follows the output of too much emotional,
or prophetic fire, as the Cumaean Sibyl felt it; the
seer Tesresia's double-sexed view of human relations
as described in Ovid; the disciples of Christ journeying to Emmaus; Buddha's fire sermon. *The Waste
Land* is, according to Mr. Graves, admirably descriptive of a glorious and complete emotional and intellectual tangle, " a-maze thick with cul-de-sacs, the
chief of which are dissatisfaction with Bostonianism,
Oxonianism, and with the crudeness of the Philistinism which denies Boston and Oxford; conflict
between theoretical hedonism and disgust of
hedonism in practice; conflict between a desire for
religious mysticism and the sophistication which
prevents him from abandoning himself to it."   It
is not possible to read this very Gravesian analysis
without a smile, particularly as the critic is supposed
to be praising *The Waste Land*, but he says enough
that is acutely true to substantiate the theory that
a spiritual harlequinade is being played out in modern
poetry. Richard Aldington's *A Fool i' the Forest*
is another clear, though less important example of
clowning in poetry; and so too is much of Humbert
Wolfe's delicate work. In France the mood has been
prevalent since the war. Jean Cocteau is one of the
poetic harlequins who outside his own country is now
                   * In *Poetic Techniques.*

associated with the *tel quel de la vie* manner of
expressing a spiritual attitude peculiar to clownship,
though the people who try to read him are fewer ·
than those who chat about him—and really one
cannot be surprised at this. Vachel Lindsay is one
of the poets of modern America who while pursuing
another aim have displayed the reason in unreason
and the splendour of the ridiculous. Because the
phantastic world where folly is wisdom and make-
believe is logic is the world of the harlequinade, the
chief harlequin of modern poetry in English is Walter
de la Mare, whether he is writing poignant lyrics
like " Motley," phantasies in prose like *The Memoirs
of a Midget*, or his incomparable poetry of childhood.
But the poetry of dream is rarely satirical ; the poet
is generally content to escape into the enchanted
wood, so that the satirical exceptions to Walter de
la Mare's dreaming poetry are rather lonely masterpieces. There is not much modern poetry which is
at once a presentation of dream and searching satire,
but a considerable proportion of Edith Sitwell's
would belong to a carefully compiled anthology of
such work. This is what has been called her witty
dream poetry.

In all three Sitwells a love of the comic and an
intellectual delight in the Harlequin, the Clown and
the Pantaloon are obvious. But their interest is often
deeper than a merely intellectual delight : this is but
a veil to more obscure purposes of the dreaming mind.
Edith Sitwell instinctively found a congenial atmosphere in the Russian Ballet, which is essentially a
form of pantomime, a sentimental harlequinade.
" Clown Pondi " has been noted as an unfulfilled

promise in Osbert Sitwell's *Argonaut and Juggernaut*, but the promise remains; and much of his satire, when the mordant wit which reminds us of Talleyrand's is discarded, becomes in part the exuberance of clowning and in part a regression to the poetry of childhood. Gino Severini, a member of the race which gave the Harlequinade and the puppet show to Europe, is a painter whose preoccupation with Harlequins and Pantaloons will be familiar to all readers of the Sitwell brothers' books of verse, for the wrappers of these volumes have shown reproductions of this modern Italian's pictures in Osbert Sitwell's possession. Sacheverell Sitwell's sympathy with the spirit of Harlequinade is revealed not only in *The Hundred and One Harlequins* but in nearly all his work, lyrical and satirical, though his expression of it does not need the furniture of the artificial paradise. It was previously said that he made the Wind into a sort of benevolent Mercury. For Mercury one could read Harlequin—the Arlecchino of magic who became so popular in England during the eighteenth century as Harlequin, invading pantomime on the major stage and slowly abandoning the Italianate show of the minor stage of the booths at fairs and pleasure resorts. The gladiators in the second of the " Two Variations on a Theme out of Zarathustra " are clowns in the arena of the circus of the wide world, and like other figures in this poet's satires they wear the mask. The modern clown's burnt cork or pigment is the substitute for the ancient mask. On a more intellectual plane where muscular action is translated into mental, the typically modern poet puts on a mask and clowns in obedience to a principle which has persisted throughout the long development of clownship.

The history of western civilisation has been to no small extent a matter of learning how and when to laugh. The principal lesson of Showmanship is, in Mr. Willson Disher's words : " Satisfy people's desire for the ridiculous and they will accept your idea of the sublime."* This has been recognised by the modern Bernard Shaw as clearly as it was recognised by the still more modern Shakespeare. In the Hebrew Old Testament there is no humour; Sarah's laugh is a bark of unbelief. In Homer the laughter at Thersites is boyishly brutal, and there is no other. Comic relief was not a part of poetry in the classical ages of Greece and Rome. The Athenian audience found relief from the succession of tragic dramas by the impersonality of the masked players and the alternating burlesques of the satirists. In Rome the mythological drama was broken up by burlesque interludes of clowning similar to that of the modern but dying pantomime. The mediæval church, first at Constantinople and later at Rome, recognized the necessity of comic relief; holy days became holidays. When the miracle plays became too comic for the taste of the Bishops a generation of lay showmen carried on the tradition of clownship. Laughter was growing satirical. In the Elizabethan drama, owing to the fact that players as well as jesters were paid servants of the court or of rich lords, the comic element was part of the play. The genius of Shakespeare drew out of this combination all the possibilities of comic relief. The combination of showman and dramatist

* *Clowns and Pantomimes*, by M. Willson Disher.

x

did not outlive the Elizabethan tradition, but many
of the minor Elizabethans' plays are little removed
from unusually well constructed pantomime. Dekker's *Old Fortunatus*, for instance, is really a glorified
harlequinade.   Old Fortunatus himself might be
Pantaloon, Andelocia becomes Harlequin, and
Shadow the Clown.   The history of the English
theatre in the eighteenth century is largely the record
of a ding-dong battle between the Elizabethan tradition (used by Pope in the *Dunciad* as a flail) and the
mixture of folklore and melodrama with the clowning
and mechanical magic of the Italian harlequinade
which ultimately developed into pantomime through
the genius of Guiseppe and Joseph Grimaldi. After
the pantomime clown came the music-hall clown, and
then, as George Grossmith described himself, the
society clown, of musical comedy and revue. Finally
we have Charlie Chaplin and the other clowns who
enlist the incomparable magic of the kinematograph.
Until the end of the Victorian Age poetry was
divorced from the art of clowning, if we except
Edward Lear.

Among living poets the Sitwells are conspicuous
for their presentation of the spiritual harlequinade.
The stage-property of their harlequinades generally
consists of satirical symbols of the world. In Edith
Sitwell's continually developing art a similar spirit
is found to persist from *The Wooden Pegasus* and
Clowns' Houses to *Bucolic Comedies* and *Troy Park*.
The deeper seriousness which seems to invade the
later work is akin to that which the poet found in
the Russian Ballet. After *The Wooden Pegasus* the
poet rarely fools lightheartedly.   Her humour in

Bucolic Comedies is comic relief from tragedy, and she is re-interpreting Shakespeare's tragic fool. A comparison of "Bank Holiday" in *The Wooden Pegasus* with "I do like to be beside the Seaside" in *Troy Park* is instructive. Similar metrical devices and queer imagery; but where "Bank Holiday" is a gay futurist picture of surfaces, the two pieces entitled "I do like to be beside the Seaside," suggested to the poet by an old doggerel tune, become an indescribable mixture of the comic and the serious, wooden stage property and remote dream. The sudden rush of words, "Light green waters swim their daughters, lashing with their eel-sleek locks," between the syncoping pauses of the "Bank Holiday" verse, is paralleled by the sudden rush of the halting rhythm of "I do like to be beside the Seaside" into

> Thetis wrote a treatise noting wheat is silver
> like the sea; the lovely cheat is sweet as
> foam; Erotis notices that she
>   Will
>   Steal
>   The
> Wheat-king's luggage, like Babel
> Before the League of Nations grew—
> So Jo put the luggage and the label
> In the pocket of Flo the Kangaroo.

If you are not content to enjoy the lilt, the pattern and the nonsense here, there is a nice task in the unravelling of the satire, the play of thought which accompanies the play of words. But the satire is implicit in the crazy jazz rhythm so that little is lost

if the verse is read as pure nonsense. " Punch and
Judy Show " and " Clowns' Luck " in *Troy Park*
remind us that the poet of *Bucolic Comedies* has
moved towards a calmer vision which is carried by a
music full of haunting sorrow and sweeps across the
tragedy of life without being engulfed in it. " Clowns'
Luck," which was suggested to the poet by the
Picasso-Cocteau-Satire Ballet " Parade," describes a
sea-side pierrot troup and the town of lodging houses
whose guests are to make an audience.   Since the
inhabitants include " generals with mayfly whiskers,
those dead ghosts," we may hazard a guess in passing
(remembering Colonel Fantock) that Scarborough
assisted the ballet in providing the stage scenery.
The pierrot-troup is the modern version of the travelling puppet-shows so popular in the eighteenth century, and of which only " Punch and Judy " survived
until the twentieth century.

The Clowns now leave the sand, like curled waves
   flow
Through the travelling theatre's portico
Where through we see the blank sea ever flow . . .

Their harlequinade becomes the microcosm of human
existence :

    What lies broken now behind
    That portico ? Strange outworn masks
    Of tragedy and empty blind
    Masks of comedy the wind
    Has torn with whispers,—broken swords
    For fighting in a vast war only

Of the spirit,—spears to fight
The empty and the hopeless lonely
Wind, or elegant scornful waves—
And that drum for Time the clown
To beat his little marches down
The vistas to the listening grave.

Is it not as if the theme, " To-morrow and to-morrow and to-morrow " has been woven into a ballet?

The actors in the booth are strangely like the pitiable puppets aping " high life " at Los Angeles studios :

    they dream
Of life in this dead pleasure land

Grown outside life for ever; if they call
Or beckon, no one answers them at all,

Our empty brains are echoing with the words
" Nothing beyond, but what our eyes have seen."

The poem is of course realistic as well as symbolic. The realism of " Clowns' Luck " is that

The audience has long been blown away
By the cold wind,—perhaps has never been.

But so interwoven are symbolism and realism that one wonders if this poet will not yet give us the first poetry of the kinematograph. Not scenario drama or spectacle but another cross-section view of the

souls of actors and spectators at the same strange
business of being alive. In "Clowns' Luck" the
actors are charged with the truth that does not pass,
while this world fades like the mirage it is, a longed-
for and disappointing mirage. The sad sands on
which they try to make laughter to buy bread are
"countries of the mind" which eventually the three
clowns leave for new spring landscapes of day-dream.

"The Punch and Judy Show" is a deliberately
subjective lyric, belonging to Miss Sitwell's witty
dream poetry. The environing world and the inner
world of the poet's heart join to make the puppet
show which is suddenly realised in a Punch and Judy
booth. Her blood

> Mimics each puppet's leap and cry
> Shrills to the Void, hung up on high,
>
> Limp in bright crackling rags of laughter,
> Ventriloquism following after
>
> Dictates of strings my ancestors
> Jerk from my memory's corridors.

This is quite close to a secondary mood in *The
Sleeping Beauty*, and we are again at the Fair which
invades the stillness surrounding the princess.

Several other pieces in *Troy Park*, notably "Three
Poor Witches" and "The Bear," bridge the gap
between the comic mood in *Bucolic Comedies*, a
sophisticated tragi-comedy, and the humorous
quaintness of dream imagery of which Walter de la
Mare is the master.

Osbert Sitwell's poetic clowning revels in the prose of " Triple Fugue," and we have seen how in verse his satire develops from bald sarcasm to a harle- · quinade of wit. He is unable to make his rhythms jazz and juggle; when he writes a " Fox-Trot " it lacks the verve of his sister's verse. But he obtains an effect of irony in the careful employment of conventional metres for very unconventional thought. This device is a reminder that the alteration of the association of ideas to which we have become accustomed is more essential to the spirit of modern poetry than changes in the form. The new orientation of the intellect which is labelled " Modernism " has produced alterations in painting and music which correspond with the changes in poetry.

" The work of art, good or bad, cannot help being the translation of law and order, or the want of law and order, in the mental composition and organisation of its creator . . . the creation is organic before it is conscious. The actual work of imagination is unconscious.; it is the result only which awakens consciousness . . . the new products are developed in their times and places out of the capitalised mental store as necessarily and naturally as the sprouting buds on the sapful branches of a tree in spring, or as complex chemical compounds. No doubt the process of the organic synthesis is a much more complex affair . . ." and there are " some special afﬁnities and repulsions connected by the term ' vital ' " of which we know little yet, wrote Maudsley in 1897,* and his remarks are helpful to-day. It must be

* " Natural Causes and Supernatural Seemings " by Henry Maudsley, M.D.

remembered that " law and order " connotes the
operation of a sound organism and the self-consist-
ency of a rational system. It may be assumed that
the greatest works of art are the product of such
" law and order " in imagination, though the organism—that is to say the mental machinery—of many
a great artist, while fundamentally sound has not
been normally healthy, healthy here meaning an all
round balanced sensitiveness to impressions. A
deviation from the normal response to stimuli may
be caused by a physically morbid or at any rate
peculiar organism, or by that acquired morbidity or
peculiarity which the modern psychologist calls a
complex. The physical peculiarity only concerns
criticism on account of its psychological consequences, which may be indistinguishable from the
signs of an emotional complex. Phthisis is frequently
such a physical peculiarity of the artist. The hunger
for love is just as frequently a psychological
peculiarity, for the artist being inclined to exceptional egoism is exceptionally liable to erotic dissatisfaction. Neither peculiarity is confined to artists
of course, but artists reflect such peculiarities in their
work, chiefly by the association of ideas.

Now ideas are associated by habits exactly like
muscular movements, and repetition makes their
grouping also more facile, while fatigue follows upon
prolonged activity of the same ideas exactly as it
does in the case of physical motions. Sometimes
ideas require as much time for co-ordination as
muscular movements. Darwin observed that a
musician could press the keys of a harpsichord in
the order of an accustomed tune as quickly as he

could run over the notes mentally. If space permitted in this book it might be shown how the disassociation of old groups of ideas have produced the wilder moments of writers like James Joyce and Gertrude Stein, and how such efforts are paralleled in music and painting. The need of making new associations, as we have seen, may come from the poet's reactions to the external world; but the abnormal response to experience is likely to owe its energy in the first place to some personal peculiarity. When Miss Sitwell in her essay on "Poetry and Criticism" pleads against the weary repetition of images and diction which were revolutionary in Wordsworth's day and became part of an honoured tradition in Tennyson's, she has the best of her own work to support her claims for new associations and for attention to the "abstract pattern" of style. But when she quotes an incoherent and incomprehensible passage from Miss Stein's prose and declares it is beautiful, we are aware of a pitfall in the argument. It is true that a great number of second-rate poets have forgotten that a poem must be unique; but the "abstract pattern," the employment of words so that their contact one with another sets up a spontaneous current of vitality, does not pre-suppose incoherence of thought or of syntax. *The Sleeping Beauty* would have been a great poem if Miss Sitwell had remembered this, and so would "Dr. Donne and Gargantua" if Sacheverell Sitwell had remembered that Shelley never wasted words and at his most subtle was never incoherent. Osbert Sitwell never loses control of the organic form, and if he has tried painfully to create the new ideal he has at least remembered that his first task is to com-

municate with the reader. Some of his most telling
satire is in the comically employed hymn-tune measures of his ancestor Bishop Heber. Whether he bor-
rowed the device from T. S. Eliot or vice versa, and
I think it likely the suggestion first came from Osbert
Sitwell's treatment of Mrs. Freudenthal's day-
dreaming, it is certainly a device belonging to the
poetic harlequinade. In *Aras Vus Pres* Mr.' Eliot
shows his recognition of the effectiveness of expressing in conventional metres the rejection of ready-
made beliefs and association of ideas. A piece
like " Burbank with a Baedeker : Bleistein with a
Cigar " is characteristic. The whole thing is a
fiercely ironical commentary on the degenerate
scum-like surface of a society based on the power
of finance. Mr. Eliot's attitude resembles James
Joyce's in *Ulysses*, but the manner is Osbert Sitwell's.

In the examination of Sacheverell Sitwell's satirical
verse, it was noted that his mood, like Jean de Bosschère's, is primarily defensive and comic irony was
used as an escape from emotion. This is especially
true of many modern Hamlets whose emotions are
more complicated than Sacheverell Sitwell's. A
remark made by T. S. Eliot in his introduction of
an English translation of Valery Larbaud's *Le
Serpent* is therefore interesting, particularly as Miss
Sitwell's " Clowns' Luck " is dedicated to Larbaud.
Says Mr. Eliot :—

" One is prepared for art when one has ceased to
be interested in one's own emotions and experiences
except as material ; and when one has reached this
point of indifference one will pick and choose accord-

ingly to very different principles from the principles
of those people who are still excited by their own
feelings and passionately enthusiastic óver their own
passions."

This is a revealing personal confession, but it is
really a reversal of the truth about the poet's
approach to art. A poet produces his first good work
as a subjective interpreter of experience. He must
be interested in his own emotions and experiences,
and this interest need not prevent him being an artist,
instead of a whiner like De Musset or a sentimental
self-glorifier like Whitman. Was the writer of " La
Belle Dame Sans Merci " not an artist?
 It appears that we must take Mr. Eliot's statement
which has been put into other words by Miss Sitwell
in *Poetry and Criticism* and by Osbert Sitwell in
Who killed Cock Robin? as an intellectual excuse for
the poet's flight from a self too unhappy and emotion-
ally complicated for any clear and sustained creative
impulse. That unconsolable misery and unresolved
complication is probably responsible for much of the
satirical clowning in modern poetry, where it has not
completely silenced intelligent poets. The importance
to creative literature of just criticism and sensitive
interpretation was never greater than it is to-day,
when the imagination has to grapple with dissolving
standards and the acolytes of beauty are, comparatively, indeed a very little clan.

BIBLIOGRAPHICAL LIST OF BOOKS BY
THE SITWELLS

By Edith, Osbert and Sacheverell Sitwell.
Poor Young People. Poems. Fleuron Press. 1925.

By Edith and Osbert Sitwell.
Twentieth Century Harlequinade. B. H. Blackwell. 1916.

By Edith Sitwell.
The Mother and Other Poems. Printed for the Author. Oxford. 1915.
Clowns' Houses. Poems. Basil Blackwell. 1918.
The Wooden Pegasus. Poems. Basil Blackwell. 1920.
Children's Tales—from the Russian Ballet (illustrated), by J de B. Lockyer. Leonard Parsons. 1920.
Façade, etc. Poems. Favil Press. 1922.
Bucolic Comedies. Poems. Duckworth & Co. 1923.
The Sleeping Beauty. A Poem. Duckworth. 1924.
Troy Park. Poems. Duckworth. 1925.
Poetry and Criticism. An Essay. Hogarth Press. 1925.
Elegy on Dead Fashion. Duckworth & Co. 1926 (limited to 500 copies) and 1927.

By Osbert Sitwell.
Argonaut and Juggernaut. Poems. Chatto & Windus. 1919.
The Winstonburg Line. Three Satires. Hendersons. 1920.
Who Killed Cock Robin? Remarks on Poetry, on its Criticism . . . C. W. Daniel. 1921.
Out of the Flame. Poems [with a Portrait]. Grant Richards. 1923. ·
Triple Fugue. Tales. Grant Richards. 1924.
Discursions on Travel, Art and Life. [Chiefly on Italy, with Plates]. Grant Richards. 1925.
Before the Bombardment. Duckworth.

By Sacheverell Sitwell.
The People's Palace. Poems. Basil Blackwell. 1916.
Doctor Donne and Gargantua. A Poem. Favil Press. 1921.
The Hundred and One Harlequins [and other Poems]. Grant Richards. 1922.
The Thirteenth Cæsar, and other Poems. Grant Richards. 1924.
Southern Baroque Art: A Study of Painting, Architecture and Music in Italy and Spain, of the 17th and 18th Centuries [with Plates]. Grant Richards. 1924.
Exalt the Eglantine and other Poems. Fleuron Press. 1926.
All Summer in a Day: an Autobiographical Fantasia. Duckworth. 1926.